DEBTOR TO GRACE
A JOURNEY IN FAITH AND MINISTRY

To my family, whose love is a manifestation of divine grace.

DEBTOR TO GRACE

A JOURNEY IN FAITH AND MINISTRY

COLIN CRASTON

Silver Fish
publishing

Copyright © Colin Craston 1998

Published in Great Britain 1998 by
Silver Fish Publishing.

The right of Colin Craston to be identified as the author of this work has been asserted by him in accordance with the Copyright, Designs and Patents Act 1988.

All rights reserved. No part of this publication may be reproduced, stored in a retrieval system, or transmitted, in any form or by any means without the prior written permission of the publisher, nor be otherwise circulated in any form of binding or cover other than that in which it is published and without a similar condition being imposed on the subsequent purchaser.

British Library Cataloguing in Publication Data
A record for this book is available from the British Library

ISBN 1 902134 04 4

Printed and bound in Great Britain by
Antony Rowe Ltd, Chippenham, Wilts.

Silver Fish Publishing is a division of
Silver Fish Creative Marketing Ltd
44c Fermoy Road, Maida Vale
London W9 3NH

Contents

Foreword	VII
Introduction	9
Foundations	13
Pilgrimage	25
Evangelicals in the Church of England since World War II	59
General Synod The first twenty-five years	121
The Anglican Communion 1981 - 1996	179
What next?	219

Acknowledgements

I acknowledge with deep gratitude the help received in enabling this book to be published. The Archbishop of Canterbury, Dr George Carey, has given warm encouragement and support from the beginning and at each stage. John Martin on behalf of the publishers, Silver Fish, facilitated the processing in a remarkably short time. William Neill-Hall, literary agent, and Canon James Rosenthal, Director of Communications of the Anglican Communion, were most helpful with advice. I was grateful to be able to check with Jill Dann memories of shared times on General Synod Standing Committee and the Crown Appointments Commission. Several other friends kindly checked other details, although I take sole responsibility for what I have written. Mention of writing leads me to express my greatest debt to Brenda, my wife, for laboriously transferring my hand-written text to disk on a rather old word processor. I am not a typist, being still in the nineteenth century. For translation to modern software I am grateful to a barrister-friend, Bob Stevens.

Foreword

Are anyone's reflections on life and ministry of value beyond a small circle of friends? Can someone who remained a parish priest throughout his ministry contribute much of benefit to the wider Church? Colin Craston spent all but two and a half years from ordination in an inner urban parish. But for much of that time the equivalent of three months a year was spent in the service of the Church of England in its national structures and in the Anglican Communion worldwide. (Rather than accepting episcopal preferment he felt called to offer his gifts in this way.)

In 1998 the Lambeth Conference meets. Knowledge of the Anglican Communion from whose Churches the bishops will come is generally very sketchy, not only among Anglicans in the British Isles but throughout its member Churches. Do we still need the Communion? How can it be held together, across many diverse cultures and containing divisive views? Answers to these questions from Craston's fifteen years immersion in the Communion's developments, particularly as Vice Chairman then Chairman of the Anglican Consultative Council, can be better informed by this book.

At the national level the Church of England is going through a reform of its structures of government to achieve greater coherence in establishing and pursuing its priorities. It must build on the basis of past lessons. Here are reflections on the first twenty-five years of General Synod, not set out in such a full measure by anyone else as yet. What the Synod succeeded in achieving, where it failed and why, may be gleaned from this frank story. Included among his observations from direct personal involvement is an assessment of the Crown Appointments Commission, with a hitherto unknown insight into the tragic death of Dr Garry Bennett, and the notorious *Crockford Preface*, just after his joining of the Commission.

Craston has lived within the Evangelical tradition all his life and understands why and how it has emerged from a marginalised ghetto into a broad spectrum. He has no doubt its stance must be Open Evangelical, not least for ecclesiological reasons. Of particular interest is his analysis of differing traditions among Evangelicals in attitudes to and interpretation of the Bible.

Reflections on the wider church are set within the framework of his own developing theology and spiritual pilgrimage, throughout which sense of debt to the amazing Grace of God has grown continually.

+ George Cantuar

Introduction

Write about your experiences in the Church. That was the advice from friends enquiring about my retirement plans. They had in mind twenty five years in General Synod, twenty of them on its Standing Committee and associated bodies such as the Crown Appointments Commission, fifteen years on the Anglican Consultative Council, six as its Chairman, long involvement in diocesan affairs, and, not least, 39 years in the same parish, St. Paul with Emmanuel, Bolton. Their kindly advice has reverberated through the reflections of the years of winding down commitments in ministry.

It has long been a habit of mind to make time for reflection. Indeed, I do not believe Christian service, particularly the ordained ministry, can be effective without it. Taking time to reflect on one's understanding of the truth, the nature and course of spirituality, church policy and effectiveness in mission has to be a priority, however full the diary. Retirement allows reflection not only greater scope but a new dimension, provided that honesty prevents a filtering out of the less comfortable memories. One can see parts of the past in a greater whole. Conclusions arrived at earlier are modified by later experience.

So what is offered in this book are reflections on life and ministry. This is not an autobiography - I have never contemplated that. God has blessed me beyond telling. I am daily astonished at his goodness. It is that experience the title of this book reflects - Debtor to Grace.

O to Grace how great a debtor
Daily I'm constrained to be!

The first lines of that eighteenth century hymn by R. Robinson are:

Come, Thou fount of every blessing,
Tune my heart to sing Thy Grace

My prayer is that these reflections will sing the grace of God, Creator, Saviour, Judge.

Reflections are always subjective, however unprejudiced and objective we try to convince ourselves we are being. I have long held that the human mind has an infinite capacity for self-deception. We readily believe what we want to believe. Perceptions are much conditioned by attitudes built over the years, past experience and inner needs. The ancient Greek adage, 'Know thyself', should ever be a guiding principle.

The reader, therefore, is owed some insight into, and assessment of, the forces that have shaped the reflections herein offered. Family background is obviously a potent influence for every individual. I was born into a Christian home, for which I will be forever grateful. Before I was born my parents followed the example of Hannah in I Samuel 1:28 in dedicating me to the Lord - 'As long as he lives he will belong to the Lord'. It was a home firmly within the Conservative Evangelical tradition of the earlier decades of this century, with a literalist approach to the Bible and the Faith generally. My mother was a warm, peace-loving person - I think I may have inherited her dislike of confrontation in relationships. My father shared with his wife a prayerful deep commitment to Christ but exercised an over-strict discipline of his children, believing it to be what God requires; though I wonder what pressures within himself it betrayed. How did I as the eldest child cope with that strict regime? By using my wits, calculating ahead. If I said, by being crafty, it would raise a knowing smile with those who have known me best. This kind of training of children, still fairly widespread in the earlier part of this century, could have harmful, lasting effects within the personalities of some, and induce an exaggerated, unhealthy sense of guilt and unworthiness. That said, however, I have much to thank God for in my parents' faith, prayers, commitment and concern to provide the best for their children. All that is best in those early days has been conserved and amplified within a loving extended family through the following years to retirement.

Such are my origins. How they have influenced my perceptions through the rest of my life I cannot be absolutely sure. My firm conviction, however, based on long reflection and such honest testing as I have been able to apply, is that the basis of my life and ministry is the redeeming and renewing Grace of God. What God has done, is doing and will do for me in Christ governs my outlook on life. Thus I must begin my reflections with two chapters: one, entitled 'Foundations', setting out my understanding of God and his saving Grace; the other, 'Pilgrimage', being the story of the way the

Christian life has unfolded for me. These two chapters will, I think, explain somewhat my attitude to life and ministry.

On the basis thus laid I will turn to reflections on the Evangelical tradition as I have known it, the General Synod (1970-95), the Anglican Communion (1981-96) and then what lies ahead in death and beyond.

Chapter 1
Foundations

A sense of God and of Jesus, crucified then risen, was planted and grew from my earliest years. I was in a community of faith - the ideal context in which to discover faith and make it one's own. I had been baptised early in infancy, and though my parents had a weaker understanding of the sacrament than I came to hold, they knew it committed them to bringing me up as God's child.

Through years at school and four and a half years in the Royal Navy there was no real questioning of inherited belief that God is, and that he saves through the death and resurrection of Jesus. In wartime particularly there were other preoccupations.

From 1946, however, with the beginning of ordination training, critical assessment of my faith had to begin. In this I was greatly helped by contact with one of the most widely-read parish priests in the Church of England. He was William Leathem, an Ulsterman, at that time Vicar of a parish in my home town, Preston. Holding firm to evangelical convictions he was yet open to truth from other traditions - a man ahead of his times in his own tradition. Within his general guidance in theological study he particularly introduced me to the writings of P.T. Forsyth. For that I will never cease to be grateful.

For some thirty years till his death in 1921 a tide of profound theology flowed from Forsyth's pen. Such eminent theologians as Emil Brunner and J.K. Mozley described him as the greatest dogmatic theologian Great Britain has given to the Church in modern times. Appreciation of his work has grown since his death. He found much to oppose in the Liberalism of his day. Anglicans in that period were more influenced by the emphasis on the Incarnation in the *Lux Mundi* essays than that of a Nonconformist theologian's on the Atonement.

But after World War II a re-issue of Forsyth's main works, and in subsequent years several books appraising his theology, have contributed to renewed interest in him. What Forsyth did for me was to deepen and expand such knowledge of God as I had and especially the meaning and wonder of his Grace through the Cross. I became ever more certain that the foundations of my life, my philosophy and purpose in life, my reason for being and my destiny, lay in who God is and what he has done in Christ crucified and risen. The past fifty years have only served to strengthen that conviction. With St Paul, I must say there is no other foundation that can be laid.

In the Evangelicalism of my early years the Cross was central to the faith and its presentation. But the method of its presentation often left much to be desired. The Gospel was sometimes declared to be that God punished Jesus, who was sinless, for us who are guilty. Undoubtedly this was intended to put over truths in Scripture. But much more careful expression was needed to avoid moral objections to such a simplistic presentation, and yet be faithful to concepts in the Bible relating to what Christ did on our behalf.

A HOLY GOD

From Forsyth I learned to start the whole story, indeed the whole story of the Universe, with a Holy God. One commentator has written, 'There is no one point at which Forsyth stood so alone as in his conscious, explicit relating of all doctrine to a fundamental understanding of God as holy'.[1] Forsyth consistently maintains that it is only as the biblical testimony to God as Holy Father, the Holy One, 'our Other' is fully accepted that God as Love can be rightly appreciated. Unless we take seriously the holiness which is absolute moral perfection and goodness, our understanding of God's love will degenerate into a sentimentality indifferent to the moral gulf between man and God. He speaks of God 'as self-complete and absolute moral personality, the universal and eternal holy God whose sufficiency is of Himself, the self-contained, and self-determined moral reality of the universe, for which all things work together in a supreme concursus, which must endure if all else fail, and must be secured at any cost beside'.[2] Holiness is not a mere attribute of God, it is his name, his being.

Forsyth emphasised the moral order of the universe based in the holiness of God. Indeed he saw the moral order as ultimately more significant than the physical order discoverable by scientific exploration. The physical order is of time, the moral eternal. The

---
1. John H. Rodgers, *The Theology of P.T Forsyth*, 1965, p.30
2. P.T. Forsyth, *Positive Preaching and the Modern Mind*, 1949, p.241.

holiness of God makes a total claim upon humanity, a claim he may in his best moments recognise but completely fail to meet. Thus God in his holiness is faced with a dilemma. His moral order is challenged, defied, by humanities sin. How may it be upheld, vindicated and not destroy the sinner made in his own image and therefore endued with glorious potential for sharing his purposes? 'The truth of Christianity', Forsyth says, 'must rest on a view of life which starts with the primacy and finality of the moral, recognises the wreck of the moral, and presents the grand problem as the restitution of the moral'.[3]

It is within that context that we can begin to understand the Love of God. Because in English the word love has different nuances even the truth that 'God is Love' can be misunderstood unless we know we are speaking of One who is perfect goodness, 'in whom is no darkness at all', 'of purer eyes than to behold evil'. His Love is Holy Love.

Holy Love is, principally, the Holy One in communion within the life of the Trinity. And when the Holy One moves out to his creature, man in rebellion against his moral rule, it is to restore relationship and to establish in man that holiness on which communion with himself must be based. 'You shall be holy, for I am holy', God says. Humanity was made for that, humanity is to be restored to that.

THE CROSS

The situation between Creator and creature must be described in terms of gulf and guilt. The latter in Forsyth's thought is not so much a sense of guilt as a state of guilt in being in rebellion against a holy Father. So man needs more than illumination, knowledge, instruction - he needs redemption. Thus we come to the very heart of God's solution, the Cross, where Incarnation culminates in Atonement.

One of Forsyth's commentators sums up his understanding of the Cross thus:

'Atonement is that act of God in Christ whereby he judges sin unto destruction and satisfies his own holy nature in the sacrifice of the Son, doing this in such a way that man is placed again in communion with himself as a penitent recipient of grace'.[4]

In Forsyth's own words, 'God's holiness issues to man in love, acts upon sin as grace, and exercises grace through judgement'.[5]

The Cross is from first to last an act of God, the Holy Trinity. Its sacrifice is rendered within humanity by the Son, but by no 'third party'. It is by God himself in his Son.

---

3. P.T. Forsyth, ed. M. Anderson, *The Gospel and Authority*, 1971, p.107.
4. John H. Rodgers, *The Theology of P.T. Forsyth*, p.54.
5. P.T. Forsyth, *The Cruciality of the Cross*, 1946, p.5.

Forsyth would have no understanding of the Atonement that undermines the fundamental unity of the Godhead, or suggests the placation of the Father by his incarnate Son.

Nor would he speak of the Father punishing the Son. He distinguishes clearly between punishment and penalty. To illustrate the point he refers to a man losing his life in trying to rescue victims of a fire. He pays the penalty of sacrifice but does not receive punishment. To suggest Christ was punished in connection with the procuring of salvation, Forsyth maintains, was to rob the whole act of ethical value. The consequence of human sin in relation to God's holy love could only be punishment. But Christ was sinless and guiltless. In sacrificing his holy life he bore the penalty. God took his own judgement. Absorbing this presentation of the Cross greatly helped me away from cruder ideas of the Atonement. Ever since, I have not only been convinced but constantly amazed and thrilled with the truth that at Calvary God, the Holy Trinity, perfectly established atonement entirely at awful cost to himself and presented it complete to the human race. There, in the Cross:

'Heaven's peace and perfect justice
Kissed a guilty world in love'.

I rejoice in other theories of the Atonement. All of them present other facets of the glorious and awesome truth of the Cross, as do the facets of a diamond. But for me Forsyth goes to its heart, Holy Love vindicating God's holy nature and rule, acting in love to the ultimate sacrifice, and saving sinful humanity into a holy communion with himself.

Even a lifetime's reflection on the Cross can never exhaust its wonder. Who are we talking about when we say, God? We are in a universe, the size and complexity of which surpasses imagination. Millions of galaxies racing away from one another, each containing billions of stars - the Hubble space telescope is detecting galaxies ten or more billion light years away. God, we say, is Creator of all these. We live on a smallish planet circling a relatively small star within one of those galaxies. The human race, chronologically speaking, has only just appeared on this planet. Each one of us is but one individual among the millions of humans. Can I really talk about my God?

What if out in the universe there are many planets where there is intelligent life, beings equally created by God? That in itself, as I see it, poses no great problem. God could relate to such creatures as he wills. As has been said, God may have other Words for other worlds, but for this world his Word is Christ.

THE ULTIMATE WONDER

Even consideration of the vastness of the universe, however, and the apparent insignificance of a single human being within it, and that person crying out 'my God', leaves us short of the ultimate wonder of the Cross. This God so loved that he gave his Son to that Cross for me, for each member of the human race. In the words of Charles Wesley:

'Amazing love, how can it be?
That Thou, my God, shouldst die for me!'

A Holy God, a God greater than can ever be imagined, giving himself to death for love of me - that must be the most amazing truth of all. And if it is true it is the fundamental basis, the only foundation for living.

The reader may ask, But what about Creation, the Resurrection, the teaching of Jesus, the gift of the Holy Spirit, the culmination of all things in the Parousia? Forsyth has been criticised for not dwelling more on these aspects of the Faith. In his defence it may be argued that the demands of his time, as he saw it, required all his emphasis on the Cross in order to correct prevailing understandings of the Grace of God. R.W. Dale, a famous preacher of the nineteenth century, could ask while Forsyth was still in his forties, "Who is this P.T. Forsyth? He has recovered for us a word we had all but lost - the word Grace". And it must be said that Forsyth often used the word Cross as short-hand for God in Christ, incarnate, crucified and risen from the dead. Undoubtedly the Salvation God offers is total in its comprehension as well as its effectiveness, embracing not only the human race for time and eternity, persons individually and in community, but also the cosmos. But at its heart, and dynamic for everything else, is the Cross where a holy God vindicated his own moral rule, judged evil and redeemed humanity. In Christ God acted to 'reconcile all things to himself in heaven and earth'.

'O for a thousand tongues to sing
My great Redeemer's praise;
The glories of my God and King,
The triumphs of his Grace.'

NEW CHALLENGES TO FAITH

Deeply grateful though I was, and am, for Forsyth's influence on my reflection on the Cross, new challenges to faith in God and the meaning of Christ and his work have faced the Christian Church in the second half of the twentieth century. All theology is done within a culture and context formed by the times. And within recent decades there have been at least two major challenges which, as I see it, have touched what I have called in this chapter my foundations. They are; our developing understanding of the nature of the universe and what it says about God as Creator; and the gigantic evils of modern times, the Holocaust, genocide in Rwanda and elsewhere, which along with more personal human tragedies and undeserved suffering reflect upon the justice of God and his moral rule.

My knowledge of physics is minimal but what I read indicates a certain randomness in the development of the universe from the first split-second of the Big Bang. If the balance had tipped the other way there would be no life as we know it. That in itself does not seem to militate against the creative activity of God. And, indeed, physicists are apparently drawn to an idea called the anthropic principle - that the earliest developments allowed for the eventual arrival of the human species. Modern science, however, indicates a less rigidly determined universe than earlier times supposed, more open in its possibilities. So, confining ourselves to the development of life on this planet, there are questions to be posed against traditional understandings of God's creative work. Evolution of species and within species is surely a convincing theory of the 'how' of Creation, even if speculation about many of the stages goes on. Man himself now can 'manage' evolution by genetic engineering. And D.N.A. studies show humanities affinity with other species in Creation. The basic genetic chemistry of humans has much in common with that of even a simple organism like yeast.

What are we to make of the dinosaurs, or even earlier forms of living creatures, wiped out apparently, by some cataclysmic event? How do they fit into a scheme of things which, in the words of the children's hymn, says, 'The Lord God made them all'? Or, to come up to date, what place in God's purposes do viruses or harmful bacteria play? The medical world grapples with continually evolving new strains immune to current drugs. Some bacteria are able to keep a step or two ahead of the latest antibiotics. Is God directly controlling the new forms of these bacteria? Are they not in fact older than the human species? And, anyway, did not all living forms begin with similar organisms?

How does the parasite in the female mosquito, responsible for malaria's mammoth toll of human life, fit in with the verdict on Creation in Genesis that God saw what he had made was good?

John Habgood, former Archbishop of York, in a book entitled *Making Sense*, says, 'The universe has revealed itself this century as much more open-textured, much less rigidly determined than the classical scientists of the previous two centuries supposed'.[6] It has seemed to me that the clue to holding together in complementary creative tension, the belief in God as Creator, and an honest assessment of how the universe and life on earth works, lies in our understanding of God as Love. If God's attitude to the whole Creation is Love, and it cannot be otherwise if that is his nature, it determines the how of Creation as well as the fact. There can be no inconsistency between his Love in Redemption and his Love in Creation. The nature of Love is never to compel or coerce what it loves. Love is ever vulnerable to the beloved, respecting the integrity of the other, not forcing its will. It allows freedom, whatever the cost.

We easily recognise that God does not treat us humans as puppets, respecting always the power of choice he has given us, and standing by the consequences. It is part of us being created in his image. While conscious of the difference between ourselves and inanimate Creation, must not God's dealing with the whole universe be of a Creator who is Love, who by his very act of creating something other than himself, accepts some self-limitation, vulnerability to what develops naturally? Natural development, evolution, does not seem to me to be at variance with the Genesis story with its emphasis on God seeing what he had done as 'good'. Good does not necessarily mean perfected, completed, incapable of development. Creation from the beginning has been, and still is, a process. Stars are created, planets spin off them, on a lifeless planet like ours life begins, its surface shifts around creating continents (and these still shudder causing earthquakes). When conditions are right, simplest forms of life eventually evolve into a myriad forms.

Without doubt deep questions remain even if these thoughts have any value. If God knows everything that happens in Creation, does that determine everything? And, if all things are moving towards a glorious goal, from the first moment of Creation to the consummation of the new Creation, as the Bible clearly affirms, is it realistic to talk of self-limitation and vulnerability of God? To this second question I believe an affirmative answer is justified. God works out his purposes

---

6. John Habgood, *Making Sense*, 1993, p. 26.

with human beings by drawing out their trusting and loving response. His way is the working of Grace, the wooing of Love crucified and risen, through which human wills gladly conform to his will. His clearest manifestation of power is a Man hanging on a Cross. A further question concerns the relationship of this way of God drawing human wills into a new Creation and his purpose for the physical order of the universe. The latter, being of time and space, will pass away as the Bible states. Its purpose will have been fulfilled. The new Creation, the nature of which is beyond imagining, will be in perfect harmony with God's love and will.

A more widespread challenge to traditional ideas about God, at any rate in the Western world, has arisen from reflection on the enormous evils and tragedies of this century, of which the Holocaust and genocides are horrific examples. For many people inside and beyond church communities, the traditional view of God's relationship with the world could be summed up in the words of the Collect in the *Book of Common Prayer* - 'O God who ordereth all things in heaven and earth'. So, personal tragedies and instances of undeserved suffering are attributed directly to God's will and either accepted as such or bitterly resented - 'why should this happen to me, or them? It is not in any way deserved'. World War I, particularly for those who had direct knowledge of the carnage and its pointless folly, did much to undermine simplistic ideas of God's ways on earth. But since World War II questioning of God's moral rule and love has intensified. Evils on a gigantic scale are portrayed, almost as they happen, on television across the world. Where once they could only be read about by a limited number of people, in newspaper reports the vivid reality is now watched by millions in the home. The accumulated effect on many thinking people is to raise doubts about a loving, just or powerful God. In a western world, at any rate, the questioning goes on in the context of rejecting old authorities.

German theologians in particular have felt the need to grapple with these problems as they have shared the guilt of their nation for the Holocaust and massacres in surrounding nations. Jürgen Moltmann in *The Crucified God* has helped me most in the theodicy issue, the moral rule of God in a world of tragedy and evil. Moltmann had been concerned with the theology of the Cross since he first studied theology, even from the period he spent as a prisoner of war behind barbed wire. By the time he came to write *The Crucified God* he believed a theology of the Cross needed in this age to be taken beyond a concern for personal salvation, true and vital though that is.

In the face of rampant evils and tragedies he saw the urgency of a revolution in the concept of God. He asks, 'who is God in the cross of the Christ who is abandoned by God?'[7] Moltmann goes on to emphasise a God who enters history and suffers it, who makes godless and god-forsaken humanity the sphere of his presence, and moves history forward by the power of suffering love. Godless and god-forsaken are his twin descriptions of humanity. Godless relates to that gulf between man and a holy God. God-forsakenness describes the experience of humanity in the world as it is. God-forsakenness is suffered by God himself in the Cross. He frequently describes the Cross as an event of 'God against God'. In the Cross God is revealed as capable of suffering - a concept rejected in former times - and as a God who experiences and overcomes the contradictions of human history within his own life of Trinitarian relationship.

An article in *The Observer* (March 3rd 1996) suggested that modern man may agree with the pained atheism of the Bulgarian, Elias Canetti: 'There can be no Creator, simply because his grief at the fate of his creation would be inconceivable and unendurable'. The Gospel says, Not so! The Creator saw it all, went through with his purpose, willing to bear the consequences in himself, and through acceptance of suffering, triumph in resurrection with a new creation offered to his creatures.

Thus Moltmann takes the cry of dereliction, 'My God, my God, why have you forsaken me?' utterly seriously. The death-cry of Jesus in his abandonment by the Father, he maintains, either makes all theology impossible or else it must itself be the foundation for a specifically Christian theology which has only this foundation. He understands the Cross as a Trinitarian event of divine suffering, which in solidarity with the world involves both the Father's grief in surrendering the Son to death and the Son's agony in surrendering himself to the Cross. Thus at the point at which Father and Son are most deeply separated they are in a deep community of will and purpose in the Spirit. His phrase, 'God against God', then, is not to be understood in terms of a loving Christ appeasing an angry Father. The Trinitarian God takes the gulf which separated godless and god-forsaken humanity into himself and overcomes it. Much is said by Moltmann about the power of God's suffering love to overcome suffering. Some argue that if God suffers he cannot be unchangeable; suffering would change him. I think such a view is no more true than that his act of creating the universe changes his essential being.

---

7. Jürgen Moltmann *The Crucified God*, Translation 1974, p.4.

Rather, we should believe, the Cross is in the heart of God from all eternity. The Son is 'the Lamb slain before the foundation of the world'. The Cross does not simply mean that God sympathises, in a weaker sense of that word. In a world of pointless suffering which cannot be justified, the power of liberation from suffering belongs to the suffering of love which leads to resurrection, the inevitable outcome of the Cross. There is a brief statement in one of the writings of Mother Julian of Norwich which beautifully sums up this emphasis of Moltmann on the Cross: 'God loves the Hell out of me'.

I do not need reminding that there is so much more to say about God and the Cross. But these concepts of God as Holy Love, upholding his moral rule and saving humanity in the Cross, as Love in creating as well as redeeming, vulnerable to the beloved, taking godlessness and god-forsakenness into himself and overcoming them by suffering love into resurrection, help me to respond to a God who is credible, the only God who is credible today. The foundations of my life are there. Everything else, as I see it, has to be based there. All else is judged and assessed and springs from these foundations. If only I could say that principle had been faithfully followed through the years! 'The good that I would I do not, the evil that I would not, that I do'. But because God is as he is in Christ crucified and risen there is no need for despair. I am accepted just as I am, ransomed, healed, restored, forgiven. And though the offering of my life to God is sinful, fallible, failing, the offering of Christ to his Father was perfect, sinless, totally obedient, and by Grace I am baptised into him. In that union the Spirit can work out the effects of the Cross. That brings me to the second basic chapter of these reflections, the way the Christian life has worked out for me.

Chapter 2
Pilgrimage

So much for the foundations, what of the building? the seventy plus years since birth and baptism? One of my favourite popular songs is Frank Sinatra's 'I did it my way'. That exposes me to the charge of self-centredness, the essence of sin against God. I ought to be concerned to do it God's way. So let it be said, every good, every truth perceived and absorbed must be attributed to the activity of the Holy Spirit, 'the life of God within the soul of man'.

What I am emphasising by reference to that song is that every pilgrimage in the Christian way is intensely personal, peculiar to the individual, even though no Christian stands in isolation. He or she is a member of the Body of Christ and needs the other members of the Body as much as sharing the life of the Spirit within. But God in his love and mercy deals with each of his children in just the way that is suited to their history, temperament and needs.

There are broad traditions of spirituality coming down to us from two thousand years of Church history - the Catholic, Evangelical, Orthodox, Monastic, Pentecostal, Charismatic, Celtic and so on. Anyone may find themselves in one or other either by nurture from early years or by conversion from a non-Christian background. And in the course of pilgrimage there can be change from one tradition to another, or, perhaps even better, while remaining in one learning and benefiting from others.

MY WAY

How has 'my way' been shaped? How has the way my life has been shaped, influenced my *Journey in Faith and Ministry*, the book's sub-title? As a child I learned to keep my thoughts to myself, partly to escape the effects of strict discipline, without, I believe, getting into a poor relationship with my parents, partly because I am an introvert. At eighteen and a half I went from school into the Royal Navy. The contrast with a sheltered Christian background was stark. As far as my pilgrimage is concerned the most significant factor was that for the following four and a half years my spiritual life had to be maintained mainly without the fellowship, teaching or worship of a Christian community, except for an odd Sunday visit to a church while in some port. Many Christian servicemen must have had a similar experience. The assurance of prayers from family and friends counted for much, as well as renewed contacts with them on leave, though the latter amounted to no more than about six weeks altogether.

Thus if I was to remain in some relationship with God through Jesus Christ it had mostly to be without direct human support. On neither of the two ships I served was there a chaplain. In these formative years, by having to work things out and find God's grace only by direct contact with him, a pattern of living became established. Demobilisation led to Tyndale Hall, Bristol, for ordination training. Although not planned as such, it turned out to be different from normal. After graduation at Bristol University, while residing at the college, there were two years left of an ex-serviceman's further training grant. They would normally have been taken up with the General Ordination Course. Instead I was allowed to read privately for the external London University B.D., for which the college was unable to provide tuition or supervision. As a result I was required to take four general papers in the long vacation before ordination, again without college tuition. In retrospect I doubt whether this way of preparation for ordination would now be considered satisfactory, but it rather followed the way life was working out for me. Fortunately, the then Bishop of Durham, Alwyn Williams, was willing to ordain me in the hope that I would later learn I had passed in the four general papers.

I joined John Wenham at St. Nicholas, Durham, and found myself in the deep end immediately as he fell ill on my ordination week-end and was off duty for my first weeks. They included having to conduct a civic service for the mayor and corporation on my first Sunday and a wedding of the Churchwarden's daughter on the first Saturday. After eighteen months John was appointed to the staff at Tyndale Hall, which meant me taking responsibility for an interregnum lasting eleven months - a valuable learning experience, supported by excellent lay leaders and the Bishop, Michael Ramsey. From there I moved to

St. Paul's, Deansgate, Bolton thinking I might stay about five years and attempt a London M.Th. In fact I stayed thirty-nine years while the parish had added to it Emmanuel and the Saviour parishes.

I have given this potted history of the thirteen years from leaving school till becoming an incumbent to illustrate the way through circumstances and developments God dealt with me, shaped my individual pattern of life. It is, therefore, perhaps understandable that I have never had a spiritual director or leant on the counselling of others. Within the evangelical tradition in earlier years in the ministry, spiritual directors as such would anyway have been unusual, nor was counselling as prevalent as now. Whether I would have become a better Christian or more effective in ministry if contrary to my inclinations I had sought out a spiritual director I cannot say. Certainly I have no problem at all with the principle of clergy or laity finding such help. Indeed in the course of my ministry I have counted it a privilege to offer that indispensable part of the priest's calling to whoever consults me.

As the Sinatra song admits, there have been mistakes. I would not dare to claim 'too few to mention'. In the end only the Lord can say. I have briefly described 'my way' to emphasise, as I said earlier, the personal, individual way in which God leads his children in their spirituality. The goal of the pilgrimage for all is the same - the perfection of God's Kingdom in his immediate presence - but the paths are as numerous as his children. Undoubtedly Christians are encouraged to follow the example of others evidently further on in the 'imitation of Christ'. St Paul urged that on his readers. The spirituality of the saints is both an encouragement and a challenge. But in the final analysis each needs to recognise that God has no mass-production techniques for making saints. He deals with us as we are with all our genetic inheritance, personal history, gifts and weaknesses, and relationships.

VOCATION

The way vocation to the ministry came to me was determinative for the rest of my life. I had an uncle ordained in the Church of England, and a cousin was about to begin in the ministry when I was in mid-teens. But the most significant factor came when I was fifteen and a half. My father was superintendent of a Mission Hall in a very poor district of our parish. One of the small committee responsible for the Mission's Sunday evening worship invited me one week to preach. Surprised though I was, it led to concentrated thinking about the future. Not long afterwards an aunt just before she died of gangrene gave me her Bible and told me she was 'commissioning' me to be a preacher of the Gospel. Thus the preaching ministry has ever since been at the heart of my work as a priest. It is not that the presidency of the Eucharist and other aspects of the priestly ministry are in any way devalued, but the 'royal sacrament' of preaching holds a central place for me. The man who took the risk of asking a lad to preach has my undying gratitude. I wonder if the Church loses many potential leaders by failing to take risks with its young people. In my second ship, an escort aircraft carrier, another crew member, also hoping to be ordained, and I requested permission from the Captain to conduct voluntary Sunday evening services while at sea. We acquired some hymn books and a small harmonium in Bombay. Soon afterwards my friend was posted elsewhere. For the next eighteen months I continued with the services, to which around 30 came regularly. It was an opportunity to build up experience in giving short addresses on the Scriptures. Fifty years later I read of another Telegraphist (my Naval branch), an Anglican serving on another escort carrier, who likewise with his Captain's permission conducted Sunday services, also using a harmonium. It is recorded of him that 'his little sermons were of matters close to our hearts in wartime'. I wonder how many others gained experience in ministry while on active service.

PREACHING

Soon after my first experience of preaching an elderly Baptist minister advised me to remember 'the only preaching that lasts is expository preaching'. That advice was in accord with Forsyth's warning against finding happy texts for the exposition of modern thought. Little did I know then that I would find myself preaching more than 3,000 sermons in the same church over 39 years. Inevitably during that time I returned to the same passages of Scripture a number of times and no doubt repeated myself - indeed I know I did because I have kept all my sermon notes written out in full. But looking at developments in style and content over the years I find I have simplified vocabulary and taken greater care to translate theological terms. In most congregations we cannot assume the knowledge of the Bible or theology that preachers of former days thought they could. I say 'thought they could' because in the 1950s I remember elderly folk in my congregation saying of a former vicar, 'he was a fine preacher, but we often did not understand what he was saying!'.

SPIRITUALITY

It was inevitable that for me the cradle of emerging spirituality was the evangelical tradition with its emphasis on daily prayer and Bible reading assisted by Scripture Union notes. Every Christian, it was assumed, could follow that pattern. Experience in the ministry suggested it was unrealistic for many. When did some busy mothers find space for more than a few minutes? Or the shift worker? Or the person whose reading habits hardly extended beyond a tabloid newspaper? I began to feel that daily personal Bible study was more likely with some sub-cultures than others, and that meeting in a small group from time to time to look at the Bible together was more effective for a lot of other people. Nevertheless, if for large numbers of Christians the practice of a daily, set-aside time with God is a lost art, the Church's spirituality and witness cannot but suffer.

As time went by I came to value increasingly the Daily Office with its comprehensive lectionary, including parts of Scripture one would be tempted to skip. I grew to appreciate the concept of joining in the worship of the Church down the centuries and in heaven, and because of its stimulus to pray when the mood is difficult. Forsyth commends the habit of an ordered religious life. Prayer entered as a duty may open out as a blessing. Omitted, we may miss the one thing that would have made an eternal difference. The role of the sacraments has also become crucial in my life. To reflect on the truth 'I am baptised' is both a challenge and a strength. It matters not that it was in infancy. It remains throughout life a personally received sign of God's covenant grace. All that Christ has done, is doing and will do, is pledged by the God whose promises never fail. With the pledge comes the challenge admirably expressed in the exhortation at the close of the Baptism Service in the *Book of Common Prayer*: 'Baptism doth represent unto us our profession; which is to follow the example of our Saviour Christ, and to be made like unto him; that as he died and rose again for us, so should we, who are baptised, die from sin and rise again to righteousness, continually mortifying all our evil and corrupt affections, and daily proceeding in all virtue and godliness of living'. Though administered at one moment in life it is in a sense timeless in its significance, reaching down from eternity unto eternity and all of life on earth, enfolding the person in God's love. Of course, the pledge in Baptism has to be personally appropriated in penitent faith. That may happen in a decisive moment or gradually, but whenever the beginning occurs the reception by faith of the Sacrament ought to go on through life. For me a conscious response to the grace pledged came at the age of five and a half, though, of course, I did not connect it with Baptism at the time. At a Beach Mission for children in Eastbourne under the auspices of the Children's Special Service Mission, I heard something that inclined me to tell my parents one evening that I wanted Jesus to come into my life. They helped me with an appropriate prayer. I have always believed in the possibility of even young children responding to the working of the Holy Spirit, as long as the issue is not forced (it can easily be) but arises from the child and is expressed in terms relevant to its stage of development. The leader of that Beach Mission, a curate at the time, later left the ordained ministry because of an extra-matrimonial liaison, but under God I owe him a great debt.

The Eucharist has become more and more precious, nevermore so than in retirement years. While it is a joyful privilege to preside, personal reflection and prayerful meditation in the service is somewhat inhibited by the need to be leading with the words and actions. Back in the pew on some Sundays now, ample scope for personal adoration and reflection is provided. Reflection on the perfect, complete atonement provided, ensuring reconciliation, redemption, acceptance, eternal life; on the receiving from the risen Lord his own life of power and peace; on sharing in the sacrament of unity with all God's people; and on the coming consummation 'at the marriage supper of the Lamb' brings tears of joy, even though I try to hide them. With advancing years I get more emotional, especially in contemplation of the Cross both in the Eucharist and in the poetry of great hymns on the theme. The Eucharist is an offering of a sacrifice of praise and thanksgiving. But it is also the opportunity of offering one's life in connection with the offering Jesus made. My own life is sinful, fallible, imperfect, unworthy of acceptance, but because I am baptised into Christ I am accepted in him and am clothed with his righteousness:

'No condemnation now I dread
Jesus and all in him is mine
Alive in him, my living head
And clothed with righteousness divine.'

So I offer my life, such as it is, in union with the offering Christ made once for all. That offering of a perfect life, lived within human existence in complete obedience to his Father's holy will is what really constitutes the satisfaction of God's moral reign. It is not so much the dying in itself, not the shedding of blood in itself, that satisfies the demands of God's holiness on humanity, but the offering of a whole life of perfect obedience from the womb to the tomb. Because the offering was for us, on our behalf, it had to bear divine judgement of all in us that is unholy, and that entailed offering up to a sacrificial death. We cannot offer Christ or his sacrifice to the Father. His offering was accepted and needs no repetition. His presence with the Father is the all-sufficient guarantee of its acceptance. As sinners we plead Christ's sacrificial obedience unto death, in the sense that we confess we rely on that alone for our acceptance, but the ascended Christ has no need to plead acceptance.

Pleading, however, is of the essence of the presence of Christ as our great High Priest in the Godhead. But the pleading, the intercession is for us. His very presence intercedes. He is there as our representative, as the fellow-sufferer who has experienced human existence, as the forerunner ensuring our arrival in glory. His all-prevailing prayer surrounds his people every moment of their lives. He has no need to beg or persuade the Father on our behalf. The Trinity is at one in love for us. The presence of our Brother, Son of God and Man, in the Godhead is itself the prayer. In *The Holy Father and the Living Christ* Forsyth says, 'Do not picture Christ as a kneeling figure beseeching God for us. It is God within God; God in self-communion; God's soliloquy on our behalf; his word to himself, which is his deed for us'.

ASSURANCE

These thoughts lead on to the matter of Assurance. Assurance is an essential part of evangelical spirituality. To some in other traditions its emphasis can sound like unwarranted presumption. Can anyone claim to know for certain that they are saved? There are warnings in the New Testament to heed: 'let him that thinketh he standeth take heed lest he fall', and 'they went out from us because they were never one of us'. It must be admitted, there is the possibility that a person may join a Christian community, learn the jargon, give the appearance of a relationship with God, and yet drift away with apparently no further interest. Many years in ministry, particularly in the same parish, convinces one that the parable of the Sower and the Soils still applies.

Yet, all that said, so much in Scripture encourages a firm grasp on Assurance. It is based not on personal performance in the Christian way, not on any degree of spirituality, not even on the strength of faith, and certainly not on merely being in a community of faith. The basis is what God, who cannot lie or break his promise, says. Assurance is simply taking him at his word. Scripture abounds with categorical promises. 'Come... and I will; Confess... he is faithful and just to forgive; believe... and you shall', and so on. How can it be presumption to take God at his word? To fail to do so is unbelief. It is not only the word of God in Scripture that encourages Assurance. The Sacraments, the word visible, the word acted, are given to assure us of our standing in God's sight, of our security on the rock, Christ Jesus. 'On Christ the solid rock I stand'.

If received with faith the Sacraments confirm God's promises to us personally. At my baptism I alone was receiving that moment the sign of the Covenant of grace. It is into my own hands the sacred symbols are given at the Lord's Supper. My faith may be faltering, weak, shot through with questions, but placed in the unshakeable word and promise of God it is accepted. It is not my hold of God that matters most, but his hold of me. To those who will take God at his word comes growing conviction that 'I am his and he is mine'. 'His Spirit bears witness with our spirit that we are born of God'.

Undoubtedly the Sacraments are actions of the whole Christian community. They are celebrations at the Lord's command by the people of God. They define its membership. But at this point I wish to stress the personal blessings by which faith is strengthened and assurance of God's acceptance confirmed.

OUR SEARCH

Over the years I have come to believe that a basic question to ask ourselves about spirituality, about our Christian pilgrimage, is, What am I looking for? Observations incline me to wonder if for some Christians it amounts to search for a personal spiritual 'feel-good' factor. In political and in social life great attention is paid to that factor. Yet as materialism and hedonism seem to rule there is increasing evidence of spiritual hunger, for the satisfaction of which many turn to a variety of pursuits other than the Christian Church and Faith. But within the Church is there a tendency to seek spirituality for the sake of one's own inner well being? We need God not as means to an end; we need him for himself. The considerable interest today in retreats, quiet days, exploration of Christian spiritualities and their methods is welcomed. But motivation is important. Is it mainly for my own satisfaction, the coping with my problems, even my inner peace? Spirituality is primarily directed towards God and others. This is not to deny personal blessing in true spirituality, but that comes as a by-product.

INSTANT ANSWERS?

Another crucial question to face in spirituality is, can I expect instant solutions to problems or needs brought to God in prayer? I have to say I believe the Charismatic Movement too readily encourages unrealistic hopes in this regard. To avoid misunderstanding, I am not antagonistic towards the movement. From the beginning of this century the Pentecostal Movement, and then in the second half the Charismatic, have been a work of the Holy Spirit to challenge the Churches after long neglect of the realised power and reviving the Spirit brings. The ascended Lord gave his Spirit to abide with his Church forever. In the course of its history new movements have revived God's people. But that does not mean the response of those affected has been in every respect infallible and without fault or distortion. In bestowing his gifts God risks their misuse. My experience has afforded opportunity to observe and study both the Pentecostal and Charismatic Movements. Three years before I was born Pentecostalism came to my home town of Preston. Some of my relations left the Church of England to join the new church. In my teens I attended with a friend some meetings of the now well established Assemblies of God. And my father, though not joining that Assembly, had very good relations with his cousins in it and with one or two of its missionaries who went to the Congo. I learned to appreciate those contacts.

In 1978 the General Synod passed the following motion: 'That this Synod, noting in recent years the Charismatic Movement within the Church of England and being concerned to conserve the new life it has brought into many parishes, asks the Standing Committee to bring before the Synod a report which will explore the reasons for this upsurge, pinpoint the particular distinctive features of spirituality and ethos which the movement presents, and indicate both the points of tension which exist with traditional Anglicanism and also how the riches of the movement may be conserved for the good of the Church'.

As a member of the Standing Committee I was asked to chair the working group to prepare the report. On the group were some actively involved in the Charismatic Movement. The report appeared in 1981. It was based on evidence from across the Church, a residential consultation of over thirty people, including ecumenical guests, and a survey of a substantial amount of literature. The two debates that followed in General Synod were of mixed quality, but I certainly had a deepened appreciation and assessment of the movement. In the Anglican Consultative Council from its fifth meeting in 1981 there was the same concern to evaluate the movement across the Communion as had arisen in England. In a book of essays, *Open to the Spirit - Anglicans and the Experience of Renewal* published in 1987, which I edited, there were contributions on the Charismatic Movement.

From this experience I have come to thank God for renewal blessings in the Churches: new faith in the power and working of the Holy Spirit, conviction that the living God transforms lives, every-member ministry, a new sense of fellowship within the Body of Christ, a deeper realisation that worship involves the emotions as well as mind and will, a flow of new songs of worship (not all of lasting quality, however) and revived interest in healing and deliverance (some of it, though, of doubtful authenticity). What I have not accepted includes a theology of 'baptism in the Spirit' as an essential introduction to a different category of Christian experience. There is one baptism into Christ, the manifold implications of which are to be explored and made real in experience throughout life. Nor can I go along with the emphasis on certain gifts and 'manifestations' of the Spirit, an emphasis which seems to stretch New Testament references beyond reasonable limits, or even take leave of Scripture altogether. I am expressing doubts about such claims as 'slain in the Spirit', 'words of prophecy', 'words of wisdom', etc., and a preoccupation with 'signs and wonders'. It may be objected that all this is to pick and choose what the Holy Spirit is giving to the Church in these days. It is rather, I would claim, the 'testing of the spirits' by the standards of Scripture. In the whole matter of strong emphasis on gifts of the Spirit, especially the more spectacular, there seems to be a subtle temptation to exhibitionism, to ego-trips, and to fascination with power. To take one example, it may be claimed that in a church meeting on policy or programme a 'word of wisdom', or 'prophecy' has resolved some indecision or difference of views. Is that to be attributed to a special intervention of the Holy Spirit any more than if at another meeting where the Spirit's guidance has been sought at the beginning someone makes a contribution which seems to point the way ahead? In both cases only time will tell if the decision was right. Preoccupation with 'signs and wonders' is, I believe, a dangerous fascination, in that it so easily feeds the desire to exercise power. Not for a moment do I doubt the ability of God to act in wonderful ways. But the power of God is supremely the outworking of sacrificial love, the drawing power of the Cross, not 'knock-down' displays of amazing signs. It is the human attitude I am on about here, not God's interventions. If I am wrong I ask forgiveness, but observation of folk in this way of thinking raises questions for me about their excitement in witnessing or involvement with 'signs and wonders' and the success factor related to them.

There is a danger, I believe, of Christian idolatry. Idolatry is the creation of a god we can manage, we can use for our own ends. It is so easy to create in our minds an understanding of God that suits our own needs and desires. That is true, of course, of all spiritual traditions, not just the Charismatic. But I suspect that some Christians are so fascinated by the prospect of being a human agent of extraordinary manifestation of God's power and of the personal satisfaction that brings that they see God as they want him to be rather than as he is.

This excursus on the Charismatic Movement brings me round again to the question of instant solutions to inadequacy and in effectiveness. Modern technology has conditioned humanity to instant solutions - convenience foods, computers, calculators. Undoubtedly God does bestow instant benefits: pardon and forgiveness in response to penitent faith, deliverance in temptation when sincerely sought and prayers for help in emergencies.

'The vilest offender who truly believes,
That moment from Jesus a pardon receives.'

There should be no hesitation in proclaiming that truth, but the Church needs to be cautious in what it claims can be instantly received. In the first twenty years of my ministry I was actively involved in several evangelistic crusades, or campaigns. Counselling by designated persons for those coming forward at the evangelist's appeal was an integral part. Records were filled in by the counsellors. In more than one of these events I was responsible for seeing that local churches followed up the records sent to them. It became apparent that some who had come forward could not be satisfactorily helped to faith in the relatively short time they were counselled by persons following a prescribed pattern given in their training. Too often they were encouraged to go away believing their needs had been met, whereas there might be deep personality problems underlying their unease and coming forward to seek help. Rather than being brought into a relationship with Christ they were soon further away because for them 'it had not worked'.

Many years later I was in Singapore, a diocese which is undoubtedly growing remarkably in numbers, mainly through the Charismatic Movement. The family I was with gave encouraging evidence of the influx of new members in many parishes. They had to add, however, that while attention was focused on those 'going through the front door', little was said about those 'leaving by the back door', disillusioned because claims of instant solutions for deep needs had not been realised. Many with crippling personality problems, hidden, buried painful memories, are not going to find some instant release. They need prolonged expert help. That is the way God is going to release them. I fear too many earnest Christians who take up counselling - almost a fashion these days - could be harming rather than helping some individuals. Discrimination between what can be instant by the grace of God and what cannot is a gift of the Spirit which needs to be developed with the aid of modern knowledge.

TAKING TIME

There cannot be instant spirituality, short cuts to godliness, any 'push-button' way to Christ-like character. Moses was forty years in preparation in the desert before God called him to be his agent in redeeming his people from Egypt. What was said of him after that long period could not have been said of him before, 'Moses was a humble man, more humble than anyone else on earth'. Paul's ministry began with an instant conversion, no doubt as a culmination of an inner work of God's spirit, but before his apostolic ministry really began he spent some time, perhaps three years, in isolation in Arabia.

Leaving the Navy in 1946, immensely grateful that I had survived when many I had served with had perished, and looking forward to beginning preparation for the ordained ministry, I was hoping for some instant blessing to make me a better Christian. With my family I attended the Keswick Convention that year. I was searching. I got the impression, rightly or wrongly, that one could by 'a second blessing' rise to 'life on a higher plane'. I got a book with that title. Experience soon taught me there was no sudden step to holiness, no once-for-all entrance to a life of victorious living. Crossing Jordan into the Promised Land was a way of describing the instant blessing. It was perhaps forgotten that the Israelites had a lot of fighting to do - and failing - once they were in the land.

THE PRIORITY

Not long after this experience I came across a pamphlet, not new at the time, entitled, *The Workman rather than the Work*. Its message was that God's primary concern is with the quality of living of his children. If he gets the workman right the work will follow. Another way of putting it is to say that in the end it is character that counts. St. Paul says, 'those whom God had already chosen he also set apart to become like his Son'. The more we become like Christ the better God is pleased with our works. I have not found that the most active Christians, or even those keenest on emphasising gifts, are necessarily the most attractive in character. They may be 'Marthas', but forget 'Mary chose the better part'. Saints are not made overnight. Christlike character is not built in one event or experience. A Japanese theologian, Kosuke Koyama, has written a book entitled *Three Mile an Hour God*. He directs attention to God's teaching of his people in the forty years while in the desert after the Exodus. In the desert the speed we can walk is three miles an hour. That, he suggests, is the spiritual speed of our walk with God in learning his way for us.

HOLINESS

So, what is the way, the pilgrim way, in Christ-likeness, spirituality, holiness? I believe we start with the call of God to his people: 'You shall be holy, for I am holy'. As emphasised in the previous chapter, God's purpose in giving his Son, supremely in the Cross, was to vindicate his holiness and in the same act to restore humanity to communion in holiness with himself. Contemplation of God's holiness evokes concepts such as glory, majesty, perfection, purity, separation from evil. We go on to recall, however, that this quality of being was manifested in a human life that experienced all the strains and stresses, joys and delights, buffetings, pains and injustices humanity faces. So holiness is also a down-to-earth quality of living. Christ-likeness cannot be copied by our unaided efforts. He alone by his Spirit within can change us into his likeness. In *The Work of Christ* Forsyth advises, 'Learn to commit your soul and the building of it to One who can keep it and build it as you never can'. Our part, I am convinced, is to make full use of the Means of Grace, prayer, Bible study, the sacraments, corporate worship and fellowship. The will, the self-discipline to do that is our responsibility, but even there grace is given 'to make us both to will and to do of his good pleasure'. No one, however, should expect that this pilgrim way will always be pleasantly smooth. There is much in Christ's teaching about conflict, suffering, sacrifice - it is the way of the Cross. Some of God's choicest saints have suffered much, with bitter experience of the 'dark night of the soul'.

> 'When through fiery trials thy pathway shall lie,
> His grace all-sufficient shall be thy supply;
> The flame shall not hurt thee, His only design
> Thy dross to consume and thy gold to refine.
> When through the deep waters He calls thee to go,
> The rivers of grief shall not thee overthrow;
> For He will be with thee in trouble to bless,
> And sanctify to thee thy deepest distress.'

In developing sainthood the crucible of suffering has a part as well as the green pastures and still waters.

ACTIVE SPIRITUALITY

Lest it be thought I am advocating passive, pietistic withdrawal from the world, or holding back from ministry and mission till some later stage of development in spirituality, I would emphasise that Christian spirituality demands involvement with the world. Jesus 'went about doing good'. Even the apparently shut-off nature of the monastic life can engage intensively in prayer for the world.

In the USA my wife and I stayed with an Episcopalian woman connected to the Cursillo Movement. Over a meal with three other women she met regularly to share three things: the moment during the past week they had felt closest to Christ; what they were currently studying in the faith; what 'apostolic action', ministry to others in Christ's Name, they hoped to undertake in the coming week. That is surely active spirituality.

A brief Scriptural sentence sums it up. 'What is required of you but to do justly, love mercy and to walk humbly with your God?' 'To do justly' - how essential it is, in an age when a healthy fear of God has gone, and moral standards exchanged for relativism chosen by the individual, that God's people should be blameless, righteous and strive for justice! 'To love mercy, delighting in mercy' - this requirement offers a lovely balance to the first. As ourselves objects of divine mercy our relationships with others are to be suffused with the same quality, forgiving 'till seventy times seven', 'blessing them that curse you, doing good to them that hate you, and praying for them that despitefully use you, that you may be the children of your Father which is in heaven'. It is worth noting there is no mention there of liking everyone, or even of natural affection towards everyone, but of blessing, doing good, praying - acts of the will. Many years ago I was helped by a sermon of H.H. Farmer, 'Judging in the light of the Cross'. We are to bring ourselves and others, however difficult and antagonistic, in our hearts and minds to the Cross of Christ and form our attitudes accordingly. We and they together stand in need of divine mercy. 'To walk humbly with your God' - what does that suggest? Walking is itself a humble way of travelling, as opposed, in Micah's time, to horses or chariots. Walking is a slow activity, one step at a time, allowing for observing the scene around and stopping to reflect. It also allows for stopping to do an act of kindness - 'inasmuch as you did it unto the least, you did it to me'. Walking is healthy - with Jesus it leads to discovery of our true selves and healing of faults and brokenness.

Walking is a leveller, open to people of all ages, income levels, skills, backgrounds. 'In Christ there is neither Jew nor Gentile, bond nor free, male nor female; we are all one in him',

> *O walk with Jesus, wouldst thou know*
> *How deep, how wide his love can flow*
> *Walk thou with him; that way is light*
> *All other pathways end in night.*
> *O walk with Jesus! to thy view*
> *He will make all things sweet and new.*

TRINITARIAN SPIRITUALITY

Christianity was a trinitarian religion before it had a trinitarian theology. Jesus' ambition for his disciples was for them to share in his relationship to the Father and his outlook on the world; and that for them, as for him, life should be finding and doing the Father's will in the guidance and strength of the Spirit. Some fifty years ago it was the writings of Leonard Hodgson, one-time Regius Professor of Divinity at Oxford, which helped me to understand that there is a social life in the Godhead into the current of which the Christian is taken up. So his or her life is of a sharer in the divine society of the Trinity, looking out on and acting in the world, from within that society. Thus the doctrine of the Trinity was the attempt to make a formal statement of the divine setting of the Christian life.

It may be that a majority of Christians know the language of the doctrine of the Trinity, but how many see how trinitarian truth can affect the vitality of their spirituality? We all need to know God as Trinity, not just because the Creeds speak in such terms, nor even just because there are pointers to such an understanding of God in the Scriptures, but because in the depths of our being we begin to know the life of God is trinitarian. So, our spirituality is not to be predominantly centred on the Holy Spirit. According to Jesus, the Spirit's role is to point to him as Saviour and Lord, and to apply his work of salvation in the believer and in the Church. Even a spirituality almost exclusively centred on Christ falls short. It is to be wholly trinitarian as the Christian life is lived out in the Godhead.

WARFARE

When John Bunyan described the Christian's journey through life in *Pilgrim's Progress* he had no doubts about the reality of spiritual warfare. There was a Devil and his wiles to be resisted. What can we say today? From reflection on the Scriptures and experience of life and ministry I have no doubt we wrestle against a kingdom of evil. I see no problem with the concept of created spirit-beings, named angels, and of rebellion occurring within their ranks, the chief rebel having different names in Scripture: the Devil, Satan, Lucifer. We avoid the charge of dualism if there is both a beginning and end of the kingdom of darkness. The decisive battle between the Kingdoms of light and darkness was fought at Calvary. Suffering, redeeming love conquered, the conclusive proof coming with the Resurrection. Though the Devil still operates we may say his number is up, the outcome in the struggle between good and evil is assured.

I have tried to emphasise in teaching that those who are in Christ, brought into union with him in his death and resurrection, have no need to ask God for victory over evil within or without, as though the answer is uncertain. The right action is to claim by faith that victory as already given. It is ours in Christ, so we thank God for it. From time to time in pastoral leadership one has sensed trouble building up in a congregation. Believing the Devil was exploiting human faults and sinful tendencies I have encouraged a few mature Christians to join in claiming the victory in faith, and rejoiced to see it demonstrated.

One name given to the Devil in Scripture points to a sinister way of crippling Christian pilgrims, Accuser of the Brethren. We see in the story of Job in poetic form how Satan tries to cast doubts before God on the man's integrity. And in a vision in the prophecy of Zecharaiah, Joshua the High Priest is accused by Satan before the Lord. The angel of the Lord rebukes Satan and orders his heavenly attendants to take away the filthy garments Joshua is wearing. He then says to Joshua 'I have taken away your sin and will give you new clothes to wear'. With God there can be no doubt about the standing of the pardoned sinner before him; he or she is clothed in the new robe of Christ's righteousness. St Paul asks, 'Who can bring anything to the charge of God's elect? God himself declares them not guilty! Who, then, will condemn them? Not Christ Jesus, who died, or rather was raised to life and is at the right hand of God, pleading with him for us'.

It is, however, not only before God that Satan's accusations are levelled, - they get nowhere there. It is also within the mind and conscience of the Christian, where the damage can be serious. When sins, especially besetting sins, and repeated failures weigh down on a sensitive conscience, despair can set in and doubts concerning God's willingness to forgive. It is then by casting all on God's mercy, and choosing to trust God's explicit word of promise rather than feelings, that the Devil can be sent packing. It may well be that an absolution by a minister of the Gospel, or a trusted experienced lay person, applying Scripture, will aid the troubled soul. Though I hold to the position of public absolution being pronounced in the Anglican Church by a priest, and I see it as a valued part of the priest's ministry to offer absolution privately as required, I accept the right of any Christian using God's promises in Scripture to assure another of forgiveness, as opportunity arises. Satan's accusations within the heart can be as firmly rebuked as they are before the throne of God,

> *Before the throne of God above*
> *I have a strong, a perfect plea;*
> *A great High Priest, whose name is Love,*
> *Who ever lives and pleads for me.*
> *I know that while in heaven he stands*
> *No tongue can bid me thence depart*
> *When Satan tempts me to despair*
> *And tells me of the guilt within,*
> *Upward I look, and see him there,*
> *Who made an end of all my sin.*

I have already mentioned my upbringing in a strict evangelical environment. Within that context a guilt-complex, and indeed an excessive emphasis on sin, can easily be deeply rooted in the personality, with sad consequences. This has required from me as honest self-examination as I can conduct. I believe, however, that over the years the biblical truths of God's complete provision in Christ and the inner peace of forgiveness have freed me from any unhealthy obsessions. It is wise to keep short accounts with God, not to delay in confessing and seeking forgiveness, getting up again quickly when having fallen. 'Where sin abounded, Grace does much more abound', though providing no excuse for sin, encourages us to see penitence for sin an occasion for magnifying Grace. We cannot fall from Grace, except by falling back on trying to keep the Law as the way of salvation. And on the other hand, it is equally good to give thanks and praise God instantly as blessings and good things are perceived. Many times a day an expression of gratitude can be lifted to the Lord. The mind can be trained to spot blessings even in little things, remembering, 'whoever offers praise glorifies me', says the Lord.

INNER INTEGRITY

It is also essential to be totally honest with God, even in our most negative experiences. Time and again in the Psalms blunt expressions of anger and complaint are directed towards God. There is no more bitter complaint against God in Scripture than we find in Lamentations 3, but the expression of it leads to a new experience of God's goodness. In counselling I, like others, have sometimes found that underlying the symptoms presented by a troubled Christian soul is an unresolved quarrel with God. An undeserved tragedy, a thwarted hope or some other bitter experience is burned into the memory. God is blamed for letting it happen, but, and this is the point, the person has never consciously expressed the anger to him. It is felt to be too shameful to do so. Like the Psalmist it has to come out before the Lord. The late Dr Frank Lake, clinical psychologist, used to tell of a prisoner given to violent rages in which God was somehow involved. He learned to cope with them by using a small metal crucifix. When the rage came on he would violently squeeze the crucifix. He would then recall that at the Cross God in Christ took all the sin, hatred and rage of humanity against himself and still loved unconditionally. There is nothing we think or feel that God does not know completely. We can express all of it to him and know he accepts us completely. A close relationship with God demands inner integrity and honesty before him.

INTEGRITY IN SERVICE

Our service for God also demands integrity - integrity of purpose. Concerning any act of ministry and indeed our life of service as a whole we need to pose the question - Why am I doing this? What is the motivation? I need constantly to have that question in mind. I enjoy the ordained ministry. I enjoy preaching. I have enjoyed taking an active part in synods, conferences and councils. If I have been privileged to help someone in pastoral care, I feel good. I am happy when I receive a word of appreciation for service rendered, a sermon preached. I was very happy to serve as a Chaplain to Her Majesty, The Queen, for seven years - a job all joy and no tears! The personal pleasure in ministry is gladly acknowledged. Am I different from other Christians, ordained or lay? So, at all times I need to take care to be open before God about this, to pray, if only briefly, before, after and even during an act of ministry, telling him his glory matters most. I am not suggesting it is wrong to experience joy and fulfilment in what we do for the Lord and for others. John Wesley designed a Covenant Service to be held on the first Sunday of each New Year. I incorporated part of it in a Communion Service for over thirty years. It reminds us that there are some duties suitable to our natural inclinations, in which we may please Christ and please ourselves, but there are others contrary to our natural inclinations in which we can only please Christ by denying ourselves. We need have no qualms of conscience if we find his service fulfilling, as long as we know ourselves sufficiently to be able to sense our motivation. When I have seen Christian workers offended because their service has not received the appreciation they sought, or been criticised, or someone else has got more attention, or (a more subtle tendency) they appear to enjoy power over others in their service, the question of motivation arises. Are they on an ego-trip, and not aware of it?

INTEGRITY OF BELIEF

Occasionally, though not frequently, I have found it valuable to reflect on the question, What if in the ultimate the faith on which my life is based is self-deception? Is it possible that there is no God, that all religion is the wishful thinking of creatures conscious of their insignificance and inadequacy and fearful in the face of mortality? Deliberately to examine the basis of one's beliefs is not unbelief. Indeed to face possible doubts with integrity and all the mind can bring to bear is a way to stronger faith and to equip oneself to 'give an answer for the faith to anyone who asks'.

I have laid stress on assurance of salvation and indeed on experience of God throughout life. Is experience, of itself, however, totally self-authenticating? Human perceptions and judgements are fallible. Within the Christian Church, not to mention other religions and all other areas of life, individuals can make enormous claims based solely on experience. How often has it been claimed, 'The Lord has told me...', concerning choices later seen as almost certainly wrong-headed?

If what we believe about God and his way in the world could be proved by some ulterior objective standard, faith would no longer be relevant. Faith inevitably involves a choice, a choice to stake one's whole existence on God, when it is possible, intellectually possible, to deny there is a God. So, when I attempt as thoroughly as possible to test my faith to its foundations, what factors bring conviction that I have made the right choice?

AN INNER CONSISTENCY

First, I believe there is within the whole framework and pattern of God's creating and saving work an inner consistency that is persuasive and self-authenticating. It is expressed in paradox which runs like a golden thread throughout. The drawing together of apparently opposing truths and holding them in balance is not, as I see it, the basis of a system of belief that human rationality would devise. The human thought processes attempt to reconcile differences in ideas. Faced with a thesis and an antithesis the search is on for a synthesis. The paradoxes of the Christian faith are not resolved away by synthesis. If they could be, it would reduce the whole faith to a tight rational system. That would incur the charge of blasphemy, claiming to encapsulate God within our framework of understanding, understanding him fully, robbing him of majesty and mystery.

Consider these paradoxes: divine sovereignty and human freedom and responsibility; Jesus Christ Son of God and Human; the Scriptures Word of God and words of humanity; the Cross, the expression of shame and glory; the Kingdom is here and not yet; the wrath of God against sin and his infinite mercy; 'the goodness and severity of God'. In his incarnation Jesus is God's revelation yet he hides his teaching in parables - 'that seeing they may not see, and hearing they may not understand'. He is emphatic that 'he who loses his life will find it'. To surrender the will to him in the whole of life is to find perfect freedom. What religious leader hoping to commend his way to as many as possible, would have established as a main principle 'that in dying we are born to eternal life', when that principle is not just about physical death but living in this world? What human system offers joy in sorrow? fighting the good fight and peace? Creation is good and every good gift within it comes from the Father above, and yet 'the whole Creation groans and travails in pain... waiting... to be set free from its slavery'. And above all there is the paradox, the mystery of the One and Only God and three Persons in the Unity. In this mystery God reveals himself and yet, in the words of Isaiah, is a God 'who hides himself'. The way of God with us is, in the words of H.H. Farmer, 'absolute demand and final succour'. I repeat, what religious leader or philosopher would launch on the world a system of belief so characterised by paradox? Yet in the faith we hold, enshrined in Old and New Testaments, stretching from Creation to the reconciling of all things in Christ at the end, revealed over a period of, say, up to two thousand years, there is this inner consistency.

THE CHURCH

At first sight it seems easy to explain the phenomenon of the Church. Other religions have their followers counted in millions. But by human standards of judgment the Church should never have survived two thousand years so far. When Jesus was crucified all that was left of his movement was a small group of disillusioned, disorganised disciples, afraid for their own skins. The bottom had dropped out of their lives, a pathetic bunch. Yet within weeks, transformed by meeting a risen Lord and taken over by his Spirit within them personally and corporately, they set out to turn the world upside down. They remain, however, a sect in the Judaism of their day, strongly opposed but growing. Before long the movement bursts its Jewish bounds, Gentiles are admitted without conversion to Judaism and gradually become the majority. If that had not happened, The Way, as it was called, could have died out, or remained just a tradition in Judaism. In the Roman Empire persecution and martyrdom abounded. Martyrdom has continued till the present day - there are reckoned to be more Christian martyrs in the twentieth century than in any previous century. But perhaps a surprising factor to consider in trying to explain the survival of the Church is the dark side of its record. The persecution of the Jews, the Spanish Inquisition, the resistance of many of its members to reforming movements such as the abolition of slavery, schism and disunity, executions and tribal massacres of fellow Christians, unChrist-like behaviour, are all to be confessed with shame. The other side of the picture redounds to God's glory - the spread of the Gospel across the world, initiatives in medical services, education, care of orphans, relief of the poor, social reforms, heroic witness and the spread of Christian standards within society over past generations. The world outside the Church, however, likes frequently to draw attention to the warts of the Church. Yet it has survived, it is more widespread across the world than any other religion, if spread through emigration alone is discounted. Can its survival be explained solely in human terms? I think not. Jesus said 'The gates of hell shall not prevail against it' and he promised his Spirit to abide with it forever. Within this Church I find again and again that my experience of God and his grace is matched by persons of every culture, language, race and background. Wherever in the world I have been privileged to go men and women have the same experiences of God. It is not just that they share beliefs such as in a Creed, they have experienced the same grace transforming their lives.

Thus bearing these reflections in mind as I try to test the foundations of faith I am convinced I am not deceived, nor pursuing a grand illusion. Indeed I become increasingly sure that above everything else I want to hang on to life with God in Christ. For nothing else would I exchange it. God's grace has made me what I am, without it I would not be me. Though I must with all my being hold on to God, it is his hold of me that matters most.

PRAYER

In one sense prayer is simple, a child talking to its parent, a conversation with a heavenly Father. We praise him, say thank you, confess the wrongs or failures, ask for help for self and others, or adore him. But in essence prayer is a profound activity, the greatest privilege humans can enjoy. We come to the Father, to the throne of grace in heaven, through Jesus Christ our Saviour, Brother, High Priest. We are bidden to come to a Holy God with boldness, astonishing as that is. He is more ready to hear than we to pray, wont to give more than we desire or deserve, incredible as that is. But often we do not know what to pray for, or indeed how to pray. In this the Holy Spirit is at hand to aid. As St. Paul declares, the Spirit intercedes with our spirit. He knows the mind, heart and will of God and asks with us for what is pleasing to God. We have thus an Advocate with the Father, Jesus Christ, through whom we pray and who prays for us, and an Advocate within ourselves who prays with 'groans that cannot be uttered' in human terms, presumably. So, prayer is really a human person being caught up into the life and communion of the Godhead, and to share in the divine purposes.

I recall an article by an eminent American doctor on the effect of prayer in healing, a matter I will return to. He had given up the faith of his childhood, being convinced that prayer had little relevance to modern medicine.

But several amazing cures, for which his medical science could offer no explanations, challenged his thinking. For those involved prayer had been crucial. In his revised attitude he remembered his childhood puzzlement at the injunction to pray 'without ceasing'. How could that be, when many hours were spent in sleep? He came to wonder if prayer might go on in the depths of our unconsciousness, even in dreams. He offered the thought that our unconscious might know how to pray better than our conscious mind. My own reaction to that is, maybe it is the Holy Spirit interceding within and for us.

An amazing promise was made by Jesus concerning prayer - 'The Father will give you whatever you ask of him in prayer'. What a reckless promise, apparently! Well, reckless or not it is not a word that slipped out without prior thought. He made the promise on other occasions 'I will do whatever you ask for in my name', so John records. In Matthew's Gospel Jesus says, 'whenever two of you on earth agree about anything you pray for, it will be done for you by my Father in heaven'. Why, then, do we not get everything we pray for? We might pray for years for some development we believe would be absolutely right, yet the answer does not come, or is long delayed and our patience is severely tried.

IN JESUS' NAME

Closer attention to the promise removes any idea of Jesus offering some magic formula, 'in my name', which will guarantee success. William Temple commenting on the verse in John 15 says 'praying in the name of Christ means praying as his representative, his representative being a disciple of Jesus in tune with his will'. The context is teaching about the Vine, whose branches are the disciples. Branches only bear the kind of fruit the vine itself produces. So, as the same passage records, 'If you abide in me and my sayings (the expression of his truth and will) abide in you, you can ask anything and I will give it'. Here, we touch again the thought of being caught up into the life of the Trinity and partaking in the divine purposes. The specific promises of Jesus must be taken with full trust but also allied with other biblical teaching on prayer. The communal relationship of life within the Godhead is the circle within which we pray in Jesus' name.

There remains, however, a baffling mystery. Why is it that so much persistent, believing prayer goes unanswered? We are concerned here not with prayers of praise, confession, adoration, thanksgiving, but with prayers begging God's intervention in our own lives and circumstances or of others, intercessions. To assert that 'No' can as much be an answer as 'Yes' is true, but it still leaves a deeper question, the question of God's intervention in the world.

DIVINE INTERVENTION

No one can read the Scriptures, or reflect on their own Christian experience, without being faced with evidence of God's intervening or guiding hand. Yet there is a major difficulty to consider, a difficulty that causes some Christians practically to doubt God's intervention. They hear others claiming divine action on a multitude of occasions, many of trivial significance, in answer to prayer - finding a parking place before someone else gets it, for instance. Critics will then ask why God did not intervene to stop the mass destruction of millions in the Holocaust? Why, in answer to the prayers of millions, did God not bring to an end the genocides in Rwanda, the Sudan, Bosnia and other places earlier than some degree of cessation actually came? I have already expressed the view that in all the suffering and injustice of the world God does not take away human choice and responsibility, does not miraculously intervene to stay the hands of Nazi butchers or other slaughtering oppressors. But, what about his intervention in the innumerable encouragements in Scripture to take everything to God in prayer - 'In everything by prayer and supplication let your requests be made known unto God'.

Two episodes in my own life may usefully illustrate the mystery of human intercession and divine intervention. In 1943 the captain of the destroyer I was serving on drafted me ashore to attend a commission board. I had not asked for it, but was not unhappy to be off Arctic convoys to Russia. I failed the board, being told I did not have enough ambition. A few months later that ship was sunk in the Aegean with the loss of most of the crew. I have a copy of the signal with a list of names lost, including the whole of my department. On the list is the name of the one who replaced me. Was God's hand in this? Relations and friends prayed throughout my war service for my safety. But, so did thousands upon thousands for their loved ones, who perished, whether they were believing Christians or not. If God's hand was in my leaving of my ship it could only be because there was something in his purposes for me still to do. For many others had God no further purpose on earth?

Within ten days of my retirement from my parish I underwent an emergency operation for a badly infected gall-bladder. In the theatre I had to be put on a life-support machine. The offending organ could not be removed, I was put in intensive care. Two months later I returned to hospital for the removal of the gall-bladder. Complications set in which took seven weeks to clear up. My wife, Brenda, and I were overwhelmed with the knowledge of intercessions from a large number of relations and friends. We have no doubt that my survival was due to the devoted skills of a surgeon and nursing staff - and to a great volume of persistent prayer. But, during that same period there were others, including a well-loved priest in the same diocese, for whom likewise much prayer was offered, who died. To these two personal events I add one other sobering story. On the Sunday radio programme on Radio 4, there was an interview with a vicar and his wife whose ten-year-old daughter had been attacked and raped. The interviewer sensitively explored the effects on their faith, and asked in particular of the effect on the child. The mother quoted the little girl's prayer, 'O Jesus, I know you love us, but why did you let this happen?' Can we doubt those parents' prayers over the years for her protection and well-being?

In my convalescence I was greatly helped by the book of John Habgood, then, Archbishop of York, *Making Sense*.[1] The chapter that made the greatest impression was 'Making Sense of Prayer'. The mystery presented in the previous two paragraphs remain, but John Habgood's thoughts are well worth passing on. 'The question insistently asked', he says, is, "does prayer make a difference?" To answer simply in terms of anecdote is not enough. Making sense of prayer, like making sense of the sacraments, needs some insight into what, so far as we can tell, is actually going on. It needs also an awareness of our own role in creating a new reality through the act of praying.'[2] He maintains that modern scientific study makes scientists less dogmatic about what can or cannot happen, because the universe has revealed itself as much less rigidly determined. 'It can be argued convincingly that in theory there is no reason why some special activity of God need not be a feature of the way the universe functions. Science, by itself, does not forbid an understanding of the universe in which prayer makes a difference'.[3] I have already emphasised that it is not God's way to intervene by suspending freedom of choice and action of human beings. With those who in faith are open in prayer to his love and working, however, he cooperates to effect what otherwise would not be. The mystery of

---

1. *Making Sense*, John Habgood, S.P.C.K., 1993
2. Ibid., p. 25
3. Ibid., p. 26

why what happens does not always accord with the desires of those who pray remains, but faith tries to grasp that some purpose, some good, will emerge. A new reality can be created through prayer.

I continue with thoughts from 'Making Sense of Prayer'. There is an analogy in human action. We find a paradox in ourselves. All our human mental processes depend on physical and chemical interactions in our brains which are capable of being explained. Yet, human beings can nevertheless make free choices. How this is possible, nobody knows. But it is a fact of human experience. And this accords with what is being discovered about the open texture of the universe. Despite Creation's overall regularities, some things, some events, are unpredictable. It is in this context there comes the principle of intercessory prayer. I quote, 'Expressions of hope and fear when laid before God can carry this message, "I am not bound by seeming inevitabilities"; despite promises or threats the future remains open; "I am not bound by my present condition"... Intercession is a claiming before God of this same openness for the future of others. It is an affirmation that freedom is indivisible, and that persons and possibilities open to them inextricably belong to each other. Intercessory prayer has often been likened to a releasing of the grace of God in the lives of those prayed for. God, as it were, needs our responsiveness in order to act, because he acts always with the forbearingness of love'.[4] In intercessory prayer God's openness and the trusting soul's openness meet within the circle of the Trinity's loving union and thus the divine purposes are forwarded. We are conscious of standing on the brink of the great mystery that is God. But what we have learned of him in the Scriptures, in Christ, and in our life's experiences of his grace encourages us to go on trusting, go on praying, even when he is 'a God who hides himself'.

HEALING

The experience of hospitalisation and surgery referred to earlier led to greater attention to God's intervention in healing. Without doubt salvation is for the whole person, indeed it is described as making whole. Each person is a psychosomatic unity, body, mind and spirit interacting. Health is when each functions in harmony with the others and with the Creator, who is not only the source of our being but sustains and upholds us every moment, as everything else in Creation, 'by the word of his power'. The Gospel assures us that the completion of our salvation will be our spirits made perfect and the redemption

---

4. Ibid., p. 34

of the body. We will have what St Paul calls 'a spiritual body', that is, presumably, a body perfectly suited to the spirit made perfect, and so we will be like Christ as we see him as he is. Without some kind of body we will not be a fully redeemed person. To be a bodiless spirit would be to be less than human.

What, then, should we expect from God in regard to the mind and the body during life on earth? Some years ago I got to know a woman with a recognised healing ministry exercised, mainly in the Manchester diocese, by laying on of hands with prayer in the context of the Eucharist. She was careful to emphasise that God's healing could be through death rather than from death. I was asked one day by the wife of a couple I had married to go with her and the woman I have referred to, for ministry to the husband. He was diagnosed as terminally ill in hospital with a brain tumour. The doctor's prognosis was of severe pain requiring massive drug doses and a death within days. During a shortened Communion service the woman laid hands on him with prayer. Within a few days he was allowed home, without pain or the heavy drugs. For several weeks, seven as I recall, he lived comfortably and died peacefully one afternoon. His wife said those weeks were among the best they had had together.

MIRACLES

However good that experience was for the couple it cannot be the full answer to the question of God's healing intervention to claim he does heal sometimes through death. We have numerous stories of healing in Scripture, notably in the ministry of Jesus. Modern times have seen a widespread revival of interest in the Church in healing. The picture is complex. Within some traditions there are dramatic, not to say excessive, claims of healing of physical disorders and deliverance from evil spirits, sometimes in the highly charged emotionalism of a public meeting. Later examination by qualified medical personnel casts serious doubts on many of these claims. Under the influence of a powerful personality, and intense emotional pressure to believe, healing is possible; the mind can so take over the body's reactions that for a spell symptoms of the illness seem to be gone. A tragic consequence of healings that do not happen is an assertion that the sick person had insufficient faith, the effect of which can be devastating. A healthier aspect of the mind's relationship to the body is apparent when relaxation counteracts pain. There are, of course, other traditions in the Church where the ministry of healing is more quietly and responsibly exercised.

I offer some reflections on healing. Starting from the basis of the Scriptures it appears significant to note three features of the miracles of healing. First, they are all instant, or almost instant, cures. Those with an element of delay occur when the sick person is healed in the act of obeying some instruction of the healer - Naaman, the leper, has to go and bathe, in the Gospels lepers have to go and show themselves to the priest, or wash in the Pool of Siloam. But the cure is not gradual as we normally expect today when we pray for healing. Secondly, healing miracles occur alongside other types of miracles, nature miracles such as the stilling of the storm and the feeding of the five thousand. Thirdly, miracles do not seem to be found uniformly throughout biblical history. There are long periods of time when apparently nothing miraculous happens. Three stages of salvation-history are accompanied by miracles. First, there is the Exodus from Egypt and the entry into the Promised Land of God's chosen people. At this time miracles are not numerous and are mainly to do with overcoming natural obstacles, like the Red Sea and the Jordan, or terrifying the Egyptians. The next development can be described as the commencement of the ministry of the Prophets, Elijah and Elisha in particular, though later in the Book of Daniel supernatural events are recorded. The third stage begins with the ministry of Jesus and continues right into the early years of the Church. Is it too fanciful to suggest that these major stages in God's saving purposes are inaugurated. so to speak, by supernatural events? In respect of the healing miracles of Jesus we see the love of God in action, making men and women whole, but his miracles are also signs of the coming of the Kingdom through him.

HEALING TODAY

From the reflections above further questions arise for our own day. First, are we entitled to expect a renewal of healing miracles at this stage in history? - I am not aware of claims of nature miracles. If so, what, following the ideas on bible history mentioned above, is so special about this stage in history? Some would claim the phenomena of the Pentecostal and Charismatic Movements amount to a new development in God's purposes for which 'signs and wonders' are appropriate. But there have been other developments before in Church history with renewing effects but not necessarily widespread miracles. Then, we may ask, if this is an age of miracles, why not nature miracles or the raising of the dead, as in the ministry of Jesus? Further, should we expect instant cures to be the norm if this age is in any way comparable with those in Scripture - instant cures that are verifiable?

The enormous developments in medical science and practice in our time are truly a gift of God to the human race. In all aspects of knowledge we are thinking God's thoughts after him. In applying that knowledge we are sharing in God's creative purposes, and in respect of medical science, in his providential and healing purposes. It is not unreasonable, therefore, to look for answers to prayer for healing for the most part through the agency of the medical and nursing profession and treatment. I am not, however, ruling out instant cures through direct intervention of God, such as defy all other known explanations. I accept there have been such, though not as many as some claim.

PERSONAL EXPERIENCE

My other reflections on healing arise from my own experience. I have already referred to a life-threatening illness after my retirement. The reason the surgeon at first could not remove my gall-bladder was the extent of infection spread across the lungs causing an inability to breathe unaided. My wife, the Area Dean and Wardens were at the hospital praying through the early hours of the morning for my survival, though I was unaware of it. I am told that in his prayers the Area Dean prayed specifically for defeat of the infection, claiming that victory, in fact, on the basis of Christ's conquest of all evil. I later reflected much on this. As I have already indicated, it had long been my practice to encourage Christians to claim in faith the victory over the Devil and all his works. Could that be extended to the 'evil' caused by virulent bacteria damaging the body? Is it possible that the Devil can use the presence of bacteria or other serious disorders to harm people? My mind then went to the healing miracles of Jesus, so many of which were said to be associated with evil spirits. Some today would dismiss the belief in harmful spirits in those days as superstition due to inadequate medical knowledge. I cannot go along with that scepticism.

Two months after leaving hospital with drainage tubes I returned for the removal of the offending organ, expecting to be out in about ten days. The reason I had to be in for seven weeks was, again, infection focused in a persistent abscess alongside the liver. Antibiotics and drainage proved unsuccessful. On Maundy Thursday the surgeon said he would have to operate a third time. My wife and I were very low in spirits. In my despair God seemed to focus my thoughts on the hymn 'Great is thy faithfulness' and particularly the lines 'Strength for today and bright hope for tomorrow'. I tried to hang on to that. With drainage tubes in place the surgeon allowed me home for the next four nights, intending to operate after the weekend. I decided to pray against the infection, as the Area Dean had done earlier. On Easter Sunday evening, though I was feeling weak, we went to a shortened service of Holy Communion. It was held in a side chapel and attended by only a few people. I came out feeling something had happened within me. My wife who had specifically prayed for healing power in the sacrament to restore me also believed the same. Less than forty eight hours later I was discharged from hospital - the abscess had completely cleared up. I have had no further trouble from that source. I am convinced that in healing God may use the sacraments. The grace received may benefit the whole person, body as well as spirit. The surgeon to whom I owe so much takes the same view.

COPING WITH LIFE

Resilience in facing the pressures of life without dependency on all sorts of aids is generally regarded as a matter of temperament. But, for the Christian believer, coping with pressures need not be merely a matter of temperament, if we take the New Testament seriously.

While writing this chapter, at one point I gazed through a window into the garden. It was a very windy day. Two birds were perching on the outer branches of a tall tree swaying in the wind. I thought how dizzy I would feel to be high up on an insecure foothold. Then the thought occurred: Birds don't get dizzy! Why? Because of the sense that if their foothold is dislodged they can simply spread their wings and take flight. They have that capacity. For the Christian believer there is also an appropriate capacity. When the pressures of life weigh in on the soul, whether in some sudden, unexpected storm or in a prolonged, wearing trial of which there seems no end, there is recourse to the ever-constant loving-kindness of God. Dislodged from apparently firm footholds in life, we can only fall into the everlasting arms underneath us. St Paul, who had more pressures than most to cope with, knew and wrote about this capacity. 'I have the strength to face all conditions by the power that Christ gives me,' he told the Christians at Philippi. To the Corinthians he explained that when he was weak, then he was strong, because the grace of Christ, known to be all-sufficient, took over to an increased degree. And in the triumphant declaration at the end of Romans Chapter 8, he could maintain 'that neither death, nor life, nor angels, nor principalities, nor things present, nor things to come, nor powers, nor height, nor depths, nor anything else in all creation will be able to separate us from the love of God in Christ Jesus our Lord'. If that does not provide the capacity for coping with life, I do not know what will. As I reflect on the pressures faced in life so far, I can only add my own humble testimony to its effectiveness.

PATIENCE

Connected with the truth just outlined is another New Testament insight. It stems from the word Patience. In modern parlance, patience may signify a dumb resignation, a passive inactivity in the face of trying circumstances. William Barclay says there is no single English word which transmits all the fullness of its meaning. The word indicates courageous endurance of toil that has come upon a person all against their will, endurance of the sting of grief, the shock of battle and the coming of death. It is spiritual staying-power that bears what comes because there is a goal of glory. Even in the darkest hour of the night, patience hopes for the dawn. It is the quality which keeps people on their feet with their face to the wind, pressing onwards. Barclay reminds us that St Chrysostom calls patience 'the queen of virtues, the foundation of right actions, peace in war, calm in tempest, security in plots'. And he refers to a prayer of George Matheson, author of 'O Love, that wilt not let me go', who, stricken in blindness and spurned in love, pleaded that he might accept God's will 'not with dumb resignation, but with holy joy; not only with the absence of murmur, but with a song of praise'. The secret of this quality is given by St Paul in Romans 15:4, and reflected in a version of the Collect for Advent II, 'that we through patience and comfort of the Scriptures might have hope'.

PEACE AND JOY

Who in the world does not long for inner peace, however busy their life or beset by pains and pressures? Peace and its sister gift, joy, are fruits of deep inner security. Peace is not merely the absence of strife, but rest at the core of one's being. Joy is not another word for happiness. Happiness depends on favourable circumstances and is transitory. Joy is a thankful serenity deep down. The basis of joy and peace, as indicated above, is inner security.

Many look for security and do not find it. Circumstances, possessions, pleasure, cannot deliver what is most needed. Even Christians can rely too much on things to do with faith - a worked-out system of beliefs, a particular form of liturgy, defined, perhaps, as the service 'we have always been used to', a never-changing church - 'when we come we want it to be as it always was'. Security is sought in things relating to the faith, but in this world changes are always to be expected. Security is more to be found in relationship. When a baby enters the world it needs above all else to feel secure in relationship to its mother, first of all, and then the closest relations. Unless a firm relationship is established with the mother as the source of its being, deep personality problems can emerge later in life, evident often in inability to enter into trusting relationships. Similarly, if a relationship with a father goes wrong, it may be difficult to trust a heavenly Father. So throughout life security is to be found in close relationships. But human relationships can also break down and are eventually severed by death. One relationship, however, is constantly open to us and cannot be interrupted by death, and that is our relationship with our God, the ultimate source of our being. That is the relationship which gives inner security whatever happens, and engenders peace and joy. A greeting of St Paul to his readers is a prayer for their 'joy and peace in believing'. He himself had learned in whatever circumstances he found himself - imprisonment, cruelty, privations, physical disability, or comfort, and full provision for his needs - therein to be content.

> *In heavenly love abiding,*
> *No change my heart shall fear;*
> *And safe is such confiding,*
> *For nothing changes here.*
> *The storm may roar around me,*
> *My heart may low be laid;*
> *But God is round about me;*
> *And can I be dismayed?*

In reflecting on 'my way', the pilgrimage in which God has led me so far, it has been necessary for me to be selective in describing lessons learned. I hope, however, that I have been able to explain why I chose the title of the book, for indeed I am to grace a debtor, daily constrained to acknowledge that debt.

The pilgrimage is not yet over, as I write. I look forward to whatever is to come. I will attempt to envisage that future in the concluding chapter.

Chapter 3
Evangelicals in the Church of England since World War II

In the summer of 1941, on leaving school and about to join the Royal Navy, I told a senior Evangelical vicar in my home town that I hoped to be ordained at the end of the war, if I survived. 'I don't know whether you should', he replied, 'Evangelicals are finished in the Church of England.' He was not the most positive of personalities. Nevertheless, his attitude was typical of Conservative Evangelicals in their darker moments between the wars. They generally saw themselves as a besieged minority.

It is not my intention to write a history of Anglican Evangelicals in the past fifty years - others have attempted that - but to offer reflections on crucial events and developments based on personal involvement and study.

A GHETTO MENTALITY

Why was the sense of marginalisation among Evangelicals so strong in the earlier part of this century? Groups within the life of the Church with such a sense place the blame on their treatment by majorities and particularly those in authority. In the 1920s and 30s the prevailing attitude towards Conservative Evangelicals was, to say the least, unsympathetic. The less acceptable characteristics of fundamentalism were ascribed to them. But there were also self-inflicted causes of marginalisation. One could argue that is generally the case. Paranoia may in part be a reaction to treatment by others, but self-examination is an essential requirement as well if the truth is to be known. Groups feeling marginalised today would do well to learn from those "under siege" fifty years ago. I see, both in a section of the Evangelical constituency today and in Catholics strongly opposed to women priests, a sense of alienation bordering on paranoia. Opposition to certain developments can be respected, but it easily leads to writing off the whole Church, and bishops in particular, as far-gone in apostasy from Apostolic truth and witness, and the 'I only am left' state of mind. The Church of England has problems today, as it has always had, but there are no grounds for despair, rather much to be thankful for.

Chief among self-inflicted wounds earlier in the century was the failure to work out a positive response to perceived threats to biblical and Protestant Christianity from nineteenth-century movements gaining ground in the twentieth. These were the Anglo-Catholic movement developing from the Tractarians, biblical critical scholarship and scientific discovery, especially Darwinism.

CHURCHMANSHIP

Threat to Protestant principles was seen mainly as touching doctrines of the Church, the Sacraments and the Ministry. Anglo-Catholic emphases were regarded as reintroducing Roman teaching. So Conservative Evangelical teaching tended to be in terms of what the Church, the Sacraments, the Ministry were not, rather than in terms of what they were. A few Evangelical theologians, such as Griffith Thomas and T.C. Hammond, could offer a positive as well as a negative response, but at parish level it was mainly the negative that prevailed. The 'true' Church was not to be equated with the 'visible'. The sacrament of the Lord's Supper was not a re-presentation of the once-for-all sacrifice of Christ, the sacrament of Baptism was not necessarily the act of regeneration. The ordained ministry was not a mediating agency with the powers Catholics claimed. In these objecting responses there was undoubtedly some defence of the Reformed position, which accords with Evangelical belief today, but a healthy theology cannot rest mainly on negatives. The failure to engage positively in the debate for the mind of the Church of England left Conservative Evangelicals in a weak position. In the resulting sense of threat, a range of symbols acquired major significance, second order practices assuming primary importance. Rituals increasingly adopted by Catholics were repudiated with fierce righteousness. The 'north end' position for the officiant at Holy Communion was a test of orthodoxy, despite the fact that in post-Reformation times the Table was differently sited and arranged. In vesture, the choir habit for clergy was the only proper use. Indeed some parishes staunchly retained the Geneva gown for preaching - its discontinuation could lead to major rows. In the 1950s it took me three meetings of a PCC to get permission for flowers in church. That congregation had been taught by an incumbent, still in office in the 1940s, that flowers in church, even on Harvest Sunday, was a step on the slippery slope to Anglo-Catholicism. Candles were taboo, turning east in the Creed unacceptable, and Morning and Evening Prayer with a substantial sermon rated as the norm for Sunday worship rather than Holy Communion. Peer pressure and fear of appearing unsound and as betraying the cause, all contribute to the bonding of a besieged minority. And so association with the like-minded in formal or informal groups, and suspicion of those outside them together provide a safeguard. When a theological or churchmanship stance is allied to a tight, pietistic aversion to what is regarded as 'worldly' - cultural pursuits such as the theatre and cinema, social activities like dancing, use of alcohol, etc, in which other Christians were regarded as lax - isolation is strengthened.

BIBLICAL CRITICISM

Critical biblical scholarship, from the Continent as well as these islands, clashed with a literalist, fundamentalist view of Scripture generally prevailing among Conservative Evangelicals. As I will argue later, there was no uniform Evangelical view on the way the inspiration of Scripture had come about. Nor was there uniformity of interpretation of Scripture. For instance, there was a division on the matter of a dispensationalist scheme in Scripture as set out in the Schofield Reference Bible. But, by and large, Conservative Evangelicals did not contend with what they regarded as 'modernist' theories of Scripture by confronting scholars on their own ground. Until after World War II they left the field open to scholars with other presuppositions, content to repeat their own positions, as though diligent scholarship could not open up new insights on the biblical text.

A most significant development in Evangelical attitudes to the Bible came to a head in 1922. Within the Church Missionary Society leadership, a crisis had arisen. The early years of the twentieth century had seen an infiltration of what were seen as liberal attitudes to Scripture within the Evangelical tradition of the Church of England, still strong in numbers and influence, as it had been in the nineteenth century. CMS was the focus of the major Evangelical missionary outreach to other lands. The use of the terms 'liberal' and 'conservative' were then, as indeed they are still today, problematical and unfortunate. They raise questions as well as answers. Certainly within CMS circles at the time they did not indicate disagreement on fundamental doctrines of the faith, on the Creeds or the thirty-nine

Articles of Religion. Concern had arisen, however, whether missionaries and teachers sent overseas might be spreading views on the authority and trustworthiness of Scripture, and of our Lord's words in endorsement of that authority, as were generally prevailing in universities and most theological colleges, which did not accord with Evangelical thought. From 1917 to 1922, efforts were made to establish a Concordat acceptable to differing convictions within the society. The more conservative members desired a tight doctrinal statement with unequivocal commitment to the trustworthiness of the Bible's historical records and the authority of its teachings, and their endorsement by our Lord's utterances. And given this, there should be the requirement to send out as missionaries only those who would believe and teach accordingly. Large numbers of CMS members participated in the debates, including leading bishops, clergy and laity. It is of significance that for some a declaration of the supreme authority and trustworthiness of Scripture as God's word written 'in all matters of faith and doctrine' as the sole requirement was not considered sufficient. Acute feelings were raised on both sides, yet all records show that every effort was made 'to arrive at brotherly accord'. A Christian spirit prevailed. In the end agreement proved impossible. A section decided to separate from CMS and form a new society, the Bible Churchmen's Missionary Society, now known as Crosslinks. Dr Daniel Bartlett, a leading negotiator throughout the debates, became the first Secretary of the new society. He was still alive when I was a student in Bristol, though he had been eased out of office, to put it kindly, chiefly because of autocratic tendencies in the war years. Someone who had close contact with him informed me that his judgement twenty-five years on from 1922 was that if only in CMS there could have been a commitment to 'the truth of all Christ's utterances', a split would have been avoided.

All this is about developments before the particular concern of this chapter, the last fifty years. But it has a significance for the situation around the time of World War II. The year 1922, marked a divide between Liberal and Conservative Evangelicals, though not all the latter moved over to BCMS. And this wholly Anglican division was not the only dividing of the ways. What became known as the Inter-Varsity Fellowship of Christian Unions had split off from the Student Christian Movement. Conservative Evangelicals, as seen in the basis of belief of BCMS and IVF, took a tighter definition of Scripture. Liberal Evangelicals were more ready to take in widely agreed conclusions of modern scholarship while holding to cardinal doctrines of the faith. Outstanding among their ranks were men like Max

Warren, Douglas Webster, F.V. Dillistone and so on, renowned worldwide for scholarship and leadership. The Anglican Evangelical Group Movement provided a focus for this tradition. For various reasons, however, the total Evangelical scene was not as bright by the mid-century as it had been at the beginning, and the conservative wing was considerably marginalised, as has been described.

SCIENCE

The third perceived threat to Conservative Evangelicals began with the writings of Charles Darwin. His researches opened up an entirely new way of thinking about the created order, the origin of species and their evolution. To Christians committed to a literalist interpretation of Scripture, particularly of what appeared to them to be narrative sections, Darwinism was seen as negating the Genesis account of creation. God's Word was being denied, his work of creation discarded. Further scientific discoveries compounded the undermining of the Christian faith, as they saw it. Understandings that the world was older than a few thousand years, that living species had common, simpler ancestors, and, more recently, had genetic affinities, were threatening to most Conservative Evangelicals, very few of whom seem to have been scientists.

In 1994 there appeared in the USA a book entitled *The Scandal of the Evangelical Mind*[1], the author, Mark A. Noll, himself an Evangelical. His opening sentence reads, 'The scandal of the evangelical mind is that there is not much of an evangelical mind'. He gladly acknowledges great sacrifices in the spread of the message of salvation, concerned activity on behalf of the needy and commitment to church and parachurch organisations, but he describes and diagnoses the flight from rigorous intellectual study. He explains how fundamentalists earlier in the century hung on to essential elements of the Christian faith but seriously damaged the life of the mind - the mind with which, along with the heart and soul, we are to love God. The greater part of his book concerns the American scene, but in considerable measure applies to the British context still today and should be required reading not least for Anglican Evangelicals. My mention of it in this chapter is because I believe it throws light on the marginalisation of Conservative Evangelicals by the time of World War II. The mind was not being thoroughly applied to the search for truth in response to perceived threats to reformed, biblical faith. All energies were bent on defending inherited positions. While firmly

---

1. Published jointly by William B. Eerdman, *Grand Rapids*, Michigan and Inter-Varsity Press, Leicester, 1994

committed to the primary and basic doctrines of the faith, the mind was not open to new insights. To the open, as opposed to the closed, mind it will be necessary to return.

It would be quite unfair to leave a completely negative impression of Conservative Evangelicalism in the 1940s. Marginalisation notwithstanding, there was much life and vitality in Evangelical parishes and organisations. Evangelism went on, both through normal parish ministry and participation in Anglican and interdenominational agencies, such as the Scripture Union and its associated body the Children's Special Service Mission, the National Young Life Campaign, and with children in uniformed organisations. The Crusaders Union and the IVF found extensive support among Anglican Evangelicals. The Keswick Convention and the Advent Testimony Preparation Movement drew their crowds, and Anglican societies such as the Church Pastoral Aid Society, the Church Association and National Church League (the latter two societies were to unite after the war to form the Church Society) existed to bind the Conservative Evangelical constituency together.

Despite internal divisions within the spectrum of Evangelicalism, its contribution to mission abroad and at home, through the CMS, BCMS, SAMS, CPAS and other mission societies, has continued throughout the century with remarkable blessing. The personal devotion and self-sacrifice of many, backed by prayer and financial commitment by thousands of Christians, led to great expansion of the Church across the world.

Whatever criticism, with hindsight, may be levelled against Conservative Evangelicals in the middle of the century, as attention is drawn to their sense of marginalisation and position of weakness in the Church of England, they did at least hang on through all their difficulties. Their commitment to the Church of England may have been reduced to a view of it as 'the best boat to fish from', but in persevering they preserved a base from which growth and increased effectiveness could happen after the war. To the turning of the tide we turn next.

TURNING OF THE TIDE

Demobilisation after the war released a considerable number of candidates for the ordained ministry, among them a good proportion with previous membership of Evangelical parishes or with a conversion experience while in the services. They brought faith tested in the intense pressures of war. In a sense they were older than their years. They had a quiet, strong determination to get on with their training for their calling. In the University of Bristol (1946-49) I heard lecturers say they had never known a generation of students so diligent in studies as those ex-servicemen and women, intent on making up for the lost time in their careers taken by the war.

Growing confidence among senior Evangelical leaders, men who had exercised their ministry during the darker years, led to an invitation to Billy Graham, by now gaining international recognition as an evangelist, to conduct a crusade in London. He had visited Britain before as Vice-President of International Youth for Christ - I recall him conducting a poorly attended evangelistic rally with Cliff Barrows in a chapel in Bristol in 1946. Crusade may not now be a favoured term to describe a prolonged series of evangelistic meetings, but the Harringay Crusade in 1954 was a remarkable event in British Christian history. The national media at first took a cynical stance but had to modify attitudes as the weeks went by. The significance of that Billy Graham mission, and subsequent ones, for the present story, apart from its boost to local evangelism, was its stimulus to recruitment for the ordained ministry. The inevitable growth in numbers of Evangelical clergy from the small minority in the 1940s to the present majority, at any rate among younger clergy, owes much in earlier decades to the impact of Billy Graham's ministry.

No tradition in the Church can flourish without a sound theological base to undergird its influence in the wider Church. It is not enough for a tradition merely to look back to and re-issue theological contributions it has inherited. Theology has to be fresh, related to contemporary needs and answering contemporary questions. From the Tyndale Fellowship, offspring of the IVF, emerged in post-war years a new series of bible commentaries. The Tyndale New Testament Commentaries, under the general editorship of Professor R.V.G. Tasker, aimed to provide a series 'written by scholars who are also convinced Christians' facing critical questions honestly.

From this beginning in the post-war period has grown a wide range of Evangelical scholarship of international renown covering biblical exegesis and theology, liturgy, church history and ethics.

A further contribution to the growing impact of Evangelical Theology came with the establishment of Latimer House, Oxford, a centre for Anglican theological research. It took some time to realise initial hopes, partly due to personality differences, but made its biggest impact when Jim Packer was its Warden in the 1960s. Weighty 'best sellers' such as John Stott's *Basic Christianity* and Jim Packer's *Knowing God*, and the Grove Booklet series, launched by Colin Buchanan, showed Evangelicals not only able to defend orthodox beliefs convincingly, but able to face with confidence new, contemporary issues.

Growing numbers of Evangelicals in the Church of England have inevitably led to a broadening of the spectrum covering all who claim to be in that tradition. The closing of ranks, strengthened bond of loyalty, strict adherence to tight formulae of expressions of doctrine and practice, all evident in a besieged minority, lose their power when numbers grow and a confident vision emerges. To that emerging vision I now turn.

EVANGELICAL VISION AND THE CHURCH OF ENGLAND

I would emphasise again that I am not attempting a history of Evangelicals in the last fifty years. Much of that is well known and has been chronicled in a number of books. Thus, references to significant events and developments during that period will appear skimpy. My aim is to pass on personal observations which may add to the general store of information and understanding. Some of those developments are touched upon in other chapters - for instance, the Charismatic Movement in the previous chapter and other matters in the chapter on the General Synod.

Among the regular events to draw Evangelicals together and promote their study inherited from before the War, were the Islington Conference, and in the north, the Southport Evangelical Conference. But a stirring of concern for some new initiative began in the north of England as the 1960s dawned. On the eastern side of the Pennines, as opposed to the north west of England, Evangelical clergy were few and far between. A feeling of loneliness and isolation prevailed. Raymond Turvey, a man himself much affected by the Billy Graham Crusades, was appointed to St George's, Leeds, in 1956. After launching some small informal meetings to draw together men in that area, he approached a few clergy on the west of the Pennines to consider a conference for the whole of the north. As a member of the steering group, I recall an early decision to plan an event without calling on any of the established Evangelical societies or institutions - typical sturdy northern independence! It reflected the feeling that all Evangelical institutions, with one or two exceptions, were London-based. The first Northern Evangelical Conference at York in 1963 drew over two hundred and fifty clergy from the Northern Province. Towards the end of it, at a plenary session, reactions were sought to the possibility of a further conference. There was widespread support for the idea, but from the floor one member, James Ayre of Cheadle, called also for a national conference. When the steering group met afterwards I was asked to raise the idea with John Stott who was due to visit my parish for a preaching weekend in connection with a centenary. This was in November 1963. He was enthusiastic. Another Northern Evangelical Conference was held in 1965 at York, as successful as the first.

KEELE 1967

In May 1964 under John Stott's leadership - just one example of the enormous contributions in leadership he has made in the past fifty years - the planning group for Keele 1967 began its work. North and south were represented, and backing from Evangelical societies and associations was readily offered. 1967 would be the year before the next Lambeth Conference. When its theme was known - 'The renewal of the Church with particular consideration of the faith of the Church, the ministry of the Church, ordained and lay, and Christian unity' - it was agreed that in the preparatory study material and in the Congress itself the same concerns should be addressed.

Thirty years on, the significance and achievement of the Keele Congress need to be emphasised afresh. There are those in recent days who have blamed what they regard as Evangelical failures and problems on the direction Keele took. As I will argue later such a judgement is mistaken. What was the mood at the time? No better assessment can be given than was voiced at the Islington Clerical Conference a few months before Keele by its Chairman, Peter Johnston. 'The Church of England is changing. Indeed, it is in a state of ferment - although it remains to be seen whether fermentation will result in a mature vintage. On the other hand, Evangelicals in the Church of England are changing too. Not in doctrinal conviction (for the truth of the Gospel cannot change), but (like any healthy child) in stature and in posture. It is a tragic thing, however, that Evangelicals have a very poor image in the Church as a whole. We have acquired a reputation for narrow partisanship and obstructionism. We have to acknowledge this, and for the most part we have no one but ourselves to blame. We need to repent and to change. As for partisanship, I for one desire to be rid of all sinful "party spirit". Evangelical is not a party word, because the Gospel as set forth in the New Testament is not, and never can be, a party matter. We who love the adjective evangelical, because it declares us to be gospel-men, must take great care, therefore, that what we are seeking to defend and champion is the Gospel in its biblical fullness and not some party shibboleth or tradition of doubtful biblical pedigree.' There is much in that prophetic word still relevant in the 1990s and beyond. Not all Evangelicals at the time would have gone along with every sentiment in that statement. There were some very disturbed at developments in the Church of England. They saw some erosion of its Protestant traditions in the Canon Law revision then before the Church. And the blandishments of Evangelicals outside the Church of England, led by Dr Martyn Lloyd Jones, to come out and form a united Evangelical Church were proving attractive. Indeed, Anglican Evangelical leaders were sufficiently concerned at the threat of defection of a number of fellow clergy that, a year before Keele, a conference was arranged at Swanwick, entitled 'Facing the Future', to persuade doubters to remain in the Church of England. Perhaps there will always be an element in the Evangelical constituency uncertain about their future in the Church of England - I came across this factor with that vicar in my home town in 1941 and it is still evident today.

Keele itself in its literature, especially the series of essays published beforehand, and its Statement reiterated the traditional Evangelical doctrines and witness. But the word that best characterised its significance and place in Anglican Evangelical history is 'openness'. Evangelicals declared themselves open to full participation in the Church of England, open to new developments as they were convinced God was leading, open to other Christians while maintaining Gospel principles. Openness presents greater demands on faith, discernment, intellectual debate and moral choices than exclusiveness and inflexibility. One of the main speakers at Keele, William Leathem, maintained that 'a closed mind is a denial of the Holy Spirit... and Evangelicals in the twentieth century have not been conspicuous for their open-mindedness'. A further quotation by the same speaker may illustrate the Conference's willingness to recognise past failures. 'Much preaching', he said, 'is too small to be believed, and too easy to be effective, and too confident to be true.' It is an observation still needing to be heeded.

Another thing Keele did was to restore a social vision to Evangelicalism. Something of the spirit of Wilberforce, Shaftesbury, the Clapham Sect and others in the nineteenth century, in applying the Gospel to social conditions and political reform of those conditions, had been lost. Keele set Evangelicals on a way of recovery.

CHANGING ATTITUDES

The launch of Eclectics for under-40s Evangelicals, chiefly at John Stott's initiative, was, as I see it (though I was too near the upper age-limit to be involved), a move to encourage openness. Within an atmosphere of confidential trust, questions could be asked about traditional Evangelical expressions of the truth and future directions. Questioning was not confined to Eclectic circles, however. At first it focused mainly on external, second-order matters, as most Evangelicals would now see them. Symbols regarded as of crucial significance in earlier years, particularly in the era of marginalisation, began to be questioned. The 'north end' position for the presiding minister at Holy Communion could be replaced by the western-facing stance behind the Table, as some came to believe. I remember a vigorous debate on this matter at the Southport Evangelical Conference. CPAS, as I recall, had published a booklet in defence of the North End and against the western position. The idea seemed to be that the position behind the Table facing the people should be 'left' for Christ, the host at the Supper, while the minister as his servant should be at the side. This seemed to be verging on the idea of a localised presence of the Lord in the sacrament which, though unseen, justified particular reverence from the worshipper looking in that direction - a concept surely unacceptable to Evangelicals. Colin Buchanan, drawing on his liturgical expertise which has since been a great boon to the Evangelical cause, challenged the arguments in that booklet and put the alternative case. To draw the Table away from an altar-position at the east wall and to 'circle' it with the President and the people was a more Reformed symbol.

Later, there was to be a less rigid attitude to vestments, helped for many by a new Canon indicating that the Church of England officially attached no particular doctrinal significance to any of the variety of customary habits, whatever individuals believed. So, stoles, coloured according to the seasons and high days in the calendar, and substitutes for cassock and surplice, such as the cassock-alb, began to be adopted. Increasingly, Evangelicals going into churches of a different tradition were willing to adapt to avoid unnecessary friction with their new congregation. This was so different from an earlier generation, when fierce rows could follow similar entrances to parishes of different churchmanship. A couple of decades earlier one staunch Evangelical could report, with a sense of triumph, that because a cross and a pair of candlesticks could not be taken out of his church he had put them in a sack out of sight above the chancel. Changing attitudes were not the result of widely agreed policy decisions. Individuals made their own minds up, no doubt in some cases after consulting trusted clergy friends. And still today some Evangelicals are more comfortable with the old ways. It was a long time before the majority of Evangelical ordinands could be content to wear a white stole for their ordination, borrowed if necessary. When I became an incumbent in 1954, it would have been unacceptable to the congregation for me to wear stoles. So, till retiring from the parish in 1993, I continued with choir habit, though it had long since ceased to be an issue. Indeed my successor came in with stoles without any protest. And when in ministry overseas, and since retirement, I have generally used them.

Changes in ritual went along with freer attitudes to cultural pursuits, social activities, both in personal and parochial life, and use of alcohol. What had earlier been castigated as 'worldly' became quietly acceptable. In the late 1950s I presented a paper at the Southport Evangelical Conference setting out a case for changing attitudes to 'worldliness'. I expected opposition, if not alarm. There was neither. Indeed the paper was accepted by the quarterly Churchman. This was in contrast with a similar attempt to question negative attitudes by my former vicar in Durham, John Wenham, who in war-time for his pains had met with opposition in IVF circles.

In the councils and structures of the Church of England, Evangelicals took a long time to recover from an isolationism bred in the days of marginalisation. Generally speaking, clergy preferred to meet in Evangelical Fellowships rather than to take a full part in diocesan structures. There were a few clergy nobly maintaining the cause in the Convocations and the Church Assembly, but in the latter body it was a band of Evangelical laity who tenaciously and with some effect defended the tradition's insights. They prepared the way for much greater representation in the General Synod.

NOTTINGHAM 1977 AND AFTER

Ten years after Keele came the second National Evangelical Anglican Congress, drawing nearly 2,000 clergy and laity, almost double the number at Keele. Study was based on three books, *The Lord Christ, The People of God*, and *The Changing World*. John Stott, in the Preface to the official Statement, reported that 'the spirit of openness and love in which participants listened to one another, learned from one another and sometimes disagreed with one another was a sign of our growing maturity as a movement'. Recognising a diversity of viewpoints, he saw the Statement as a stimulus to continuation of the debate.

Among the twelve 'Declarations of Intent' adopted by the Congress 'with virtual unanimity' at the final plenary session were the following significant admissions; an unhappy distancing from fellow Evangelicals in other denominations, regrettable past indifference and ill-will towards Roman Catholics, lack of urgency in mission, lack of concern for social responsibility issues and political involvement, and for stewardship of the world's resources and the welfare of and justice for all, a neglect of study and Christian learning, low standards in worship and apathy in spiritual life. All these admissions were accompanied with pledges of reform and renewal. There was commitment to the goal of visible unity of Christ's Church with a common confession of faith in Christ leading to unity at the Lord's Table. Basic to other points in the Declaration was the pledge 'to proclaim, explore and defend against current misconceptions the biblical faith in the deity of Jesus Christ and in his role as the only Saviour of Men (sic) through his death in our place and his risen life' - inclusive language was not yet a determinative matter.

From this summary of the Declarations I have so far omitted one very significant point. It was number two of the twelve. 'We acknowledge that our handling of inspired and authoritative Scripture has often been clumsy and our interpretation of it shoddy, and we resolve to seek a more disciplined understanding of God's Holy Word.' It is an admission that would hardly have been contemplated twenty or thirty years earlier, but it gives no impression of the controversy that has followed Nottingham 1977, and still prevails.

The issue is Hermeneutics, the principles of biblical interpretation. Tony Thistleton, now an internationally recognised authority on Hermeneutics, had introduced the subject at the Congress. Any attempt to summarise his presentation must be inadequate, but it recognises the need to bear in mind two cultures in rightly understanding the Scriptures, the culture of the original writer and that of the reader today. Both cultures have their different horizons. With an increasing number of Evangelical scholars in Universities and Theological Colleges, the concern for sound, defensible understanding of Scripture has developed. But the way the development has gone has divided Evangelicals. Some, arguably a minority, have seen it as a betrayal of what they are pleased to call 'classic' Evangelical use of Scripture. Among these there was already some dissatisfaction with the stance adopted at Keele. Indeed a revisionist attitude to Keele, blaming it for what they disapprove of in the broad range of Evangelicalism, is even more apparent today than in the years immediately following Nottingham.

Dissatisfaction with trends in Evangelical theology and biblical interpretation is not the only cause for complaint. Criticism is also levelled at Evangelical performance in the Church's synodical structures as not being robust enough. One of the bodies where dissent became focused was the Church Society. Formed after the war by a merger of the Church Association and the National Church League, the society was intended to be an effective instrument for Evangelical unity and joint action. The aim has never really been realised. Any hope that it might be was shattered in 1983 when it was taken over by a hard-line faction which dismissed the editorial board of the Churchman, the journal it had fostered, because of the publication of certain articles on biblical interpretation deemed to be too liberal. The result was the founding of Anvil with the support of a wider range of Evangelical leaders.

Another focus of dissent has been the 'Proclamation Trust'. Originating as a society devoted to the admirable aim of promoting the preaching of the Word as a priority for Evangelicals it had also acquired a critical stance towards the wider Evangelical scene both in theological and ecclesiastical matters. Charismatics have been a particular target. More recently, since the passage of legislation for ordination of women to the priesthood in 1992, the formation of Reform has attracted opponents of that development which they see as but one sign of the failure of the Church of England to remain true to its biblical and Reformed commitment.

For many years now the Church of England Evangelical Council has been a forum in which the different interests, societies and groupings of Evangelicals have sought harmony of thought and action. I served on it for a spell. It seemed then to have little success in reconciling different views. Looking now from the outside, one would have to regard the Council as still failing to heal divisions.

In 1995 and 1996 Evangelical bishops, in the wake of the launch of Reform, called a conference of Evangelical Leaders. The first in January 1995, though providing a platform for some valuable papers, did not go far in reconciling Reform to the rest of Evangelicals. The second conference twelve months later may have been a bit better in establishing understanding and mutual trust. The need for mutual trust is one of the crucial concerns of the present situation. To this we will return after consideration of other matters of major importance.

THIRD NEAC AT CAISTER

Eleven years passed after Nottingham before another national gathering of Evangelicals took place. This time it was at a Norfolk holiday camp at Caister and drew several thousands with a high proportion of laity. The style was very different from Keele and Nottingham, being more of a celebration, less demanding intellectually, though there were numerous workshops tackling contemporary issues. The worship continued to reflect developments, particularly in music and song, influenced considerably by the Charismatic Movement and widely accepted in the Church of England. Of major significance was the address of the Archbishop of Canterbury, Robert Runcie. He was thankful for the 'new identity' of Evangelicals secured at Keele in 1967, which was 'both Anglican and Evangelical, needing to apologise for neither'. He praised the contributions of Evangelicals in ecumenism, liturgical change, social action and sacramental life. Then, on the basis of shared discussions with leading Evangelicals before the conference, he challenged Evangelicals on their understanding of the Church and the question of authority in the Church. He felt Evangelicals had far too long neglected the doctrine of the Church, yet they had a great deal to offer. 'I hope and pray', he said, 'that this great celebration will not merely be an expression of joy about the new and vigorous life in so many Evangelical Churches, but it will look beyond its own tradition to see how the whole Catholic Church of Christ can equally be renewed and the Gospel more faithfully proclaimed to the glory of our Lord Jesus Christ, the Saviour of the world and the Lord of the Church.'

As one looks back over the past fifty years, it is possible to recognise three major developments in Anglican Evangelicalism. There has been the Open Evangelical development, sometimes unfairly described as Liberal (whatever that means), gaining increased support. There has been the Reformed Constituency, deriving strength from a position on Scripture held by Warfield and Hodge in the nineteenth century, and generally leaning towards a Calvinist approach. Of that tradition Dr Jim Packer has been a greatly respected leader. And in the last twenty-five years or so there has been the Charismatic Movement, not confined, of course, to Anglicanism. I have written at some length on this in the previous chapter. I would further acknowledge here its influence in making Evangelicals more sacramental in theology, more colourful and less restrained bodily in worship and more committed to lay ministry than they ever were in practice, whatever they said in theology, and supremely in spiritual renewal personally and in ministry of laity and clergy. A most significant influence in the movement was David Watson, whose early death robbed the Church on earth of outstanding leadership. The influence of churches like Holy Trinity, Brompton, and the Alpha course flowing from it, and indeed the greatly used Anglican Renewal Ministries, belong to this tradition.

I believe it needs to be said that, ten years after Caister, Evangelicals have still to come to grips with the ecclesiological challenge. What is our understanding of the Church and of the exercise of authority in it? The present divisions in their ranks will not be effectively addressed without agreement on such an undertaking. But, again, more of that later.

THE BIBLE: CAN EVANGELICALS AGREE?

Throughout more than a hundred years, a debate about the Bible has gone on among Evangelicals, emerging into prominence at different times. The debate is not about the fact of Inspiration. The provision and subsequent preservation of the record of God's revelation in history, and supremely in Christ, by the inspiration of the Holy Spirit in conjunction with human writers is common ground. Argument centres round words such as 'verbal', 'plenary', 'inerrancy', 'infallibility' and 'autographa' (the original texts of Scripture no longer available to us). In other words, debate is on the method and result of inspiration.

Ranged on different sides from the late nineteenth century were Hodge and Warfield in America and Denney and Orr in Britain. Hodge and Warfield defended the idea of verbal inspiration, though careful to repudiate any 'misapprehension because of the extremely mechanical conceptions of inspiration maintained by many former advocates of this term "verbal".'[2] Orr, on the other hand, could say, 'The phrase "verbal inspiration" is one to which so great ambiguity attaches that it is now very commonly avoided by careful writers'.[3] He went on, to express the idea of inspiration which pervades all the parts of the record, the word 'plenary' is more suitable than 'verbal'.

It is when we come to the concept of inerrancy, however, that a greater divide is seen. In 1881 Hodge and Warfield made this claim: 'The historical faith of the Church has always been, that all the affirmations of Scripture of all kinds, whether of spiritual doctrine or duty, or of physical or historical fact, or of psychological or philosophical principle, are without any error, when the *ipsissima*

---

2. *Presbyterian Review*, April 1881, p. 233
3. *Revelation and Inspiration*, 1910. p. 202

verba of the original autographs are ascertained and interpreted in their natural and intended sense.'[4] Two observations may be offered at this stage. They gave no indication of the way, or the certainty, of ascertaining the original autographs. It is also worthy of note that even such a firm commitment to inerrancy and interpretation in 'natural sense' did not preclude an understanding of the early chapters of Genesis allowing for evolution as the way of creation. Mark A. Noll in *The Scandal of the Evangelical Mind* quoted from Warfield's writings on evolution and the age of the earth at some length.[5]

Orr and Denney were blunt in their reaction to the concept of inerrancy. First, Orr: 'It is urged, for example, that unless we can demonstrate what is called "inerrancy" of the biblical record, down to even its minutest details, the whole edifice of belief in revealed religion falls to the ground. This, on the face of it, is a most suicidal position for any defender of revelation to take up ... Such "inerrancy" can never be demonstrated with any cogency which entitles it to rank as the foundation of a belief in inspiration'.[6] Denney is on record as follows: 'The infallibility of the Scriptures is not a verbal inerrancy or historical accuracy, but an infallibility of power to save. The word of God infallibly carries God's power to save men's souls... That is the only kind of infallibility I believe in. For a mere verbal inerrancy I care not one straw. It is worth nothing to me; it would be worth nothing if it were there, and it is not.'[7]

I turn to those stalwarts of former days because I am convinced that the differences revealed in their writings have persisted among Evangelicals to this present day. Indeed there are those in current debates who look to Warfield as chief mentor and guide in their attitude to Scripture. Yet no one can read the theology of Orr and Denney and deny their thorough Evangelicalism. Even in pre-Keele days I knew very well Evangelical stalwarts who found those two theologians more convincing than Warfield. And on BCMS Committees, on which I served for twenty-eight years, there were a few who followed the preference for plenary rather than verbal inspiration.

SPECIFIC BIBLICAL ISSUES

Warfield's followers attach great importance to the autographa, the original texts of the biblical authors. These are claimed to be inerrant in every respect even when, as with historical books of the Old Testament, the ultimate compiler is using existing records. Mark Noll, in his book quoted earlier, says, 'When fundamentalists

---

4. *The Presbyterian Review*
5. op. cit., pp. 206, 207
6. *Revelation and Inspiration*, pp. 197-9
7. quoted by A.B. Bruce in *Inspiration and Inerrancy*

defended the Bible, they did so by arguing for the inerrancy of Scripture's original autographs, an idea that had been around for a long time but that had never assumed such a central role for any Christian movement.'[8] The presuppositions in the claim concerning autographa can be summarised thus: God is perfect, his revelation is perfect, by his Spirit he ensured a perfect record when written down. It is thus a doctrine accepted by faith, deduced from certain presuppositions. It would seem to depend on a theory of the Scriptures as verbally dictated by the Holy Spirit - an idea that Warfield certainly did not hold. Be that as it may, there seems to be an insurmountable obstacle to accepting the claim. If God took the step of so controlling the human writers as to ensure that every single detail was without error, why did he not ensure the same inerrancy in the transmission of the texts over succeeding generations?

What we are actually faced with are variations in various manuscripts, omissions in some manuscripts and frequent uncertainty as to what extant texts mean. In the Old Testament, footnotes have often to admit 'Hebrew unclear'. When IVF drew up its basis of belief, it deliberately claimed 'infallibility of Holy Scripture as originally given'. I have not been able to accept such a high claim for something we have no access to. The only Bible we have is a translation of a range of manuscripts, most of them copied down over generations. Undoubtedly there has been a providential maintenance of a trustworthy record of the original revelation, but it requires a leap of faith to hold to a doctrine of inerrancy in the autographa, a leap of faith which the texts themselves do not require.

Yet there are Evangelicals today who regard adherence to their understanding of the autographa as a touchstone of true Evangelicalism. In the correspondence columns of the Church of England Newspaper, after the first Evangelical Leaders' Conference in 1995, I was told that I excluded myself from the ranks of Evangelicals by not accepting the IVF (now UCCF) basis. I said in reply that I found this astonishing, and enquired if an Anglican Evangelical, totally satisfied with what the thirty-nine Articles affirm on Scripture, has to accept without qualification the doctrinal basis of a voluntary organisation formed in the twentieth century.

In 1977, I asked a New Testament scholar of firm Evangelical convictions when biblical scholars like himself might produce a book on the scriptures that took into account the trustworthy findings of modern studies already acknowledged in their commentaries on the books of Scripture. He

---

8. op. cit., p. 133

told me that such a project was in hand at that very time. A series of essays, all by Evangelical scholars, edited by Howard Marshall, was to appear with the title *New Testament Interpretation.* Among the authors, apparently, there was an expectation of criticism from sections of the Evangelical world for accepting too much of modern studies - hence, a symposium by 19 scholars rather than a single author who might more easily be dismissed. Although emanating from the Tyndale Fellowship for Biblical Research, the book was not published by the Inter-Varsity Press - was it regarded as too liberal? - but by Paternoster Press. In the Editor's Foreword, Howard Marshall states, 'We have written as conservative evangelicals who combine a high regard for the authority of Scripture with the belief that we are called to study it with the full use of our minds.'[9] In his own essay he says, 'Belief in the "truth" of the Bible cannot be a substitute for historical study. We may wish... that God had given us a Bible that would be instantly and correctly understandable by any modern man. But he has not done so, just as he has not given us a Bible with a guaranteed text (instead of one that has to be determined by the techniques of factual criticism).'[10] In the same book Ralph Martin says, 'The transmission of the New Testament text has been affected by the contingencies of historical circumstances, and since we do not possess the original autographs for inspection, it is incumbent upon us that we use all the means available to recover the text which stands nearest to the original.'[11] That means we do our very best, but absolute certainty eludes us.

Another problem for upholders of autographa inerrancy is surely the harmonisation of biblical documents. It arises in the historical books of the Old Testament and particularly with the Gospels where, apparently, contradictory details of the same events, admittedly of small significance and not affecting the main purpose of the narrative or its truth value, can be seen.

Arguments can and do range over explanations offered and objections raised, seldom leading to agreement, because one side must for prior reasons maintain a position to which the other side is not committed. Quoting Howard Marshall again: 'Harmonisation is legitimate, but only when the hypotheses necessary to establish harmony are not more unlikely than the hypotheses of non-historical reporting in one or more of the sources.'[12]

TEMPERAMENT - A CONTROLLING INFLUENCE?

Surveying the divisions concerning Scripture within Evangelicalism through modern Church History to the present day, not to mention

---

9. *New Testament Interpretation,* The Paternoster Press, 1977
10. Ibid., p. 132.
11. Ibid., p. 222.
12. Ibid., p. 133

differences between Evangelicals and other traditions, one question demands attention. Is it simply a matter of truth versus error? Are those, for instance, who at present claim to be upholding the 'classic Evangelical' understanding of Scripture and its interpretation simply being loyal to the truth, and those who are not averse to a more open stance drifting from the truth, indeed into error, as has been suggested? Could the reality be more complex, and does a person's temperament have a controlling, or at least a significant, influence in the stance they adopt?

There is in all of us a disposition to regard ourselves as uncomplicated personalities, unless we are wracked by deep-seated problems. We want to feel we have got our act together, to be sure where we stand. But recognising that most of the mind and the forces that shape us are below the conscious level, the task of truly knowing ourselves is no simple quest. Why do I react as I do? What do I really want in any endeavour? What is my real motivation? Why do I accept the intellectual position I do? These are questions not answered off the top of my head. There are systems which aim to help self-knowledge - the Myers-Briggs and the Enneagram methods of analysis, for instance - which some find useful.

Applying the questions raised to the different Evangelical stances, I return to the influence of temperament. Are some strongly inclined by their make-up to need for inner security a tight system of belief - in the matter under discussion a rigid view of Scripture? From an incontrovertible presupposition they deduce a logical conclusion - God is perfect, his revelation must be perfect, the Scriptures as a record of that revelation must be perfect. Using the analogy of a wall, remove one brick (we cannot be certain of the text at all times, or there appears to be a factual error) and the whole wall will collapse. Or, to change the metaphor, take one step on a slippery slope, and you don't know when you can stop. On the other hand, we need to ask different questions of those with a more open stance. Do they naturally shy away from controversy and confrontation? Does uncomfortable contention for the truth disturb their desire for peace? (I have already admitted at the beginning of the book my own dislike of confrontations.) Does their commendable search for truth in all its fullness, their recognition that the truth is bigger than the human mind can grasp, make them less concerned, or even careless of details? So we might go on.

The answer to these differing approaches is surely not to try to change personalities, nor for one approach to triumph over the other. Both need each other. Within Evangelicalism, one side witnesses to the need for firm anchorage in revealed truth and confidence in it, the other side to the wide range of all God's truth and its application to the complexities of human life and society. Both sides acknowledge the authority of Scripture in matters of faith and behaviour; they may differ in application. Because of mutual need, mutual respect is a Christian requirement and mutual learning an enrichment in obeying Christ. It follows that some ostracising tendencies in recent days are, to say the least, unhelpful.

THE AUTHORITY OF SCRIPTURE

One of the slogans so easily and frequently bandied about, particularly by Evangelicals, is the authority of Scripture. Yet there are very few types of Christians who can not claim to accept it. Far more Christians than Evangelicals, for instance, are content with what the thirty-nine Articles affirm on Scripture, testifying to its authority. In fact, however, the authority of Scripture is Scripture as interpreted. We may posit by faith a statement of its objective authority as the divinely-given written Word of God, authoritative whether we accept it or not. But for practical purposes it is as interpreted in the Christian community or in the individual's life that its authority becomes effective. To illustrate, I read in the Old Testament that certain meats are forbidden, or more seriously that an adulterer should be stoned to death, or in the New Testament that I should as a man not have long hair, or that women should not say a word in church. I do not take these expressions as literally a word from God to be followed without question by me today. I have applied principles of interpretation to Scripture, while recognising its overall authority.

There is for very many people, especially those with busy lives, an understandable yearning for knowing the truth in a simple and uncomplicated way. We see this in the case of prominent, intelligent laity, pressurised by full lives, who are attracted to the Roman Catholic Church because, as they admit, they want the Church to decide their Christian faith for them; or, those who are attracted to a fundamentalist expression of the faith based on a literalist approach to Scripture. Give it me straight and simple, is their request. Mark Noll, in the book already quoted warns of the danger of teachers convincing people (in the case he is dealing with, the teachers are Creationists) that 'simple conclusions from the Bible' are being offered, 'when they are really contemplating conclusions from the Bible shaped by their own understandings of how the Bible should be read.'[13]

---

13. op. cit., p. 198

In interpretation of Scripture there can be no substitute for rigorous intellectual endeavour. A prayerful attitude and willingness to submit to God speaking through his Word are, of course, essential but these are to be allied with intellectual integrity. The Anglican emphasis on Reason and Tradition, that is, the accumulated wisdom of the past in understanding the Bible, in the service of present-day interpretation, makes that point. Mark Noll quotes a Canadian scholar's assessment of an Evangelical weakness: 'The Evangelical Protestant mind has never relished complexity. Indeed its crusading genius, whether in religion or politics, has always tended toward an over-simplification of issues and the substitution of inspiration and zeal for critical and serious reflection'.[14] While Noll himself maintains, 'Fruitful Evangelical thinking at the end of the twentieth century must come to grips not only with the excesses of the fundamentalist past but with the compounded damage done when those excesses were grafted on to even longer-lived intellectual weakness.'[15]

SOME PRINCIPLES OF INTERPRETATION

There seem to be certain principles of interpreting Scripture which are particularly relevant today. In naming three I am not implying they are the only ones, nor am I suggesting they are novel.

First, we need to recognise the Bible as containing a progressive revelation. At every stage in the historical process there is the divine initiative in addressing the human agents, whatever the mode, vision, event and guided reflection on the event, voice or growing conviction. But there is also the human side, the perception. Perception can only be within the framework of the knowledge and understanding of the person concerned at that time. What is revealed by God will expand and burst the boundaries of current understanding, but it will still be within the capacity of that person at that stage in history to grasp. The full implications of what is revealed may not be seen until later generations, but what is grasped at the time will be recognisable as truth and relevant to current understanding. In the process of revelation, concepts within the framework of understanding inherited from the past may be left behind as untrue, only partially true or no longer relevant. Revelation, then, is a progressive, educational process initiated and directed by the Spirit of God, perceived and received by the human agent.

So, for instance, in the Levitical Law presented in the Old Testament there are very many injunctions relating to human

---

14. op. cit., p. 12
15. op. cit., p. 130

behaviour and the ordering of society. Reason enables us quickly to see which are no longer relevant to our day, either because later parts of Scripture guide us or because common sense tells us. Even in the later parts, in the Epistles for instance, reason informs us that the issue of long hair for men, or veils for women in church, no longer applies because the culture has changed. But regarding some clear directions in Scripture concerning behaviour, different conclusions may be reached by persons accepting the Bible's authority. Capital punishment for murder is one example. What of the wide range of human sexuality matters, heterosexual, homosexual, marriage? Can we still read off every single text dealing with these issues as determinative today without distinction or qualification? There is much concentration today on verses relating to homosexual acts, with many but not all very sure of their clear directions. Yet there is not equal certainty about prohibitions relating to women's menstruation times. Why, and by what criteria, are distinctions made?

A second principle, and one that derives from the first, is the concept of development. We see development within the Bible, including the New Testament. Inspired Apostles grew in knowledge of the significance of the Christ-event, his life, death and resurrection. For instance, they grew in knowledge in regard to circumcision and the keeping of the Law of Moses, and thus of the place of Gentile believers. And to the end of their ministry, some had wider and some narrower views. In the process of growth they could make mistakes, disagree among themselves. So development of the implications of what had earlier been revealed went on.

Development of understanding of God's revelation still goes on. The canon of Scripture is complete. No further Scriptures can add to those writings, not the Koran or the Book of Mormon or any other book. But though the canon is closed, development of understanding of its teachings, and drawing out of its implication, cannot be halted. The doctrine of the Trinity is a development of what is found in Scripture. The ordained ministry, as we have it in different branches of the Church universal, represents variations in development - showing that Christians do not always agree in development. The ultimate abolition of slavery was a development of scriptural ideas, resisted at first by many Christians. In the New Testament the institution of slavery is not challenged. No instruction for its abolition is given. Christian slaves and Christian masters are to behave in a Christ-like way within the institution. But eventually, in later centuries, when the Christian conscience, influenced by biblical insights, and indeed that of non-Christians too, awakens to the iniquity of the system, and the times are ripe, abolition can be effected. Many Christians have seen the ordination of women similarly as a development of biblical insights for which the time has come - but more of that later!

The third principle may be called that of congruity. All the truth we discern in Scripture must be congruous with all the truth discovered in creation and the history of humanity. We recognise here the indivisibility of all truth. All truth is God's truth, so we must aim for congruity in our understanding of it. We must not be content to keep different realms of truth in distinct compartments in the mind, unrelated and unreconciled. I find James Denney still relevant here. 'The doctrine of God, in the very nature of the case, is related to everything that enters into our knowledge; all our world depends on him; and hence it follows that a systematic presentation of the doctrine of God involves a general view of the world through God... All that man knows - of God and the world - must be capable of being constructed into one, coherent intellectual whole... The world is all of a piece; man's mind is all of a piece; and those easy and tempting solutions of the hardest problems which either arrange the world, or the activities of the mind, in compartments, having no communication with each other, are simply to be rejected.'[16]

A recent study of Richard Hooker, the sixteenth-century theologian with a major influence on Anglican thought ever since, reveals support for this approach to truth. Kenneth A. Locke in an article in *Anvil* (vol 14 no. 3 1997) drawing on Hooker's Laws of Ecclesiastical Polity writes: 'Hooker rejects the notion that scripture is and must be treated as the only source of human wisdom and knowledge. To limit oneself solely to the scriptures is to cut oneself off from the many other ways God imparts his will to humanity.' (referring to passages in Laws). 'Again, Hooker's respect for human reason and his belief that God may be known through ways other than scripture reveals the strong incarnational bent of his theology.' Locke adds a caveat that for salvation Hooker sees the Bible as the only source and guide.

Mark Noll quotes Jonathan Edwards, the outstanding mid-eighteenth-century Evangelical, as maintaining that true knowledge was 'the consistency and agreement of our ideas with the ideas of God' ... 'all the arts and sciences, the more they are perfected, the more they issue in divinity, and coincide with it, and appear to be part of it'.[17] Christians need to affirm these truths with renewed confidence in post-modernist days when objective truth is denied and relativism

---

16. *Studies in Theology,* James Denney, 1895, pp. 1 & 4
17. op. cit., p. 50

rules - everyone deciding what is true for them. But the relevance of this principle of congruity to interpretation of Scripture also needs to be seen. A denial of it is evident when apparently intelligent Christians refuse to accept scientific and verifiable discoveries about the age of the Universe, and of this planet, about fossils, genetics, DNA similarities between species, and so on, preferring a literalist reading of Genesis 1, 2 and 3. To compartmentalise truth, or deliberately to refuse the attempt to integrate it, is to fail to honour the God of all truth with the mind. One area of human knowledge, continually advancing, which can enrich our understanding of truth in Scripture, is discovery relating to the human psyche. This contention should not be taken as suggesting the infallibility of scientific discoveries, but there are clearly established facts in which we are actually thinking God's thoughts after him.

THE PRINCIPLE OF AUTHORITY

The Evangelical claim for the Bible as our final authority in all matters of faith and conduct needs some unpacking. Clearly it testifies to the need for the Church and the human mind and will to be subject to God's Word. Though the Church, the People of God called and redeemed in both Old and New Covenants, existed in time before the Scriptures, it was itself brought into being by the divine Word. Created by the Word, it only remains true to the divine purpose as it lives by and is obedient to that Word as preserved in the Scriptures and rightly understood. So, while the Church has authority to adapt its ministry, worship and ordering of its life as it believes the Holy Spirit leads, it may not require of any, or itself teach as an article of faith or necessary requisite of salvation, anything which is not read in Scripture or may not be proved thereby (Articles of Religion,VI).

It is clear from these affirmations that, strictly speaking, our final authority is God. But because the Bible is the only record of the redeeming love of God, as opposed to what is revealed in Creation, because in the Bible alone God draws near to humanity in Christ Jesus and declares his will for our salvation, the Bible is the medium of his authority.

Humanity today is contemptuous of the authorities that formerly held sway and rejects them. Can we 'come of age', manage without a final authority? Fifty years ago, the convincing answer to that question came for me from P.T. Forsyth in his magisterial book, *The Principle of Authority*. He maintains that the principle of authority is ultimately the whole religious question, and that the Christian faith alone can provide an authority whose very nature creates freedom. Expounding his concept of authority, he is certain that authority cannot simply be external on the one hand, or simply objective on the other. 'A real authority', he says, 'is indeed within experience, but it is not the authority of experience; it is an authority for experience, it is an authority experienced.'[18] So the authority is nothing in us, but something in history, given to us. What is in us can only recognise it, and the conscience that now recognises it has been created by it.

Here it is useful to ask the question, Why do I believe? Why do I believe God is our final authority? Why do I believe salvation is mine through the death and resurrection of Jesus Christ? The answer Evangelicals readily give is: 'Because the Bible tells me so.' But that prompts a logically prior question: Why do I believe the Bible on these matters of faith? Forsyth would answer: 'Because God, the Holy God coming to mankind through Jesus Christ, redeeming and renewing through the Cross, coming to the soul, breaking it down in grace and restoring it in grace, has established his authority within.' The final authority, then, is not just God in the abstract, but the word of God in Christ, recorded in Scripture, subduing and liberating in the same act. Forsyth calls this the evangelical experience, though the adjective there is not a churchmanship label, but an indication of experience of the Gospel. Our authority is not just God, objectively over against us, but God in Christ, our Redeemer and Conqueror. This expression points to a fundamental aspect in the nature of authority. True authority is not only that which ought to rule a person, but which does in fact rule them. The Bible is called by Forsyth the sacrament of God's reality and power. His authority is objectively established there, but to be that which actually rules in the life of a person the Word of the Cross in its redeeming and regenerating power, must convict and evoke faith.

Members of the Church of England and all other Churches need to hear this clearly. The Christian faith is not just a matter of believing certain truths, not just a personal benefit from a certain style of worship, not just a feel-good factor from drawing aside into a sacred building, not even appreciating the company of Christians, but a life-changing matter of experiencing a saving God at the centre of one's being. The principle of authority is the experienced work of a Saviour.

---

18. *The Principle of Authority*, Independent Press, 1952, p. 75

TWO DIVISIVE ISSUES

Disagreement over the application of Scripture to issues facing the Church at the end of the twentieth century have been, and are, the ordination of women to the priesthood and homosexual activity. Division runs across the whole Church of England, and indeed the Anglican Communion, as well as Evangelicals. I do not intend a comprehensive treatment of either subject. On women's ordination I will simply offer my reflections on some 30 years of thought that led to strong support in the votes for it. On homosexual issues I will only offer a few considerations - I cannot claim any expertise.

Ordination of Women

In 1969 the Bishop of Manchester (William Greer) asked me to take over the chair of the Diocesan Council for Women's Ministry. At my first meeting I had to face the question: 'What do you think about the ordination of women?' It had not yet become a burning issue, except for a minority in the Church. I promised to give my mind to it. As an Evangelical, the principal study had to focus on headship. I soon became aware of the other arguments for and against, which I will touch upon in the next chapter on the General Synod.

It was in fact the need to examine what the Scriptures had to say about headship, whether it was God's unchanging will for men to be in the 'head' position, in the Church, that concentrated the mind on principles of interpretation of Scripture. A wide sweep of the Bible clearly reveals that a patriarchal system is common to all the cultures in which the Scriptures emerged. All the books appear to be written by men and, until Jesus began to make a difference, women were very much under male leadership, if not the property of men. Yet there are some notable exceptions in the Old and New Testaments. Deborah (in Judges), Huldah (II Kings), Phoebe, Priscilla, Lydia were in leading positions. The early chapters of Genesis seem to offer insights on the relationship of men and women. They are together in complementary parity in the image of God (Genesis 1:27). In the second story of creation in Chapter 2, companionship and partnership in marriage is the heart of the matter. The woman being a 'help' does not indicate subordination, for the same word is used of God elsewhere. Only when we come to Chapter 3 and the Fall does the notion of subordination arise, and then as a dire consequence of sin. I could not see that so far as Genesis is concerned, the subordination or subjection of woman to man is a fundamental part of God's purpose for humanity.

It is with Paul, principally, that exegesis of the Bible's headship teaching becomes more difficult. Taken at face value, our English versions of I Corinthians 11: 3-16 appear to subordinate women to men, or at least wives to husbands, but everything depends on what Paul means by 'head' - the head of woman is man, the head of man is Christ, the head of Christ is God. I was convinced by the commentaries of F.F. Bruce[19] and C.K. Barrett[20] that head means source. That makes sense, in that following Genesis 2 the source of woman was the man, and man has his source or origin in Christ, the Eternal Word, and the source of Christ is God the Father. I was aware that some people opposing this interpretation had ranged through all the uses of the Greek word for head and found very few indicating source. But, though writing in Greek, Paul's mind was steeped in Hebrew thought and terminology. And in Hebrew the directing centre of the personality was not in the head, as we understand, but in the heart and guts. 'The head is not regarded as the seat of intellect controlling the body, but as the source of life', so the *New English Bible Dictionary*, published by the IVF in 1962 affirms (p.508). We talk of the head of a river, meaning its source, and indeed that use of the word in Hebrew is found in Genesis 2:10. To continue the *New Bible Dictionary* quotation, 'when man is spoken of as the head of the woman, the basic meaning of head as the source of all life and energy is predominant'.

It seems to me to be truer to our understanding of the Trinity to regard Paul's statement of God being the head of Christ as indicating source or origin rather than subordination. Christ in his incarnation certainly submits to the Father, but in his essential nature he is 'equal to the Father as touching his God-head' (Athanasian Creed), as the Prologue to John's Gospel and Philippians 2 make plain. C.K. Barrett says Paul is referring to the Father as the *fons divinitatis* (fount of deity).[21] As the Nicene Creed declares, the Son is God of (from) God.

There are other passages in the Epistles to weigh, but I believe an honest and credible interpretation, consistent with the view adopted above, is possible, which I have offered in other publications, for example *Biblical Headship and the Ordination of Women* (Grove Books, 1st Ed 1986; 2nd Ed 1988).

Homosexual Issues

I would prefer to dodge this matter. As mentioned earlier, I claim no expertise as I have not studied it thoroughly enough, and I want to avoid off-the-cuff dogmatic assertions. I took a long time working

---

19. F.F. Bruce, *1 & 2 Corinthians*, 1971
20. C.K. Barrett, *A Commentary on the First Epistle to the Corinthians*, 1968
21. op. cit.

out from Scripture what my attitude to women's ordination should be, and would be equally careful in this regard. But it is becoming an even more divisive issue than the ordination of women. What is happening in the Episcopal Church of the USA and in Britain will assume major proportions for the whole of the Anglican Communion at Lambeth 1998. Barring some miracle of understanding and agreement, the clash between some American and some African bishops, with others drawn in, could be damaging.

When at the age of eighteen, I joined the Royal Navy I had never really had to face the fact or implications of homosexual orientation or activity - being at a day Grammar School was obviously in those days different from a Public School. In the Navy I judge there was more talk about homosexual genital acts than actual practice. Nevertheless I developed a deep emotional aversion to the idea of homosexual relationships and physical expressions of them, even in milder forms, which remains with me to this day. To see two men kissing each other on the lips sends a shudder through me. So to take the strongest of lines would for me be very easy.

In recent years, however, as the issue, particularly in relation to clergy, has come to the fore I have had to admit that negative emotional reaction is not enough. No moral problems can be solved by the emotions alone, though I suspect that for many Christians they play a bigger part than they care to admit. I recognise that we must start with the Scriptures. There is not a great deal to go on, but taken at face value the direction appears very clear. At the time of writing I have not had the opportunity to study the different interpretations of the biblical evidence.

I have, however, already emphasised that, in the interpretation of revealed truth in Scripture, certain principles of interpretation are essential - the principle of a progressive revelation, the principle of development and the principle of congruity. These must apply in discovering God's will in this moral, human area as in every other challenge confronting us in modern life. The principle of congruity seems to me to bear particularly on this matter. On that I tentatively offer a few considerations needing to be weighed, accepted or discounted, before conclusions are reached.

In relating biblical truth, to the rest of truth so far as we can with confidence discern it, we must assert that the natural, divinely-intended purpose of sexuality is the bonding of a man and a woman in marriage with the possibility of procreation. It now seems pretty definite that human sexuality exists on a spectrum. In everyone there are male and female characteristics, in hormones, in genes. For most people there is no doubt to which part of the spectrum they belong, they are therefore heterosexual in their basic drive. But others are nearer the centre of the spectrum. Indeed, a very small number are so constituted that they are at war in their inner selves rebelling against the sex there were registered as at birth. Christian reaction cannot afford to dismiss these uncomfortable facts if we want to look at our problems with God's eyes.

Does, then, the fact of the sexuality spectrum inevitably mean that some are genetically determined as homosexually orientated? The answer may seem obvious, but I raise it because I believe environmental causes may also be recognised. Unfortunate relationships of child with mother or father, which I would take could eventually be 'remedied', may lead to homosexual inclination. Then, it also seems true that young people in puberty and teenage, while their sexual sense is developing, are the target of propaganda and active attention by gay or lesbian activists. There can be nothing but condemnation for such exploitation of the young.

If these considerations have weight, what is to be the Christian attitude to those born and unalterably homosexual? First and foremost, acceptance as with every other child of God. Homophobia must be eschewed, whatever our emotional disposition. Then, I would affirm the possibility of long-term relationships with friends of the same sex gladly accepted within the love of God. Now the crunch questions arise.

In what ways may two persons of the same sex, deeply committed to one another, express their affection? At this point most people appear to assume that sodomy and sodomy alone will be the expression - if they are men, but what if they are women? Suppose there is genital expression short of sodomy, oral intercourse or mutual masturbation, for instance, does that make any difference? In answering that question I imagine emotional reactions come strongly into play with many heterosexuals.

In my lifetime I have known deeply respected Evangelical clergy who were obviously homosexually orientated, who had young men, perhaps students, or one man friend, living in the vicarage. In decades past folk, at any rate in Evangelical circles, did not seem to subject them to suspicious comment. Years ago in my own parish there lived a retired priest, mostly confined to the house, who shared his home with a man from one of our congregations. In the other congregation two women unrelated by blood who shared one home. They are all dead now but as a pastor I never thought I had the right to question their relationships.

That brings us to pastoral policy bishops should follow with homosexual clergy. If a man is thought to be, or in confidence admits to be, homosexual and in a long-term relationship, has the bishop the right or the duty to probe concerning what goes on behind his front door? If so, on what grounds, and what has changed since former days? No doubt the bishop could be anxious about possible scandal, but should he bar the man from ordination just on the basis of a possibility? The same questions would apply to women. No one can assume that all activity between a man and a woman in a marriage accords with everyone else's standards. But if they are Christians we leave it to their conscience before God how they conduct their intimate life.

There is nothing in Scripture by way of a code of practice for sexual activity between a husband and wife. Couples may vary considerably in what they find acceptable and desirable. Would a bishop be justified in similarly leaving a homosexual pair to their conscience? What he and the rest of the Church will have an eye to is the scandal that might arise. The evidence suggests it does not arise in every case. If it does, then clearly disciplinary action must be taken, not on the basis of mere gossip but with fair, pastoral examination. I am very uneasy about double standards in the Church. Certainly those ordained to leadership or, for that matter, laity in leadership positions must be "examples to the flock". The ordination service, following Scripture, makes that very clear. But there cannot be two standards of Christian behaviour, one for leaders, one for the rest. I wonder how many of those taking the strongest line about homosexual clergy are prepared to tackle directly the intimate lifestyle of ordinary lay members in a committed relationship, by interrogating them?

In (self) righteous indignation some Evangelicals have asserted that no homosexual in same-sex genital activities can expect to be in the Kingdom of God. Are they equally prepared to exclude from the Kingdom those who are jealous, envious, bad-tempered, quarrelsome? (Galatians 5:16-25). I believe some Christians need to ask themselves why sins touching our sexuality arouse fiercer reaction than other sins.

None of these considerations, individually or collectively, should be read as advocating one line or another. All too easily parts, individual sentences, can be extracted from an article or speech, particularly by the media, to highlight a controversy deemed newsworthy. Because any venture into this emotion-stirring debate may easily be misrepresented, I emphasise these are relevant considerations to be faced. But unless they are fully addressed, along with most careful interpretation of the Scriptures, a credible Christian solution for these days will not emerge. I emphasise these days, because it must be remembered that the Christian Church down the centuries has a faulty record in dealing with sexuality issues. We have only to think of attitudes to women in earlier times, not least by the Fathers of the Church, or in modern times of stumbling efforts to come to terms with methods of contraception. And in such matters Scripture was used, or abused. Let Evangelicals in particular remember what has been drawn earlier from the book by Mark Noll about applying the mind with integrity. And, within that integrity, let them ask why they do get so emotionally worked up about sexual matters when the Scriptures list so many breaches of God's will for humanity which do not similarly excite their righteous wrath.

EVANGELICALS AND THE CHURCH

What do Evangelicals want for the Church of England? There is a prior question to that: What is their doctrine of the Church? - a question to which I will come in due course. But for the present I wish to concentrate on attitudes to the Church of England. In the doldrums of the second quarter of this century, probably the most positive Evangelical attitude was that already mentioned - 'the best boat to fish out of'. Towards other traditions in the Church, particularly Anglo-Catholics and 'Modernists', suspicion and alienation prevailed. For the Church as a whole the fond hope was for a re-run of the sixteenth-century Reformation. Now that so much has changed, growth in numbers, in theological competence, in influence, what do they want to see? We can get into that question by examining their attitudes to other Anglican traditions. Are they really content to live with them, to co-operate with them to the fullest extent short of denial of what is deemed to be essential to the truth, and to learn from them in mutual trust? The last point there sharpens up to a challenge I would put to those most critical of the present state of affairs in the Church. It is whether they believe they have a monopoly of the truth and whether they wish to see the whole Church of England Evangelical. The challenge may be regarded as unfair and a misrepresentation of their position, but it does sometimes seem that nothing will satisfy short of synods, bishops, dioceses and the other traditions following a firm Evangelical agenda. The same might be said, of course, of groups in other traditions, but they are not in the compass of this chapter.

In my early days on BCMS General Committee there was a tense debate on whether the society, committed to Conservative Evangelical principles, could conscientiously embark on a policy of 'diocesanization'. It meant putting our missionaries at the disposal of a bishop and his diocese overseas for deployment instead of sending them to existing BCMS stations, as hitherto. A positive answer, reached by a majority, with some still opposed, was only possible by giving an assurance that the only diocese to which it would apply was Central Tanganyika where the bishop, Alfred Stanway, an Australian, was 'one of us', a Conservative Evangelical. In the light of at least thirty or more years, and the change of attitudes and policy, that debate now lacks credibility, but to recall it has relevance for today's disagreements.

At the 150th anniversary of the Evangelical Alliance, Archbishop George Carey urged Evangelicals to avoid believing they alone have the whole truth about God, and that therefore the whole Church of Jesus Christ should be like them. He acknowledged that their witness and life in the Church was more extensive and confident than it had ever been, but they needed to avoid past attitudes that equated Evangelicalism with the 'true Church'.

The Church of England, and the Anglican Communion, is a broad Church, comprehensive of the traditions that have developed over nearly five centuries. The clock cannot be turned back to any former age. No Church can do that. Developments within its life are not necessarily wholly good, even good developments may have flaws, but a Church that does not relate to a changing world, while holding on to 'the faith once delivered' is a dead Church.

MY OWN DEBT

I intend now to give my own answer, arrived at over the years, to the question about attitudes to the Church of England and its different traditions. Evangelicals cannot have a monopoly of truth. No one tradition can comprehend the sum of God's purposes and will. I am now less sure of some things I was certain about when I began in the ministry, but more sure of the cardinal truths as Evangelicals see them, which I have tested in ministry and personal pilgrimage. But the need for a humble reverence before the awful majesty of God and the mystery of his ways, and the recognition that the more one knows the more one realises there is far more beyond, has grown with the years. I also recognise that God's people can never be fitted into one mould, whether in worship, spirituality or approach to the truth. There are different traditions in the Church because for one reason, people need there to be.

I have learned from contact with liberal (for want of a better word) Christians. Their openness to new directions, new ways at looking at our theological and ecclesiastical heritage, has been a challenge, a stimulus to using the mind. Every generation brings new problems and new opportunities for the Church, as the world and society changes. It is not enough for the Church to stamp its foot and shout old answers, whatever truth they contained. Without any disloyalty to revealed truth answers appropriate to the situation are called for. Even when disagreeing with liberal expressions of faith there has been benefit in the challenge to rethink and honest debate has often revealed substantial agreement on essentials. Scratch a liberal and find underneath someone quite conservative, is often a cliche with some truth.

DEBT TO CATHOLICS

I value also what I have received from the Catholic tradition in the Church of England, despite firm disagreement, for instance, with a section of it on the ordination of women. On the sacraments I have moved considerably from the mainly negative expression of their meaning surrounding me in my youth - 'the sacraments are not this and not that'. I do not say my sacramental theology would get a hundred per cent marks in Catholic circles, but I have learned a high doctrine of the sacraments, as I have tried to explain in the previous chapter.

For Evangelicals in the past, and for many of them still today, a description of the ordained ministry entirely in functional terms was sufficient. The ordained were to preach, pastor, lead, counsel. They could at times in fact act like little popes in their parish, but any thought of Catholic understanding of the priesthood was repudiated. I learned in friendly acquaintance with Catholics that a purely functional understanding of the ordained ministry was inadequate. As my appreciation of the value of the sacramental principle in God's dealings with humanity, more evident in Scripture than previously recognised, developed, so I saw its relevance to the ministry. I can best illustrate this by reference to a book published in 1970.

It was a joint production by four authors, two Anglo-Catholics, and two Evangelicals (Eric Mascall and Graham Leonard, Jim Packer and Colin Buchanan). At the time there was some shared opposition to the Anglican-Methodist proposals for unity. The authors offered an alternative set of proposals for a united Church of England, which came to nothing. But the first part of the book contained their theological argument on Scripture and Tradition, God and his Grace, Church and Sacraments, Episcopacy and Ministry - Evangelicals and Catholics in total harmony nearly thirty years ago! Indeed they say in the Introduction: 'We cannot accept any suggestion that there is something dishonourable in men who have apparently been opposed to each other seeking to discover how far this is really so'.[22] And they go on to declare, 'we are all four committed to every line in the book ... and we are determined that no wedge should be driven between us'. I am not sure whether Graham Leonard, now in the Roman Church, would hold entirely to everything in the book, but I value what he put his name to then.

I sum up what the authors say about ordained ministry with this quotation, 'All ministerial oversight embodies an authority which stems from Christ as Head of the Church, and witnesses to his Lordship over his Church, including its ministers themselves. And we may further say that, though New Testament presbyter-bishops were not Apostles, yet the authority of their office was identical with the authority exercised by the Apostles - namely, the personal authority of the Lord.'[22] Witnessing to the Lordship of Christ, embodying an authority stemming from him, those words describe ministerial oversight as a sign, a God-given sign, a sacrament. They do not, as I see it, make ordination a sacrament comparable with the two dominical sacraments, though the action of laying-on-of-hands with prayer is a sacramental action, but are indicating that the presence and ministry of those ordained in the Church signify Christ's lordship. The authors continue: 'So there is more than simply a difference of function between ordained ministers and other churchmen and the assertion of (Paul) Tillich that a minister is simply a layman with a special job to do, who differs from other laymen only by his professional training, cannot be accepted.'[23]

The sign emphasis can, I believe, be legitimately carried further in accordance with New Testament teaching on authorised ministers. The ordained are to be a sign to the rest of the Church of its witnessing, reconciling, serving and pastoral responsibilities, a reminder in visible form (a sacrament) of what the whole Church is to be about. The whole Church is to witness, to be a reconciling agency, to serve within and outside the fellowship, to pastor and care for all members. Contrary to a popular misconception from the past, it is not just the parson's job. Ministers themselves, in accepting the sign their

---

22. *Growing into Union*, S.P.C.K., 1970, p. 74.
23. Ibid., p. 74

ordination gives them, must remember that the authority they signify is the authority of self-sacrificing service, demonstrated by Christ in the role of a slave washing his quarrelling disciples' feet.

In 1984 Garry Bennett, a fellow member of the General Synod, invited me to bring a couple of Evangelicals to New College, Oxford, to share with him and two other Catholics in unhurried discussion on our understanding of Priesthood. A considerable degree of agreement emerged, largely reflected in the foregoing statements. Two years later the General Synod debated the Faith and Order Advisory Group's report The Priesthood of the Ordained Ministry. It was what I had gained from the Growing in Union book and that New College discussion that led me to take a somewhat different line from other Evangelicals in that debate, but in support of three Evangelicals in FOAG.

Calls for Lay Presidency by Evangelicals do not accord with the understanding of ordained ministry outlined above. The need, urgent in some places, which it would address is not in dispute. Where congregations are denied the Eucharist because of shortage of priests, or one man has to dash round two or three congregations arriving in time for the Thanksgiving prayer, or in times of sickness or holiday having to import a stranger priest, dissatisfaction is justified. Why, it is asked, may not a lay person be authorised to preside? Presumably it would be someone accepted as a lay leader, to some degree associated with the parish priest in the managing and pastoring of the congregation. So, the logical step might be to incorporate such persons into the Local Non-stipendiary Ministry. LNSM is already well established in a growing number of dioceses. A prerequisite should be that the Incumbent already has gathered a team of lay leaders, sharing responsibilities. The person concerned would need a sense of vocation to the ministry, but the initiative for the vocation may come from the Church as well as from inner conviction. The LNSM solution should never be just for meeting Eucharistic demands, but to make more effective the ministry in the parish, getting away from the one-man-band pattern.

Clearly Readers would be among those considered. Authorisation to preside, presumably by the bishop, seems to be on the way to ordination, in that the bishop is sharing his presidential responsibilities. Training for LNSM is currently organised differently from that in colleges and courses. Advocating this solution is not, for Evangelicals, on the basis that an ordained priest has special powers to effect a valid sacrament. Rather, because the Eucharist is where the local church is sacramentally identified as the Body of Christ in that place, the ordained leadership, representative of the bishop as the focus of unity and representative of the priesthood of the believers gathered there, is the right agent to preside. For the ordained ministry is guardian of the teaching, pastoral oversight and discipline of the Church.

The third area in which I have appreciated Catholic emphasis is Ecclesiology, understanding of the Church. That I will come to shortly, but before I do I will comment on what I find unconvincing in the Anglo-Catholic tradition. It is in the realm of Ritual. I am referring to a range of ritual actions that have spread widely across the Church of England since the nineteenth century. I appreciate that some Catholic clergy, influenced by modern liturgical studies, not to mention Roman Catholic priests for that matter, have simplified ritual activities.

RITUAL HABITS

There appears to be an attitude that the more elaborate the ritual the greater the reverence. I fully accept that some personalities are helped in worship by ritual more than I am. And the way some Evangelical worship, almost devoid of any ritual, is conducted, reverence is a casualty, the faults lying with both clergy and laity - why do some of the latter have to gossip while the administration is going on?

Ritual, I submit, should be unobtrusive, should not draw attention to individuals, whether officiants or assistants, but above all should be expressive of truth in worship. On the last point, I recognise different understandings of aspects in worship, particularly in the thanksgiving prayer in the Eucharist, and thus there will be different practices. But I question excessive waving about of hands. Some celebrants in the Eucharist never have their hands still for more than a few seconds, employing them in exaggerated gestures. When Series II and III services of Holy Communion came in, a Catholic friend, an acknowledged liturgist well versed in the early Church liturgies, instructed me that consecration of the elements is not by the priest waving his hands over them, but is by act of thanksgiving said by the president on behalf of the whole congregation. Hence, ever since, the manual acts of the *Book of Common Prayer* have not been prescribed ritual.

There are four actions in the consecration: taking of the Bread and Wine, for which a visible act is obviously appropriate; the giving of thanks - a verbal declaration; the breaking of the bread, inevitably to be acted and seen; and the distribution. Would not that four-fold structure be better grasped by confining ritual expressions to the four points? I appreciate the value of the sign of the Cross for many

Church folk, reminding them of their baptised status and commitments, but is it overdone by some? What is it actually implying if repeated frequently in a service?

I have no problem with turning east in the Creed, if it is a reminder of an early Church practice and worshippers know why it happens, but I cannot see a true reason for a special act of reverence to an altar. Of course, if a Catholic sees it as a place of a localised presence of Christ, and also there is a tabernacle for the reserved sacrament, I understand the ritual. But I cannot share that understanding. There is a whole debate here about sacred objects and places. I have no problem with set-apart, consecrated, material buildings and furniture, but in a Reformed approach are the lectern bearing the Bible, the pulpit for the exposition of the Scriptures, the font, to be less regarded with reverence than the holy table? I hope I am expressing a Reformed Catholic point of view and not merely a negative Protestant objection.

A last question on ritual! What is the justification for quite elaborate ritual attending the reading of the Gospel in the Eucharist? I am thinking of a procession led by a crucifer to the chancel steps with elaborate ceremony, candles, book-carrier and three-fold sign of the Cross by the reader. We are bidden to say, 'This is the Gospel of Christ', and often, but not always, it includes reported words of Christ. Leaving aside the question whether they are the very words or a summary by the evangelist, are not other parts of Scripture also the Gospel of Christ? In the Epistles are explanations of the death and resurrection of Christ, the heart of God's saving work, which could not be explored till after Pentecost. The Gospel is not only the deed, in Christ crucified, but the Word giving the divine explanation through the Apostles. Are not many chapters in the Epistles, as well as sermons in the Acts, as clear presentations of the Gospel as passages from the Gospels? And the Gospels themselves are not just accounts of the life and teaching of Christ but also contain post-Pentecost interpretations - witness the Prologue to John's Gospel. None of this is an attempt to start a campaign. It is to say there are some legacies of the Anglo-Catholic movement I consider unhelpful, and to plead that in defining our ritual in worship we avoid the fussy and ensure it expresses truth.

Having expressed these personal observations on the ritual legacy of Anglo-Catholicism, I welcome, in contrast, the possibility of Catholic renewal. For too long the energies of Catholicism in the Church of England have been largely absorbed in opposing developments - ordination of women, Church unity schemes with non-Roman denominations, re-marriage of divorcees in church. They would strongly maintain it had to be; they had no option. Nevertheless, when a tradition in the Church is too long on the defensive, it not only inhibits positive theological thinking about evolving situations but inculcates a sense of marginalisation. I have suggested this was the experience of Conservative Evangelicals between the wars. May Catholics take heart from the developments Evangelicals have experienced since the last war, and thus contribute to the total well-being of the Church of England. In the emergence of Affirming Catholicism is hope of renewal, though a substantial number of Catholics at present do not agree.

ECCLESIOLOGY

When Archbishop Runcie challenged the Evangelical Anglican Conference at Caister in 1988 to develop the understanding of the Church, he was touching a neglected study among Evangelicals. The general attitude in former decades was to concentrate on the mystical, invisible definition as the company known only to God of those truly regenerate, and to play down the importance of the visible, institutional Church. Indeed membership of the institutional Church was often disparaged - it could lead to false assurance. I have often listened to sermons emphasising it is not enough to be baptised, to be confirmed, to receive Communion, and so on. The motive may have been commendable but over-emphasis on the negative was, to say the least, questionable.

Shared insights with Catholics have certainly led to a richer understanding of the visible Church through the centuries, with its ordered life structured on the historic ministry, and defined by and administering the sacraments. The Church is both a divine company and a human institution openly recognised in the world. While the New Testament recognises - and Anglican formularies reflect the fact - the possibility of the institutional Church being a mixed company, wheat and tares, the general assumption in the Epistles is that those baptised, those in the eucharistic fellowship, are in the Body of Christ. To be in Christ is ipso facto to be in the visible Church. The Church is not an adjunct to the Gospel, a company a person 'joins' after conversion. The Church is part of the Gospel.

Holding fast to these New Testament principles, however, does not provide us with a full ecclesiology for today. Jesus certainly did not prescribe a full understanding of the Church for all time and did not lay down a structure of ordained ministry. He promised his Spirit to guide his Church, and after Pentecost a process of development went on. A wide range of gifts and ministries emerged, but gradually the oversight, episcope, at first exercised by the Apostles was delegated by appointment. The development did not finish with the passing of the apostolic age. Episcopal oversight by bishops in key churches, sharing responsibility with presbyters and deacons in surrounding churches, became an established pattern. The bishops were to be guardians of the apostolic faith, a focus of unity and a transmitter of authorisation in ordination.

The authors of Growing into Union provide a strong justification of the historic episcopate and development of the three-fold order, not as something absolutely necessary or as commanded by Christ, but as 'fitting', to exhibit the ministry of Christ in special fullness.[24] 'The historic episcopate - which, as such, must be sharply distinguished from the corrupt prelatical forms it has too often taken - is a pattern of apostolic ministry. It is not the visible Church's heart, nor the principle of its circulatory system, but (if the phrase is not over bold) it is a part of the visible Church's developed bone-structure - no more, and no less.'[25] 'As president of the Eucharist and representative both of the universal Church to his own diocese and of his diocese to the universal Church, the bishop appears as a constitutive and focal element of the Church's visible oneness, just as Christ is the constitutive and focal element of that spiritual oneness which the Creed predicates of the Church, not by sight, but by faith.'[26] So, they maintain, the historic episcopate should be maintained and valued.

There are many reasons why I am glad to belong to the Anglican Church, but one of them is its retention of its historic heritage and continuity with the Church down the ages, with its ordering in dioceses for which the bishop is a focus of unity. I have a criticism of a trend among Evangelical clergy; there often seems a lack of appreciation of that heritage and over-emphasis on the 'here and now' of the Church's life. To be 'with it' seems a matter of priority. One manifestation is the abandoning of canonical vestments for lounge suits. It is a second-order matter, but what does it signify? There is no difference between the ordained and lay membership? That new members will be put off by robes as a relic of former times? I personally do not accept either of those points. In other realms of life, authorised persons are accepted to be in a certain dress - police, judges, barristers, the military, mayors and so on - are any put off? I suspect a fashion has developed on inadequate grounds, and it is

---

24. op., cit., pp. 75-80
25. Ibid., p. 77
26. Ibid., p. 76

symptomatic of a failure in Evangelical congregations to pass on the value of the Anglican heritage, particularly to new members.

On the basis of the ecclesiological approach briefly outlined above, I see certain consequences relevant for Evangelicals at the present time. First, not all the questions about the Church can be answered directly from the New Testament. There is no going back to the first century. The Holy Spirit has been with the Church for the past two thousand years and, while the Church has often been disobedient and failed, God has remained faithful and his Spirit has continued to inspire and guide. All that has not been contrary to Scripture can be valued. Then, in the Anglican tradition the basic unit of the Church is the diocese, a number of churches in fellowship with the bishop. The local congregation is in the frontline, the place of witness, nurture, worship and service for most Christians and most of the time - there are also occasions for the essential Church activities in the wider Church. But it should be remembered that diocesan people, including the bishop, and agencies are also engaged in frontier action. All the areas of human life - work, civic organisation, community services (education, health, security, social support) - are not confined within a parish's territory. The powers 'that be' must be addressed with Gospel imperatives; society at national and regional level needs to be challenged with the demands of the Kingdom of God. We are not congregationalist in our ecclesiology. Very few, if any, parishes are self-sufficient for maintenance of ministry or in resources to engage, every aspect of the Church's responsibilities. Even the wealthiest and biggest congregations, tempted to think they can meet all their needs and, further, subsidise others, still benefit from diocesan structures and resources. They have confirmations, help with schools, legal services, pastoral care when needed. Because dioceses in England, and elsewhere, are generally large, the deanery as a smaller fellowship of local churches within the larger diocesan fellowship is an appropriate way of co-ordinating the Church's responsibilities.

I regard the deliberate withholding of parish shares in the diocesan budget as a failure in Christian fellowship. Of course, diocesan and national budgets have to be stringently related only to essentials. And those essentials need to be established by consent of parishes through representatives. In my experience, dioceses are making great endeavours to match up to those requirements. But it seems to me a deficient understanding of the Church to withhold financial support because some aspects of diocesan policy are not approved of by a parish. If a parish believes it cannot meet its requested share in the budget, I would question whether it should continue to be an independent parochial unit, or be rather a part of a larger parochial grouping. I am sensitive to the fact that sometimes huge fabric costs descend on a congregation, or there may be a need to retain a poorly attended church for pastoral reasons in a remote district, and so special help should be provided. Maybe twenty years as an Area Dean has inclined me to be tougher with parishes defaulting on payments than bishops feel they can be. In the 'middle-management' role one can be more informed about parishes' willingness and ability to pay, and wrong perceptions that prevail.

Finally, I see no justification in Anglican ecclesiology for calls for a Third Province from those, Evangelicals among them, dissatisfied with the present situation in the Church of England. To give allegiance to a supposed Province, superimposed on and/or permeating the two Provinces of Canterbury and York, being no longer in fellowship with one's diocesan bishop, is, I submit, a negation of Anglicanism. The Provincial Episcopal Visitors, 'flying bishops', come near to such a negation - some say it is a negation - but at least they work with the diocesan bishops and some responsibilities remain for the latter towards all parishes in their dioceses. If a Third province is seen by any as the only way they can remain in the Church of England, then I think they should examine their position and choose between being Anglicans and some other Church affiliation.

For an Anglican understanding of the Church, I confess myself much in debt to Bishop Stephen Sykes and his book, *Unashamed Anglicanism*.[27] His arguments, chiefly in Part II, that there is a distinctive Anglican doctrine of the Church, are to me totally convincing. I cannot attempt to summarise them, but I warmly recommend their study by Evangelicals. I will return to this matter in Chapter 5.

A CRISIS FOR EVANGELICAL COLLEGES

An important development for Anglican evangelicals arose from a crisis at the end of the 1960s involving two colleges in Bristol, Clifton Theological College and Tyndale Hall. Their separate existence within the same city was the result of a split in the 1930s. The Principal of the Bible Churchmen's Missionary and Theological College, founded by BCMS, had been Dr Sydney Carter. Unresolved differences on policy led to him resigning and heading a new college not far away, with himself as first Principal. After the war relations between the two Colleges improved. In the mid 1950s there arose the possibility of uniting the Bristol Colleges. The vision owed much to John Wenham

---

27. Darton, Longman, Todd, 1995

at Tyndale Hall. Representatives of both Councils, encouraged by the respective staff meetings, accepted the vision, but it was subsequently abandoned by both Councils. Nevertheless, out of what John Wenham had envisaged came a substantial sharing of facilities - lecturing was shared, joint staff meetings held and library acquisitions harmonised. These developments were halted in 1965, but then in the mid-1960s there came from outside the local situation increasing pressure for the colleges to consider uniting. There were too many places in the Theological Colleges overall for the number of ordinands coming forward. Two colleges, identical in principles of churchmanship and fundamental theological convictions, in one city no longer made sense. The House of Bishops, with whom responsibility for recognition of the colleges rests, was bound to tackle the situation.

In the late 1960s, therefore, the councils of the two colleges opened negotiations, and progress seemed likely to lead to success. But outside the two Councils all was not well. On the staff of Tyndale Hall were some members of outstanding academic calibre who became alarmed at the proposals for the structuring of the proposed united college. They had been witnesses of an earlier serious crisis affecting the staff at Clifton. Its council at the time was like those of other colleges self-appointed, with only the Principal from the members of staff serving on it, despite a request from other members to be able to attend. This put the Principal in a similar position to an Incumbent of a parish with his colleagues as curates, and junior curates at that - though a junior curate could at least be on the PCC. This kind of arrangement for a college staff did nothing to encourage gifted scholars making a career in theological education and specialising in their subjects. Tyndale Hall had itself lost two such members some years before, Dr Geoffrey Bromiley and Dr Philip Hughes, both of whom ended up in North America. Within the Clifton staff, the Vice-Principal, Alec Motyer, and his colleagues found this system of college government increasingly unacceptable and their unease was given as the reason for their dismissal in 1965. The Revds Peter Dawes (later Bishop) and Michael Farrer were also dismissed with Alec Motyer, and two other members of staff resigned in sympathy, the Revd Jim Innes and Dr Graham Windsor. Rightly, as is now recognised, they wished to have a proper share on the Council in the policy and administration of the college.

Around 1968 it became clear that the united College was to be structured in the old way. The following year a crucial factor came into play. By the constitution of Tyndale Hall the consent of the BCMS General Committee was necessary to any union with Clifton.

Canon William Leathem and I were members of the General and Executive Committees, both of us alarmed at the proposals now before BCMS. There may have been others, but the two of us talked much about the line to take. What complicated the matter was that some of the Tyndale Hall Council were on the BCMS Committee, and friends at that. The decisive meeting was to be in May 1969. Canon Leathem decided to vacate the chair in favour of the President of BCMS, Sir Norman Anderson. The structure of government in the proposed college was not the only cause for concern. A changed Basis of Belief from that of BCMS, to which Tyndale Hall was committed, was disturbing some members on the General Committee. And it appeared that preliminary proposals for the staffing of the united college could end up with a less academically qualified staff than was available already in the two colleges. The seriousness of the step of seeking to persuade the BCMS Committee to withhold approval of the merger on the proposed terms weighed heavily - certainly it was one of the hardest decisions I have had to make. Ending of the merger negotiations could result in the loss of both Colleges, and indeed of the Women's College, Dalton House, the sole surviving women's institution recognised for training Anglican Parish Workers for the Inter-Diocesan Certificate, as well as missionaries for overseas. There was, however, another factor which could not be introduced into the debate in the B.C.M.S. Committee.

In January of that year I had learned from Dr Jim Packer that his time with Latimer House was coming to an end and he saw no future in England for his main vocation in life of ministerial training. He would probably go to the North American Continent. In confidence I asked his reaction to the possibility of returning to Bristol in a leading role, if some option other than the proposed merger opened up. Fully recognising the tentative nature of our ideas he expressed warm interest.

The result of the lengthy and emotional debate in the BCMS Committee was a vote to withhold approval of the merger. As a consequence the whole of the Tyndale Hall Council felt it had no other option but to resign, the principal, Canon J. Stafford Wright, included. Before resignation took effect, Jim Packer was invited to become the principal. I was asked to chair a working party to create a new structure for Tyndale Hall with Jim Packer and members of staff and others participating. The working party soon became the new Council. The reorganisation, in which Jim Packer played a dominant role, continued through 1970. At his invitation, Alec Motyer returned to Bristol to be deputy principal. All the staff would serve on the council, an Association of all wishing to support the college would be formed, from whose members some would be elected to serve on the council. Thus the staff would have collegial responsibility, like fellows of a university college, and have a more secured future, to develop their scholastic gifts.

Meanwhile the House of Bishops was not the only body to be anxious about an excess of places in colleges. The Church Assembly in February 1970 asked the Bishops to prepare a report. A working group, chaired by the Bishop of St Albans, Robert Runcie, presented a report to the colleges in October of that year. It could not dispel the growing anxiety across the colleges, indicating as it did the need for some closures. Indeed the original reports recommended withdrawal of recognition from Tyndale Hall, and the merger of Clifton with Wycliffe. There was no hope of that being in Bristol. Dalton House, the BCMS Women's College, indicated that the closing of the men's Colleges in Bristol, robbing them of teaching support, would effectively close them.

In the Spring 1971 sessions of the General Synod, Bishop Runcie spoke of his group's 'principal desire to keep a college in Bristol' by a union of Tyndale and Clifton... 'if there could be a new start based on reconciliation'; of the latter he still saw insufficient evidence. So the bishops were offering a last chance for continuation of theological training for Anglicans in Bristol by amalgamation of the three colleges. He recommended teaching staffs and existing Councils to offer resignation and the forming of a negotiating body. Later in the debate, in my first speech in General Synod, I urged the Bishops to allow time for another attempt at reconciliation and merger, for which I could report wholehearted support from the newly formed Tyndale Association and from substantial numbers of former students of both colleges as well as present students. I also indicated the desire of Dalton House, the BCMS Women's College, to participate in negotiations. It was now known that the Bishop of Bristol, Oliver Tomkins, was ready to chair a negotiating body. He was to play a decisive, tremendous part, at all times characterised by good humour and patience, in the prolonged negotiations. It is hardly possible to exaggerate the debt Evangelicals owe to Oliver Tomkins during those many months. It was a privilege to witness his wise chairmanship.

From the start and for a long time the clash between the new Tyndale and the old Clifton approaches to college organisation held up progress. There were also strong differences over pooling of assets, especially buildings. Some on the Clifton Trust, not themselves on the negotiating body, were reluctant to hand over their property, and so charged a rent through the early years. BCMS likewise felt obliged to hang on to the Tyndale site till sure of the principles on which the new College would be established, but gave its use free of charge. Eventually, however, it was agreed to form an Association (to be known as Trinity Association) from which there would be election of some members to the new Council, where they would join all the staff of the new Trinity College. Much controversy focused on staff appointments, and particularly on the post of Principal. From the Clifton side there was opposition to Jim Packer. Suggestions by the Clifton delegates were unacceptable to the Tyndale and Dalton House members. Eventually the Clifton members agreed to the appointment of Alec Motyer as Principal - a delicious irony - and Trinity, Bristol, was born with its leadership vested in Alec Motyer along with Jim Packer as Associate Principal, Joyce Baldwin (from Dalton House) as Dean of Women and Gervais Angel (from Clifton) as Dean of Studies. To the praise of God the College celebrated its 25th anniversary in 1996.

What is the significance of this complex and at times traumatic story - apart from ensuring a successful college in Bristol? It marks a turning point in ordination training in the Church of England. Other Colleges also reformed, some enlisting the support of, and establishing some form of accountability towards, an Association of supporters. Teaching staffs were strengthened both in numbers and academic qualifications, thus enabling individuals to specialise and engage in research. With larger staffs, colleges could offer courses to students other than Anglican ordinands, many from Third World countries. Whereas student numbers before the 1970s were around forty per college, later they were generally well over 100 in evangelical colleges. It is arguable that the growing influence of Evangelicalism in the Church of England in the last twenty years owes much to the developments in the tradition's colleges, not least with their contribution to the growing strengths of evangelical theology. Out of deep division and struggles the Lord brought good.

EVANGELICALS AND EVANGELISM

I was born and nurtured in an Evangelical culture totally committed to evangelism through interdenominational campaigns - 'crusades' had not yet been adopted as their description. Indeed it was through that medium most conversions were expected. My father had taken part in two such campaigns by Fritz (later, Fred) and Arthur Wood (father of Bishop Maurice Wood) in Preston, one before World War I, one after. The brothers Wood were to found the National Young Life Campaign. Most of the Christians I knew of my father's generation had come to faith in those campaigns. One of my earliest memories is as a three-year-old being propelled across the stage of a theatre in Preston in 1926 with a bunch of red roses to present to La Marechale on the last night of her evangelistic campaign - she was the grandmother of my friend and bishop, the late Stanley Booth-Clibborn.

Nothing was more likely, then, that taking up an incumbency in 1954 in Bolton I should be much involved with a succession of such evangelistic events. They included Billy Graham Crusade Relays, a town-wide Crusade led by Eric Hutchings in 1958, and then the Billy Graham North of England Crusade in Manchester, 1961. Being on the Executive Committee of the latter, I had ample time and information to help my parish prepare to make maximum use of the opportunity. We had a number of counsellors prepared, others committed to the choir, and for five months beforehand visited every home in the parish each month with literature and an invitation to join us on a free coach journey any evening of the Crusade. Our folk worked and prayed diligently. In the twenty-one nights only thirteen non-church members accepted the invitation, and so far as we could tell none made a commitment to Christ. I fully accept that the experience for many other churches in that Crusade, and indeed in a number of subsequent similar events, including Mission England, was different. And I have already testified to the contribution of the early Billy Graham Crusades to the turning of the tide for Evangelicals in the Church of England.

The 1961 experience, however, forced me to think afresh about evangelism. Clearly there were sub-cultures then, and even more so now, apparently impervious to big event 'evangelism'. To take just one example, the working class culture, whose men hardly lift their horizons beyond work, if they have it, the working-men's club, Labour club or pub, a football match or bowls. It takes a mighty, revolutionary step for an individual man to step out of his peer group and even go into a church - except for rites of passage - let alone take a journey to an evangelistic event. How different from the middle-class suburban father used to taking independent action! Are there forms of evangelism for some sub-cultures that are more tribal than individualistic? In my visits to Sabah (previously North Borneo) I have been impressed by the policy of the Sabah Anglican Interior Mission among the animistic tribes of the interior. In any village approached, the aim is to convert the headman and after that to baptise the whole village, because whatever the headman's religion so is that of his village. Direct comparisons with England are out of the question, but I believe community involvement is a prerequisite for evangelism in many parishes, as well as being in its own right part of the Church's mission in caring and striving for justice.

Evangelicals are evangel-people or they are nothing, so should be to the fore in re-thinking the evangelistic task. That seems to me to demand serious reflection on at least two areas - ways and means, and message-presentation.

WAYS AND MEANS

On ways and means, many were helped by the publication in 1992 of the results of research carried out by Canon (now Bishop) John Finney, then Church of England Officer for the Decade of Evangelism in Finding Faith Today - How does it happen?. Most people become Christians gradually over several years, largely through the influence of relatives and friends. Serving the same parish over thirty-nine years my own experience certainly confirmed that judgement. Only four per cent in the survey came to faith through evangelistic events. 'Evangelisation needs to be founded on fact not fantasy,' John Finney maintained. He also laid stress on the services of the local church, especially baptisms and eucharists. Books, films and plays were prominent for some in their journey to faith. My hunch is that the role of the occasional offices in evangelism varies from culture to culture. My experience has been that the order of effectiveness is funerals, then baptisms some way behind, then weddings. If families are determined simply to make use of the parish church they seem not to hear what is said in preparation, although occasionally one gets a pleasant surprise, maybe years later.

On the whole, however, Finney's report underlined the strategic role of the parish unit in evangelism. I am still not ruling out the place of the mission, either parish or more widely based, but I want to stress the key role played by friendships and relationships. What I believe needs careful monitoring is the use of enthusiastic young persons in reaching out to their peers and school children. Their enthusiasm is not the problem, indeed their warm desire to commend Christ is to be greatly welcomed. But their method of preaching can be less than wise. Use of shock tactics in their presentation, trying to instil fear, copying of the ways of older evangelists, over-simplification of the message - 'accept Christ and all your problems will be solved', for instance - all need kindly, different advice. That said, one cannot but be aware of the enormous, widening gulf between the culture of most young people today and the Church. At my age I have nothing to offer, but I greatly admire those churches and groups trying to bridge the gap and present the Gospel in the youth culture, even if, as in the case of the 'Nine O'Clock Service' sometimes it goes wrong.

John Finney's successor as Decade of Evangelism officer, Canon Robert Warren, has continued to stress the role of the local parish unit, but rightly emphasises that to be effective it must be built into a missionary congregation. Very many congregations have a desire to see the Decade successful but do not know where or how to start. They may not yet realise changes have to begin with them. Is their congregation a company others would want to join? If outsiders come in are they struck by the realisation, 'God is here!', as St Paul said should be the case? Are they prepared to take a radical look at the pattern of their activities, dear to them and hallowed by time, and make changes if necessary?

At the Mid-term Review of the Decade of Evangelism for the Anglican Communion in Kanuga, North Carolina, in September 1995, the Bible Study notes focused on the Eucharist as the time and place where the congregation is principally confronted with the Gospel. Before it can evangelise effectively the congregation itself must be evangelised. The implication was not that it consisted of unbelievers who need to come to faith, though there may be some of those, but rather that the Gospel needs to challenge, permeate and change as necessary all that it does in worship, organising of its life, fellowship and witness. Metanoia, a change of mind and attitudes, is called for. Believers need to become disciples. Risks need to be taken.

One of the greatest encouragements in evangelism in recent years has been the launch from Holy Trinity, Brompton, and their proliferation across the world and denomination, of the Alpha course and other similar introductions to the Christian faith. Instruction in the basics of the faith in a friendly atmosphere has touched a spiritual vacuum in large numbers of all classes in society.

CROSSING FRONTIERS

In stressing the role of the local parish in evangelism, it is obvious that the greater part of the responsibility lies with the individual lay members in their relationships and friendships. Those relationships will be in the context of work, social associations, civic groups and neighbourly contacts where being Christian, acting and serving in a Christ-like way, has to be the basis of any witness. The values of God's Kingdom have to be manifested in a way of life. Friends and neighbours need to catch a 'whiff of heaven'. Many clergy, too, find fruitful ministries in secular associations. Two spheres have proved well worth while being involved with, in my experience. They are the Cadet Services and ex-servicemen's organisations. In thirty-four years as chaplain to the Air Training Corps I never failed to find the utmost co-operation from officers and other ranks. A clear role for the chaplain is laid down in the regulations. In the time I was Wing Chaplain, I found that some clergy felt they did not have time to fill vacancies on local squadrons. But the duties involved offer a unique opportunity to serve alongside groups of lads and girls in their formative years in the context of training for responsible citizenship. In terms of evangelism the effect of this ministry may be largely pre-evangelism. I would warmly encourage clergy who have the opportunity to take up chaplaincies.

There is also a much-needed ministry, again with unique opportunities, among ex-servicemen's organisations, particularly those of veterans from World War II. It can be argued that, with a growing proportion of the population in the senior-citizen bracket, the Church has an increasingly demanding ministry to old people, many of whom once had some church connection but slipped away. Those who served in the forces through the war now have, I find, special needs.

I draw my conclusions from acting as a chaplain to the North Russia Club, an association of some 2,000 men, formed within recent years of those who served the Arctic convoys to north Russia between 1941 and 1945. The longing for a service of worship on appropriate occasions is quite remarkable. A combination of factors seems to contribute to the welcome of spiritual input. As they have reached retirement, free from the demands of a job, their minds turn more than ever before to what for so many was the most significant time of their lives. Memories of dangers and privations flood back one of the most insistent questions that haunts them is, Why was I spared when friends, mates I was close to, were not? There is almost a feeling of guilt. This now increases their sense of mortality. I would urge clergy who are ex-servicemen to use retirement years in ministry to these associations, if qualified to join them - they usually advertise their meetings.

MESSAGE PRESENTATION

Message presentation, I am convinced, needs more serious study than it appears to be getting in Evangelical circles. Our age in the western world is increasingly influenced in culture, the media, education by post modernism. The modern gods, or authorities, that had been thought to have displaced religion and God - namely, Science, Rationalism, Education - have been found wanting. They have not been able to meet the world's needs. So now, we are told, there are no absolutes at all. Truth is what each person decides is true for themselves. Relativism reigns. We must all do our own thing. We can be grateful for what Christian leaders like Lesslie Newbigin and others, including Graham Cray at Ridley, Cambridge, are doing for us in this intellectual ferment.

I suspect, however, that though post modern ideas may reach the general public through culture and the media, the vast majority do not confront them at the intellectual level. They have ideas about supernatural forces, even vague ideas of God who might look after our interests - 'someone up there' - and who will see us right in the end, if there is a life after this. What they do not find relevant or convincing is Church talk about God. To quote the old adage, we scratch where they do not itch. The remarkable, widespread reaction to the tragic death of Diana, Princess of Wales, revealed a deep hunger of the spirit, not least among young people starkly reminded that death can suddenly strike the young and beautiful. Expressions of sorrow and loss owed more to wishful sentiment and a vague search for comfort than to Christian convictions and Gospel assurance, but it all exposed a spiritual vacuum needing to be filled.

I am convinced that one of the greatest needs of the Decade of Evangelism is to rethink how we can talk about God. Men, women, young people will always be brought to faith in Christ through the work of the Holy Spirit, even in response to a simplistic presentation of the Gospel. But we generally raise unnecessary barriers in evangelism by not taking care to present a God who is relevant and credible. I touched on this in my first chapter. If we speak of God as in complete control of everything that happens in the world, backing it up with anecdotes of his interventions in our own lives, and then something like the Dunblane massacre in 1996 happens, or a little child is murdered by a sex fiend, or there is genocide in Africa, how are our claims going to be received by secular people? Part of the answer is about the free will God has given humanity, but it is not enough. Where was God, they ask, when it happened? Far off, unconcerned or unable to do anything? The message of the Cross comes right to the heart of the agony. Most people are not bothered about sin as such. Traditional biblical terms, such as redemption, the Cross, being born again (except in a half-humourous description of becoming religious or turning over a new leaf) are language of another world. But concepts such as justice, reconciliation, pity and sympathy, even sacrifice, are still able to touch people at the depths of their beings, despite whatever post-modernism says about there being no absolutes or objective truth. Here, surely, are inroads for the Gospel.

In May 1996 there appeared in the *Daily Telegraph* weekend supplement a very moving article by a writer, Martyn Harris, described as 'by nature an atheist, by profession a cynic'. He was in a long fight against cancer, suffering relapses. He had been brought up a Methodist but abandoned that commitment. He wanted, as a teenager, to hear arguments about things that mattered, such as the existence of God, the truth of the resurrection, the problem of evil. But 'there wasn't much intellectual meat in chapel, the ministers never seemed to deal with the basis of belief... It was as if science and the modern world had terrorised religion out of tackling its own central mysteries.' Yet he was never quite an atheist. The triumphalism of science, he says, seemed quite as silly as the foam-flecked enthusiasm of fundamentalist religion. Coming to terms now with his mortality, he had had second thoughts about Christianity. He had begun to read the New Testament, though at first embarrassed to be seen doing it, and had been impressed above all by the force and authority of Jesus. Among other books he studied were those of C.S. Lewis. The message of love at the heart of all that is good and cherished drew him. He still faced the mysteries of the cosmos. He said that ultimately he could not simply argue himself or anyone else into faith, but he was making his choice, and could even face death 'without the spiralling panic it once evoked'. He has since died.

This article reminds me of the need for intellectual integrity in presenting the Gospel - I recall the quotation from the Keele platform, 'much preaching is too small to be believed, too easy to be effective, too confident to be true'. It also shows the need for empathy with folk in the titanic struggles they face. And, consequently, it must be recognised that all who hear the message are in widely different personal circumstances. Coming to faith is by a multitude of roads.

WHITHER NOW?

Here are Evangelicals approaching the new millennium, stronger in numbers than for perhaps a century, a broad spectrum, more influential in the structures of the Church and in theological circles - where are they going? As has been said, the ball is at their feet, what are they to do with it? Before answers can be given, another element in the present reality has to be faced. They are divided, arguing among themselves. It is not about the Person and Work of Christ, Salvation, Grace, the Trinity, the Gospel, but chiefly about two things - interpreting Scripture and the state of the Church of England. Interpretation of Scripture focuses on the leadership of women in the Church, not particularly their ordination but them being 'heads', and on homosexuality matters. To those Evangelicals distancing themselves from the rest, interpretation differences have been construed as touching the Bible's authority. I will say no more than what I have said already in this chapter.

What of the state of the Church of England? Clearly there are substantially different perceptions. On the one hand, there is talk of serious doctrinal drift, of failure of Evangelicals to stand for the truth in synodical structures and especially in the House of Bishops, of unhealthy centralisation and burgeoning bureaucracy, and capitulation to liberal standards in faith and moral issues. Speaking for myself, on the other hand, and I believe for many others, I just don't see the same picture. 'Two men looked through prison bars; one saw mud, the other saw stars.' So far as doctrinal standards are concerned, I see much to encourage. Of course there are adherents of the Sea of Faith practising in the Church, and in recent times bishops questioning the corporeal resurrection of Christ and the Virgin Birth. But such theological questionings and even denials are not new in our time. There was much ferment in the 1960s, Bishop Barnes before the War, bishops who appeared to be not much more than Deists in earlier centuries. The Church of England has survived. And if one follows through successive reports of the Church of England Doctrine Commission, each one in my judgement getting better than its predecessors, there is real cause for thanksgiving. The latest, The Mystery of Salvation, deserves wide acclamation.

I would be expected, as one who was heavily involved in synodical structures till 1995, to defend the record of Evangelicals. Inevitably, with hindsight, mistakes may have been made, opportunities missed, but they have pulled their weight to say the least, in a comprehensive

Church. And it is not necessarily a measure of faithfulness to fall out with other traditions. As for bishops, I think it is often forgotten by their critics that in accepting their office and responsibility they undertake to be a focus of unity for all traditions in their diocese. As one of the foremost Conservative Evangelical bishops once said to me, 'We find ourselves doing things we would not do before becoming a bishop.' Collegiality is not a dirty word. It is a way of collective leadership worth striving for, but it cannot be an easy road on which all will applaud their efforts. Holding divided groups together while a common mind is sought requires skill and patience.

Instead of increased centralisation and a growing bureaucracy I do, in fact, see the opposite trend both at national level and in many dioceses. Devolution wherever possible seems now to be the aim. And streamlining at the centre is, as I see it, in order to be more efficient in serving the whole Church, dioceses and parishes.

Frequent references are made by discontented members of both Evangelical and Catholic traditions to the 'Liberal Establishment'. Having been in a position to observe closely what goes on in central structures, including the appointment of bishops, I do not understand the complaint. Perhaps I am regarded as being part of it!

I come back to the question at the beginning of this section - where are Evangelicals going? It remains for me a question without an answer as yet, for much depends on finding a way to build up mutual trust and to live with differences. In 1987 Archbishop Runcie, in introducing a report on the divisive issue of women priests quoted from Henry Newman, 'You cannot have Christianity and not have differences'. And a careful study of the New Testament reveals the early Church as exhibiting unity in diversity. As I have tried to show Evangelicals, for as long as they have been recognised as such, have had different opinions and policies on the Bible and on many other things. For a comprehensive study bearing out that view Mark Noll's book, already frequently quoted, cannot be bettered.

I see the Council of Jerusalem in Acts 15 as a guide for the present situation. Much was at stake in the controversy that had arisen, indeed the integrity of the Gospel of grace alone by faith alone, and the future of the Church either as a branch of Judaism or a Church for all nations. A compromise was reached. There must have been some give and take. It was a compromise that did not undermine the Gospel, but it was apparently sufficient to avoid a split. It does not seem to have been a compromise that lasted very long. St Paul, in writing to the Corinthians on matters dealt with in the Jerusalem statement, does not quote it or keep strictly to it. Sometimes compromises in the Church last only for a time, and are no worse for that. What is most significant in the Council of Jerusalem, apart from safeguarding the Gospel for all, is not just what was decided, but the spirit in which the decision was made. No doubt the debate was vigorous, but Christian love and mutual trust prevailed. The Gospel is truth, but truth in love. In Philippians 4:5, Paul urges Christians to let their 'moderation' be known to all. It is well nigh impossible to find one English word for the one he used. Some commentators offer 'sweet reasonableness', others 'mildness', 'big-heartedness', or 'graciousness'. William Barclay relates it to situations when action 'may be legally completely justified and yet morally wrong'. If only Evangelicals would keep in mind there are times like that, and cultivate the quality Paul advocates.

Thirty years ago, when some Evangelicals were being very critical of the Church of England, using hostile expressions, an elderly Evangelical clergyman said to me, 'I could not talk about my mother like that. I love the Church of England as a mother in God.' That is how I feel about the Church of England. She has her faults but I will stay with her.

The author with his daughter Carolyn and son Andrew pictured after the conferring of his Lambeth DD, 1992.

The General Synod of the Church of England sitting in Westminster. The author is seated at the end of the second front row.

The author with the Archbishop of Armagh, Robin Eames, at the 10th meeting of the Anglican Consultative Council, Panama, 1996.

Debtor to Grace 117

The author with the Church of England delegation to the meeting of Anglican Consultative Council, Wales 1990 (Archbishop Robert Runcie, Dr Margaret Hewitt, and the Revd Michael O'Connor).

As chaplain of the North Russia Club conducting a service on HMS Belfast marking the fiftieth anniversary of the outbreak of World War II.

The author addressing the ACC 8th meeting of the Anglican Consultative Council, Wales, 1990.

HMS Eclipse off Iceland, 1942. The ship was sunk soon after the author was transferred, with much loss of life, including his replacement. This episode raised many important questions for the author about the providence of God.

Archbishop William Temple boards HMS Eclipse, accompanied by Lt Commander Mack.

Seated at the organ for a service aboard the aircraft carrier HMS Shah, Colombo, 1945. It was a rare chaplain's visit. Normally the author would conduct ship-board services.

The author addressing a session of the General Synod in York.

Chapter 4
General Synod: The first twenty-five years

One thing this chapter will not be is a history of the General Synod from 1970 to 1995. Who would have any interest in such an enterprise? *The Reports of Proceedings*, the Synod's 'Hansard', run to 75 volumes, and a lot of the verbatim record of speeches is eminently forgettable, except, perhaps to the speakers concerned, if still alive. And even they might at least wish they had said something different.

I cannot, however, follow the example of some ex-Synod members in their largely negative assessments of an institution which brings together bishops, clergy and laity in the exercise of authority in the Church. The way this consultative and legislative body conducts its business needs considerable improvement, but of its place in an Anglican ecclesiology I believe there is no doubt - a point I hope to develop in the next chapter.

What I offer here are reflections on some of the main issues and developments through the first five quinquennia, based particularly on personal involvement. There were some major matters, liturgical revision among them, on which I have nothing of interest to contribute, even though I listened and voted. From the beginning I decided it was not possible to be thoroughly acquainted with every item and report in each group of sessions. I imagine most members take that line; a plethora of documents descend on one before sessions. There will be on every item of the agenda some who know what they are talking about.

AN EVOLUTIONARY PROCESS

A spirit of reform permeated the first five years of the Synod. The initiative sprang from the newly formed New Synod Group, later to be re-named Open Synod Group. It was natural that those most enthusiastic for the the inauguration of synodical government, the essence of which, at national level was the integration of the House of Laity with those of bishops and clergy (the Convocations), should have an agenda of reforming measures. Though there was a general welcome for synodical government in the Catholic and Evangelical groups on the Synod, the mood in these traditions was more cautious. Both of them contained a considerable proportion of their membership opposed to the proposals for Anglican-Methodist unity already moving towards a final decision. The New Synod Group, ready to welcome members of any tradition - hence, its later change of name - strongly supported the Anglican-Methodist scheme and looked for further moves towards Church reunion. It also advocated reforms of the way clergy were deployed, employed, paid. Two previous reports, one by Leslie Paul and then one of a group chaired by Dean Fenton Morley, had advocated wide sweeping changes. The latter report had been voted down in the dying stages of the old Church Assembly, but it had been decided to continue the search for reforms. There was strong support for the ordination of women in the New Synod Group, and a concern to change or modify the Convocation Regulations denying any remarriage of divorcees in church.

This agenda of changes being advocated put the Catholic Group and the Evangelical Group on General Synod (EGGS) on the defensive, at any rate as far as many of their members were concerned. Even proposals to change the way clergy are appointed to parishes were seen as a threat, in that the existing patronage system was held to be a defence of distinctive churchmanship in parishes. Progress in achieving the New Synod Group's reforms was limited in the first quinquennium. Indeed, the Anglican-Methodist scheme collapsed through failure to achieve the required majority of votes in General Synod, though having been approved by the Methodists. Some other objectives were fulfilled, either then or in later quinquennia, such as the ordination of women, while others though unresolved are still on the agenda. One, perhaps unexpected, change was the approval of a new canon to allow Christians of good standing in other Churches to receive Holy Communion on occasions in Anglican churches. The move owed much to Professor Geoffrey Lampe, but it was strongly backed by Evangelicals with their commitment to the Open Table.

In reaction, to a first quinquennium agenda raising the possibility of reform and change the elections to a new General Synod in 1975 showed something of a backlash. Catholics and Evangelicals, the latter still not as strong in numbers as they were later to become, made strenuous efforts to increase their representation. Thus the debates in the next five years revealed a more conservative Synod. And as the General Synod has evolved, elections have continued to be dominated by emerging key issues - church unity proposals, women's ordination, sexuality matters, etc. Candidates, for change or against, have been required to state their position in seeking election, though it is surprising that some get elected on the basis of election addresses mainly consisting of vague generalities - support for apple pie and motherhood - as though afraid of putting anyone off. In these cases the deciding factor may be the character of the candidate - no bad thing! - or friendship, or assiduous canvassing.

Synodical government rests on the dual principle of episcopal leadership and consultation of bishops with clergy and laity, bishops in council. In the first five years of General Synod, the House of Bishops appeared somewhat uncertain of their role. One occasion when they tried to exert their influence by reversing a decision of Synod on an addition to the Church's calendar, they got their knuckles rapped. This seemed to cause them to lie low for some years, except on matters where constitutionally they had a right to act. Gradually, however, the role of the House of Bishops in General Synod, in addition to their constitutional provisions, became clearer and generally welcomed. Over the last ten to fifteen years, when the Synod has found itself bogged down over prolonged, divisive debates, it has turned to the House of Bishops for a lead. This has happened with legislation for the ordination of women, the marriage of divorcees in church, the homosexuality debate, lay presidency of Holy Communion, 'extended Communion'. The two other Houses have not always welcomed what the bishops have come up with. It has to be remembered, however, that their House contains differing strong convictions while striving for a united voice, and that as bishops they have to be a focus of unity amid the diversity of views in the Church. If the House of Bishops is effectively to fulfil a leadership role in the General Synod, and beyond in the Church, time and space must be afforded by lessening demands elsewhere, and adequate resources on theological and moral concerns provided from outside its own membership.

CHURCHMANSHIP POLITICS

Reference has already been made to three distinctive groupings in General Synod from its beginning - the Catholic Group, the Open Synod Group and the Evangelical Group in General Synod. They have their separate meetings, and they play a major part in elections. Some

Synod members belong to no group and are proud to say so. Some attend more than one group meeting, some are even paid up members of all three, either because they want to express breadth of sympathy, or like to know what the others are up to. It would be a mistake to think there is hostility between the groups, indeed General Synod is a friendly club, especially in the refreshment rooms and even more so at the residential sessions in York University. Debate in the Assembly is much more courteous and charitable than in the House of Commons. Just occasionally, in highly emotive debates, the boundaries of charity may be breached, and in private conversations unfair assessments of those of opposing convictions are expressed, but that is true throughout the Church and simply illustrates the truth of the Article that 'infection of nature doth remain, yea even in them that are regenerated'.

From the beginning the Standing Committee has reflected the three groupings in its own membership. The single transferable vote had ensured this result. And the Committee itself, through its Appointments Sub-Committee has sought to ensure that in all appointments to the Boards and Councils and nominations to other bodies within and outside the Church of England, a balance of churchmanship is secured. That, in itself, would be no easy task, but it is complicated by also having to achieve fair representation of bishops, clergy and laity, men and women, north and south, with due attention to age, if possible. There can be no sense, therefore, of the Standing Committee being like the Cabinet of the Government, all of one party, even though a Cabinet may not always be united. If courteous charity generally characterises debates in Synod, it is perhaps more so in the Standing Committee. Mutual respect prevails. But because pressure of time in a heavy agenda sometimes curtails discussion before decisions are taken, dissatisfaction can ensue. In my twenty years on the Standing Committee, the best meetings have been residential and thus more leisurely. The Policy Committee has generally been an overnight meeting. But the meeting that stands out most clearly as rewarding and fostering unity was a residential one where the greater part of the time was given to exploring our theological convictions on an issue before the Church at the time and relevant to Synod debates.

When courtesy and charity have been duly recognised, however, the existence of churchmanship politics almost inevitably draws out the time taken for the Church to make its mind up. There is a sense in which this is no bad thing. Rushed business is unwise business, generally speaking. Widespread support for a new initiative does take time. Minorities have a legitimate objection to being bulldozed. But the very notion of politics can convey attitudes and tactics out of keeping with a Christian assembly. If the Church is to conduct its business in a Christian spirit, it needs to avoid ways and means all too evident in secular politics.

For me, the best expression I recall of the way any debate should be conducted came in 1988, in a debate on the notorious *Crockford Preface* by the late Dr Garry Bennett, itself an issue that touched churchmanship issues in an emotive way. The then Bishop of Guildford (Michael Adie) introduced a report on the matter by the Standing Committee. In the course of his speech he maintained that the Preface and the sad events that followed 'should give us pause now to recognise that the traditions within the Church of England need one another.' 'We cannot evade decisions', he continued, 'we do not avoid conflict; but we can listen to one another, recognising that we are together the body of Christ, the Church'. He then quoted Bishop John Taylor, formerly of Winchester, who had recently commented that our 'quasi-parliamentary structure and its permanent staff tempt the members of Synod, and the parties within it, to gain the decisions they hope for by manipulation, lobbying and tactics. This creates an atmosphere of confrontation and even of conspiracy, and argument tends to use the logic of power or expediency rather than theology'. Michael Adie went on to remind Synod 'we are not, as in Parliament, different parties sitting on benches opposite one another and opposing one another; here we recognise that God works through the whole Church, even in those with whom we disagree, and our job is not to exploit our power to block the views of others but to work together to understand and, wherever possible, to discover agreement behind our controversies'. A question now facing the Synod is, could the reforms arising from the Turnbull report provide a context for greater understanding and co-operation between the traditions, as well as a more efficient system?

A LOOK AT OURSELVES

Businesses have the need for regular stock-taking. In 1979, General Synod began a process of spiritual stock-taking. That is, admittedly, a loose way of describing the Partners-in-Mission Consultation agreed to after initial resistance and misgiving. The PIM Consultation process had arisen within the Anglican Communion from a concept first articulated at an Anglican Congress in Toronto in 1963 - Mutual Responsibility and Interdependence in the Body of

Christ (MRI). A directory of projects in Mission across the Communion had emerged from the acceptance of the MRI principle. The underlying thesis is well described in the second meeting of the Anglican Consultative Council Report (Dublin 1973), itself called *Partners in Mission*. 'The responsibility for mission in any place belongs primarily to the church in that place. However, the universality of the Gospel and the oneness of God's mission mean also that this mission must be shared in each and every place with fellow-Christians from each and every part of the world with their distinctive insights and contributions' (p.53). So, from 1973 onwards Churches, Provinces and individual dioceses had held consultations in which they invited Anglicans from other parts of the Communion, representatives of other Churches in their area and in some cases representatives of secular bodies, to assess current mission programmes and needs still unmet.

By 1979 some parts of the Communion had held more than one Consultation. England and Scotland were the only two Churches not to have agreed to one, even though the Church of England had sent, as requested, representatives to others' Consultations. Fourteen dioceses in England had set up a PIM Consultation. Why the delay and initial resistance to one for the Church as a whole? There was, I believe, an emotional barrier to overcome. As the mother Church of the Communion we find difficulty in relating maturely to children when they have grown up; could we really learn from them? We have not yet surmounted this emotional barrier. A slightly more respectable hesitation focused on other questions: Can partners from other Churches and cultures understand our problems and pressures? Is not our situation unique? We have structures deeply rooted in history, an established Church, a complex legal framework tied into Parliament.

In introducing a report of the Standing Committee advocating a national PIM Consultation, on the advice of the Board for Mission and Unity, I invited the Synod to accept 'that it is a distinctively Christian exercise to allow other Christian partners to share in a review of one's work, especially in carrying out the mission of the Church'. I quoted an ACC statement indicating that listening to the Holy Spirit speaking to us through others could have painful and exhilarating consequences, but that was the essence of discipleship, obedient discipleship. It had to be emphasised that a Consultation is not simply a means of administrative and management reform, to enable us to do better what we are already doing. It is about the meaning of mission in an area and renewed obedience to mission.

Two year's preparation under the leadership of the Archbishop of York (Dr Stuart Blanch) led up to the Consultation in June 1981. The Synod had decided that the Consultation should concentrate on the work of official (statutory) and voluntary bodies operating at national level, though the dioceses and their structures were not to be neglected. Fifty-five Internal Partners, representing fifteen official Church agencies and twenty-eight voluntary organisations, joined seventeen External Partners, nine of them from other Anglican Churches, four from other overseas Churches and four from other Churches in Britain. External Partners visited Church House, Church Commissioners, Pensions Board, the Voluntary Societies, the British Council of Churches, Lambeth Palace. That took ten days. Over two weekends they split up to visit seventeen dioceses. Their meetings with the Internal Partners spread over six days.

On a Sunday afternoon in the York Group of Sessions, immediately following the Consultation, its findings were presented. There had been frank exchange of views and assessments, much difficulty in reaching an agreed statement, some unresolved disagreements, but overall a series of challenges to the Church of England accepted by the Internal partners. They touched a general failure to establish a shared ministry between the ordained and the lay, a need to cast off the trappings of privilege and stand in solidarity with the poor and underprivileged, the need for reform of General Synod with merging, ending or creating boards and councils in obedience to mission, the need for more flexibility in the voluntary societies, the recognition of failure towards young people, a revitalising of the local church with a sense of gospel-urgency.

Two areas where the greatest gap between Internal and External Partners emerged were in the evangelistic task in England and the Church Commissioners. A general reaction to the External Partners' view of evangelism in England was that it was too simplistic and failed to appreciate the secular and materialistic atmosphere here. On the Church Commissioners, the External Partners advocated a transfer of the vast resources from maintenance to mission with a phasing out of subventions to parishes by 1995. Told that the law prevented this they urged the changing of the law. It is ironic that seventeen years later, without any willingness or attempt to change the law but by a combination of factors, including inflation and unwise investment, the burden of maintenance has shifted heavily to the parishes.

Summarising the main challenges of the Consultation is not just a matter of historic interest. What is more important is to ask to what extent the challenges have been met. When the report of the Consultation, *To a Rebellious House?* - the question mark is important - was debated in 1982 there was a general concern to respond positively. In the following years we have seen a growing advocacy of shared ministry, a standing by the marginalised and the poor in Faith in the City and its follow-up, attempts to reform the Synod and its associated bodies in the Infrastructure Review and now the Turnbull proposals, more co-operation and flexibility of missionary societies in the Partnership for World Mission and a succession of conferences between the Synod and voluntary agencies, a more serious attempt to grapple with responsibilities to children and youth, and in the Decade of Evangelism, a new approach to evangelism through the attempt to build up missionary congregations. In different aspects of the Church of England's mission, together with partner Churches in Churches Together in England, good theory still has to be translated into effective practice in the way the Consultation envisaged. It might be argued that developments in the years since 1981 would have happened anyway, but on reflection, and bearing in mind agendas within the Standing Committee since then, I would claim the national PIM Consultation had a considerable impact at national level. It was sobering to see ourselves as others saw us, and not less important was the opportunity for a wide range of our own official and voluntary bodies to stand back and review together our common mission.

SYNOD AND THE SOCIETIES

There was a period in the development of the Welfare State when statutory bodies, national and local, had little or no partnership with voluntary agencies meeting similar needs in the community. The same was true for the General Synod and Anglican voluntary societies until the mid-70s. Reference has already been made to the participation of a wide range of voluntary organisations in the Partners-in-Mission exercise. I recall a meeting in the preparation period of representatives of these organisations with the Steering Group. It was for many, if not most, the first time they had been in the same room together, nor had they ever contemplated such an event. The exceptions were the overseas missionary society representatives. Although autonomous, accountable only to their own constituencies, there had been limited relationships. In 1976, however, a working group was set up under the chairmanship of Sir Norman Anderson which led two years later to the creation of Partnership for World Mission. Synod and missionary society representatives shared in the working group.

Though coming to the group from the Synod side, I had already served twenty-four years on a society General Committee and knew how far there was to go in real partnership between the societies themselves. And from that side there was suspicion about the consequences of entering into a partnership with the General Synod. Would it blunt their effectiveness in world mission? Would they lose control of their own affairs, and thus forfeit the confidence of their supporters? A major question to be faced was, should the Church of England leave all its overseas mission outreach to the long-established voluntary societies? Other major Churches of the Communion have Boards of Mission as part of their synodical structures through which they relate to overseas Churches. Clearly there was no possibility of winding up the voluntary structures, or any serious thought to do so. Nor was the Synod likely to become itself an agent for overseas work. Yet the Synod greatly needed to be better related to the challenges and opportunities of world mission. So Partnership for World Mission was launched with the support of Synod and the missionary societies. It was deliberately a hybrid sort of body with nominations from both sides of the partnership and accountable to both. The cost of operating is shared.

No one, I think, would claim that the partnership has been free from problems, or even that the high hopes of the enthusiasts at the beginning have been fully realised. But there should be no turning back to the previous wide gap between Synod and societies, and one hopes the eventual Turnbull provisions will allow for the partnership to continue.

THE INFRASTRUCTURE REVIEW

The PIM Consultation had raised the possibility of reform of the General Synod's Boards and Councils in order more effectively to fulfil the mission of the Church at national level. At parish level there is widespread ignorance of the Church of England's national role. The Council for Education must relate directly to government agencies as well as serving the dioceses. The same is true of the Board for Social Responsibility on a wide range of social and ethical issues. Initiatives for consultation often arise from the Government. The National Health Service pays for hospital chaplaincies - our Chaplaincy Council must work with the service on policies and practical matters. Synod representatives collaborate with our ecumenical partners in Britain and Ireland in mission responsibilities. The major question to be faced, therefore, is: Are the subordinate structures of General Synod best suited to the national responsibilities as well as serving the internal life of the Church as represented by the members elected to Synod?

To try to answer the question the Infrastructure Review Group was set up in 1985. It was a small group under the chairmanship of the late Dr Margaret Hewitt and was serviced by John Shirley, seconded from the Church Commissioners. In the days before General Synod there had been earlier reviews of the infrastructures, one in 1956 and the other in 1970, on the eve of the inauguration of General Synod.

An unexpected death robbed the Synod of one of its most effective and colourful characters in Margaret Hewitt, always distinguished in the Assembly by her array of hats! Thoroughly committed to all she saw best in the Catholic tradition, she was ever cheerful, fair to all and astute in her assessments, never more so than in chairing the Review Group.

Policy and Finance

Without minimising the importance of other aspects of the Review Group's proposals, a crucial question related to policy and finance. From its inauguration the Synod had a Standing Order (146) which laid down that the Standing Committee is required 'to set priorities (for all the Synod's subordinate bodies) and co-ordinate all work done in the Synod's name'. Those twin aims had not been realised. Priorities, the essence of policy-making, and finance are inextricably linked, so long as finance is limited, as it has been and is likely to be. The Standing Committee, responsible for priority decisions had, however, to recognise that management of the Synod's finances was in the hands of the Central Board of Finance, an independent body which ante-dated Synod. There was a link between the Standing Committee and the CBF - the Joint Budget Committee. In theory, the latter was the forum in which to marry priorities and finance. In practice it was not.

As a member of the Review Group, I brought the experience of nine years on the Joint Budget Committee. I had found it the least satisfactory committee of Synod I served on. That was not the fault of successive chairmen. Of the other members, three came from the CBF and three from the Standing Committee. The former were expected to provide financial expertise, the latter to bring agreed priorities from the Standing Committee, even though its Policy Sub-Committee offered little or no guidance. Only on votes for allocations to other Anglican and ecumenical bodies were guidelines given. The result was that each member of the JBC applied his own judgement, even prejudices, in discussion as to how the available financial cake should be divided up. Over a period of two or three days, the chairmen and secretaries of each spending body would appear in turn before the JBC to be questioned on their budgets. The JBC, following regional conferences with Diocesan Board of Finance chairmen and secretaries, would have a ceiling figure for the finance likely to be available. That figure was compared with the higher total of the submitted budgets and a percentage cut right across the board agreed. In often quite arbitrary ways, the representatives of the Boards and Councils had to agree to cuts. It is no wonder they found the exercise demoralising. There had been no clear establishment of priorities between different aspects of the work of the different spending bodies, only the individual choices of seven individuals. If a budgeting process is to be fair, heads of spending bodies should all be present at the same time even if they do not have a vote.

The successful marrying of policy and finance is a difficult task, not only at General Synod level but also at diocesan level, parish level, in all church organisations, and indeed at Anglican Communion level. But it has to be achieved or there is dissatisfaction and disenchantment at all levels. The Review Group, in the words of Dr Hewitt, was 'fully convinced that the time has now come for the major work of the Central Board of Finance to devolve on the Standing Committee, and for that committee to have its own finance committee to manage Synod's finances'. In the subsequent debates the CBF successfully defended its corner, persuading the Synod to retain it 'broadly in its present role and form'. In the interval between publication of the report and the debates, strong opposition had built up in the CBF to its demise. Every Diocesan Board of Finance was represented on it. There was a fear that such hold as the DBF representatives had on the Synod budget would be lost. Understandably, their concern was for the levy on their own diocesan budgets. Yet many of them were not members of General Synod and thus never heard the debates that went to shape policy. Keeping the budget down seemed the only concern.

Priorities

Leaving aside the finance side of the policy-finance equation, there was a pressing need to discover a way for the Standing Committee to establish priorities within Boards and Councils and across them. It had to be done without undermining the rightful authority of each Board to respond to its terms of reference in its constitution. The Review Group proposed a Programme Committee in place of the Policy Sub-Committee, on which the major Boards would be represented but without voting powers. The Synod preferred to call it the Policy Committee. It was hoped that this would be the body to advise the Standing Committee on priorities to be fed into the budget process. I served on it for the first five years of its life, to 1995. It achieved a way each year of prioritising all new items of work, and thus expenditure submitted by the Boards, and it did it with their chairmen present so they could share in the debate.

What the Policy Committee did not do in the initial period was to establish priorities in all the existing work going on. Certainly each Board was reviewed in depth in turn, and no doubt this could lead to some internal Board decisions on what could be done. But a thorough prioritising process should require all existing commitments along with new items to be on the table for assessment. One appreciates that this can affect contracts of individual Board secretaries, if a person is tied to a particular and possibly specialist task. But some flexibility could be required in staff employed. The Standing Order already referred to requires the Standing Committee not only to co-ordinate and supervise the work of Boards and Councils, but to 'curtail, expand or modify their activities' where necessary.

A task the Policy Committee just began to deal with in its first five years was to decide in conjunction with the Business Sub-Committee what reports produced by Boards should be debated in Synod. As chairman of the Business Sub-Committee - a responsibility I tried to avoid - I sought the Policy Committee's guidance to take back to the BSC. Over the previous years, all reports landed up in Synod. Boards obviously sought maximum publicity for them, even if no decisions were needed beyond referral to dioceses and parishes. But often the debates on the reports lacked vitality; they could have been referred to dioceses without debate. Some reports it was clearly useful to debate - the Church and the Bomb report, for instance - because they were addressed to society at large. But if the Synod itself is to have priorities in the agenda of its debates, and thus conserve time and money, the Standing Committee must choose reports really needing debating. With the closer working with Boards and Councils, early advice can be given on the destination of a proposed report. I realise in all these observations I am dealing with the structures still existing at the time of writing, and what emerges from the Turnbull provisions may be different, but I believe similar policy and priority control will be needed.

Mission and Unity

The Infrastructure Review Group stirred considerable opposition in recommending the division of the Board for Mission and Unity's twin responsibilities. It was not for any failure to appreciate that mission and Church unity are inextricably linked. Division in the Church's mission in the world contradicts its Gospel message of reconciliation in Christ. But it needed to be recognised that there were aspects of mission covered by Boards other than the BMU - BSR and the Council for Education, for instance. Nevertheless, the agenda for the BMU was overloaded. It was so in my membership of it in the first ten years of the Synod, and there was evidence it was still so ten years later. Pressing and continuing demands on the ecumenical front crowded out mission concerns, and that was so even though the Decade of Evangelism was soon to be launched. On ecumenical matters, the Standing Committee relied on the BMU for information and advice, and in this respect had a more direct relationship than with other Boards. In the end the Synod agreed to divide the BMU, creating a Board of Mission and a Council for Christian Unity, the latter continuing to relate directly to the Standing Committee. The hope was expressed that the Board of Mission would, through the Policy Committee, promote theological reflection on the nature and prosecution of mission through all the Boards.

Other Changes

Ministry, like mission, is a portmanteau word. So much can be put into it - the ordained ranks, Readers, other accredited lay ministers, those in specialised ministries like hospital chaplains, chaplains to the deaf, chaplains to prisons and to the armed forces, not to mention the laity as a whole. The Review Group considered it would be beneficial to bring into closer relationship at least some of the bodies at national level responsible for ministry. The Advisory Council for the Church's Ministry (ACCM) was renamed the Advisory Board of Ministry. The Synod decided to include the Council for the Deaf under the new Board but resisted the proposal to add the Hospital Chaplaincies Council. Previously, an ACCM committee had had a link with the Central Readers' Conference but, in revised terms of reference following the Synod debate, the Advisory Board of Ministry took responsibility for the oversight of the work and training programmes for Readers.

Communications was an area in need of review and reform. The Synod agreed to combine the Press and Broadcasting Departments in a single Communications Unit.

For some time there had been a degree of dissatisfaction in some quarters at the way the Appointments Sub-Committee nominated members to Boards and Councils. No doubt an element of personal disappointment obtains here. In their difficult task the ASC cannot please everyone. The Review Group was disinclined to go for a system of election by Synod of members to the Boards. The Synod revealed an ambivalent attitude to the issue, accepting the principle for one Board and not another. In the end it was decided to experiment with election to a section of all the main Boards.

CONFOUNDING THE ESTABLISHMENT

In all the twenty-five years since Synod began, there has never been a more embarrassing story than the 'Millbank Project' - embarrassing, that is, for the top brass in the Standing Committee and Church Commissioners. The Corporation of Church House, in whose trust the ownership of the House is placed, was also involved, but emerged without blame, unless its policy of generosity in allowing the Synod and its staff to live in the building rent free and so having insufficient funds for essential refurbishment was blameworthy. The story so far as the Synod was concerned, spread over almost two years. In fact it started six years earlier than 1987, the year the Synod got involved.

The Standing Committee's first report to Synod in February 1987 made recommendations on the future housing of Synod and of its staff. It was based on prolonged investigation and debate involving the Church House Corporation, the Church Commissioners and the Standing Committee, A basic consideration was that Church House needed to be redeveloped at considerable cost (28 million was suggested) if it was to meet modern standards and continue to attract rent-paying tenancies. The Commissioners were unwilling to pay for that - it would mean a substantial loss in annual income for the Church. Instead, they invited the Synod's staff to join them at 1 Millbank - hence the name 'Millbank Project'. Normal meetings of committees could be held there, but not the sessions of General Synod. For the latter, other venues would need to be hired. Kensington Town Hall and the Queen Elizabeth Centre in Westminster were investigated. The loss of the Assembly Hall at Church House for Synod sessions would be sad, and at either of the other two venues considered the nature of the Synod's debates would inevitably be changed, it was believed. A major plus was the possibility of the staffs of Church House and Millbank being under one roof. Ten years earlier a working group had advocated the bringing of the central institutions of the Church into closer relationship.

So the establishment approached Synod with a united front. But that united front, so far as the Standing Committee was concerned, did not represent the total conviction of all members. The fact was - I speak for myself and others, as I believe - we were much at the mercy of experts, I knew nothing of planning permissions, property development, conference facility prospects in central London, renting possibilities. In introducing the Standing Committee's report to the Synod, Professor David McClean confessed, 'Very few of us can claim any expertise in property development and its financing'. He claimed reassurance on the rightness to relocate the Synod staff at 1 Millbank from six years of 'drawing on their skills and expertise of several different groups of professional advisers'. Notwithstanding the difficult position David McLean found himself in on that occasion, his contribution to General Synod, particularly as Chairman of the House of Laity and in all legal business, was outstanding. His calm, astute, always clear and eirenic presentations enriched the debates. In retrospect, with the assurance of hindsight, I would say that blinded by science we nearly made a tragic mistake.

In the February 1987 debate, in spite of attempts to consider re-location away from London and to delay discussion for further investigation, the Synod with great regret agreed to the Standing Committee's proposals. The staff was to be rehoused, but no decision taken about venues for future meetings of Synod. Among the voices raised against accepting the proposals as they stood was that of Mr Roy Lyon, a lay member from the Liverpool diocese. He had two main problems. Despite the project having been considered behind the scenes for six years, the Synod was asked to make a decision that day as a matter of urgency. Furthermore, there was insufficient information about the possibility of redevelopment of the Church House site with the private sector, if necessary along with 1 Millbank. He was told that all commercial possibilities had been considered.

I knew Roy Lyon well. He worked in the Planning Department in Bolton Town Hall and over several years had sought my co-operation as Area Dean in the Church's part in town planning. Some time after the debate he asked me to his office. Usually he was bubbling over with enthusiasm; this time he was obviously worried. In contact with Westminster Planning authorities and other bodies in central London, he believed he had overwhelming evidence that Church House could be redeveloped to provide new, attractive conference facilities able to draw in substantial income. There were other details from his investigations. It appeared that a quite different set of financial and other factors from those given in the debate now obtained. He was convinced, also, that a very substantial offer could be made for 1 Millbank. He mentioned the possible buyer, but I cannot disclose it. What I believe is true is that the Commissioners would have been unwilling to sell.

Possessed of all his verifiable information, his quandary was whether to attempt a Private Member's Motion to re-open the whole Millbank Project. He was, he said, only a back-bencher, he never willingly made trouble. He learned from me that the Standing Committee was proceeding with the Synod's mandate, but I felt he had no option but to attempt to seek a new debate. In July 1988 he presented his motion and despite heavy opposition from establishment figures, persuaded the Synod by one hundred and 92 votes to 78 to have the project reconsidered as a matter of urgency.

A small working group chaired by Dr Christina Baxter was appointed by the Standing Committee. It reported by November of that year. It was a full frank exposure of mistakes, wrong conclusions, errors of judgement. Never has there been a debate in Synod with so many apologies from members of the Standing Committee. Archdeacon David Silk, Proctor for the Canterbury Convocation, in introducing the debate offered on behalf of the Standing Committee 'a full apology for any statements that have been misleading, and accepted full responsibility for the fact that it was itself misled'. In the course of the debate it became clear that it would have been a better course to have had the Synod set up a working party right at the beginning to consider the whole matter, rather than keep the investigation secret, even though some aspects required confidentiality. Once again senior establishment figures attempted to get Synod to remain with the original proposals. But in the end it agreed to stay in Church House and accept any financial consequences. It was a close vote, two hundred and forty-one to two hundred and eight. It further approved a motion inviting the Church Commissioners and the Pensions Board to move their staffs in due course into Church House, and asking for plans to have both bodies along with General Synod housed in the House complex (modified as necessary) by the years 2000-2005. Whether the outcome of the Turnbull proposals will eventually lead to such a result is not known at the time of writing. A further motion to have the elected members resign, on the principle of accountability, so that Synod's confidence in them could be tested by an election, was defeated.

There was a sad irony to the concluding episode to this story. Roy Lyon was absent through illness, an illness that proved terminal. On partial recovery, however, he was invited to join the Corporation of Church House, a privilege he deeply appreciated, and began to see his optimistic forecasts of the viability and success of the House as a conference centre being fulfilled. If he had felt like David taking on Goliath, he enjoyed similar success.

MINISTRY MATTERS
Terms of Ministry

An unresolved set of issues, bequeathed by the expiring Church Assembly in 1970, concerned the terms of service for the ordained ministry - namely, deployment, pay structure, retirement age, method of removal from a benefice when pastoral relationships have broken down. The Leslie Paul report and then the Fenton Morley report (*Partners in Ministry*) had introduced radical ideas affecting the centuries-old pattern of appointment by patronage, to which only modest changes had been made in earlier decades. The Church Assembly was not ready for radical change. A survey of the dioceses had revealed a strong desire for reform but not according to the Partners in Ministry proposals. The General Synod Standing Committee appointed a 'Terms of Ministry Committee', under the chairmanship of the Bishop of Manchester (Patrick Rodger). I found myself on the Committee, probably on the basis of a pamphlet I had written in 1969 entitled Patronage Reformed for the Seventies.

The Terms of Ministry Committee proposed changes in five main areas, but not in a package deal. Each was dealt with separately by Synod. That was as well, because one area took fifteen years to reach some conclusion. On payment of clergy, the Synod approved proposals to set up a Central Stipends Authority, vested in the Church Commissioners. Hitherto there had been in effect forty-three independent and autonomous stipends authorities. To enable the new system to work, it was decided to pool benefice endowment income and transfer the ownership of glebe to dioceses. Of late, some parishes have complained bitterly of what they have described as the central Church's theft of their resources, and thus of their parochial independence. Without these reforms, however, the aim to achieve some degree of equality in clergy stipends and to maximise income from glebe would have been impossible. Dioceses, drawing on relevant expertise, have considerably increased glebe income.

Another successful proposal was to establish a retirement age for clergy at seventy years. The measure to effect this was finally approved in 1977. Anyone taking up an office after that date was affected; those in office before were not. A persistent concern over previous decades, taken up by Leslie Paul and Fenton Morley, was deployment of clergy across the forty-three dioceses with a fairer distribution. The TMC proposed, and Synod agreed, that the Bishops should appoint a working group to devise a scheme to that end. Furthermore, an adviser on clergy appointments should be appointed by the Archbishops. Both these ideas were later brought to fruition. A further proposal was for a Measure to dissolve pastoral relationships in cases of disability or ill-health or pastoral breakdown, but it later proved a burdensome piece of legislation, involving huge expenditure by the Church in respect of a couple of cases. The threat of its use, however, has been sufficient to bring to an end some irredeemable pastoral situations.

The fifth proposal, the reform of the Patronage system, proved a bridge too far. It had appeared to be top of the list of needed reforms over previous years, and was the first of the TMC's terms of reference. At first, signs of progress seemed encouraging. It was proposed that at a vacancy in the benefice a small ad hoc Parish Appointment Committee should act. Three parties would be involved - the patron or representatives, the bishop or his deputy with possibly another diocesan representative, and two persons from the PCC. To some in Synod this reform did not go far enough; it did not sufficiently take account of the need for efficient deployment of clergy across a diocese. Reform of patronage should be in the light of that need. So, on a successful amendment to its proposal, the TMC was asked to think again. It fell to me to introduce the committee's second thoughts.

It was necessary to distinguish between deployment and staffing. The former was the responsibility of the Diocesan Pastoral Committee in identifying spheres of service across the diocese and determining the number of posts. Staffing is a confidential exercise involving discussion of names, capabilities and movements. The TMC, therefore, wished to stay with the Parish Appointment Committee proposal. Those most insistent on the deployment need, however, could see no way through, short of abolition of patronage altogether. An amendment to that effect failed by the narrowest of margins. The Houses of Clergy and Laity voted for abolition, there was a dead heat in the House of Bishops, 14-14, an indication of the strength of support for radical reforms in the first quinquennium. From the more conservative section of the Synod came a move to get rid of the idea of a Parish Appointment Committee method. It too failed. Yet when the time came to vote on the TMC motion unamended, a majority was against - not the only time in the Synod's life it has landed in a contradictory position.

The Standing Committee, picking up the bits, appointed a working party to consider further the appointments to benefices - the TMC now being discharged. It proposed alternative systems, A and B, which parishes could decide on. A was a modification of the patronage system, to ensure the concurrence of the PCC and bishop to a patron's nomination. B was a modification of the earlier PAC idea. There would be three Selectors, the bishop, a nominee from the PCC and a nominee by the PCC from outside its membership - if desired it could be a former patron. The hope was that gradually, if not immediately, parishes would move to alternative B. Attempts to eliminate each alternative failed, and the Synod agreed to set in motion a Benefices Measure based on the alternatives.

In 1978, in a new Synod, the Measure received general approval. In the revision stages I found myself involved again as chairman of the steering committee. But it was not for long. I felt compelled to resign - the only time in all my ministry I have resigned from a committee because of differences in policy. There were two developments that seemed to undermine what I, with others, had striven for since the beginning of Synod. One was provision for a parish, once it had opted for alternative B, the Selectors system, to reverse the decision later. The other was an imposed requirement of a two-thirds majority on the PCC in favour of B before it could be implemented. This clearly tipped the whole Measure in favour of the existing patronage system, despite the Synod overwhelmingly approving a balanced dual system by a total of 328 to 51 votes in 1975 and another vote at general approval stage of 327 to 87. In my view it was turning the clock back in the long struggle for a better system of appointment. For over ten years I had sought a system that ensured full common discussion and partnership in decision making by the diocese, represented by the bishop, by the parish by representatives and by the patron, or some other representative of the wider Church, with all sides together through the whole process. Whatever benefits might be claimed for parishes in ensuring the maintenance of their particular churchmanship by the patronage system, I could not see any justification for it on any biblical principles. With the changes proposed in the Revision committee, it would be harder for a parish to leave patronage and easier to return.

The following year, 1980, from the floor of the Synod, I attempted to remove the reversibility provision and the need for a two-thirds majority - an idea nowhere else required at parish level - but the Synod was unconvinced. Between the Revision stage and Final Approval, the Draft Measure was referred to the dioceses. The result was the removal of alternative B, the Selectors system, in 1983. So the Benefices Measure became law in 1985. In terms of substantial, even if evolutionary reform, fifteen years of gestation in General Synod may be said to have brought forth a mouse - an improvement on what had been inherited, undoubtedly, but if the Selectors system had survived would it not have increased the participation and confidence of the laity? I did, however, get some personal satisfaction within my own parish. At a stage of pastoral reorganisation, bringing two parishes into unity, a provision of the Pastoral Measure was used to remove the respective patrons and create a new body consisting of the bishop, one representative from each congregation and a fourth person chosen by the PCC from the General Synod. The parish welcomed the change.

THEOLOGY OF ORDINATION

Through the greater part of the Synod's life up to 1995, understanding of what ordination is or is not has underlain our most divisive debates - relations with the United Churches of the Indian sub-continent, the Anglican/Methodist scheme, the Covenant proposals relating to the Free Churches, the ordination of women to the diaconate and then priesthood. Anyone with foresight could have expected this. Long-standing differences between the Anglican traditions on the meaning of ordination and ministerial priesthood were not going to be laid aside in the interests of merely making progress on contemporary issues.

When men and women have been nurtured spiritually in one of the traditions, particularly Catholic or Evangelical, they cannot lightly contemplate apparent denials of aspects of their tradition. For example, a devout Catholic cannot bear to have a doubt about the validity of the sacrament being received, because he or she knows that in a true sacrament comes assurance of complete acceptance by God. Just so a devout Evangelical must have no doubt about the authority of the Word written or spoken in order to be assured of complete acceptance by God. The two approaches are not incompatible, for Word and Sacrament are joined together by God, but it is easy for each to be critical of the other, or at least to feel superior to the other.

Behind the differing understandings of the ordained ministry lie different but complementary understandings of the Church - at least they should be seen as complementary. The Protestant emphasis is on the invisible company of all believers justified by grace, drawn to God by the Word in Christ. The Catholic emphasis is on the visible Church down the ages in continuity with the Apostles, defined by sacramental membership in the Body of Christ and sustained by God through the ordinances administered by his ordained servants. A full and true doctrine of the Church is not realised by one emphasis overcoming the other, or digging in against the other, but by holding both in creative tension. In an earlier chapter I wrote of the paradox running through the Christian faith. The faith is not a matter of thesis and antithesis creating a synthesis, in the sense of a mixture of common features and elimination of differences. This is not to say there are no errors or false notions on either side; human grasp of the truth is never infallible. So the concern is not Protestant versus Catholic, but Reformed Catholicism.

In the light of these thoughts I have turned again to an important, but not very satisfactory, debate in 1986. It was a report produced by the Faith and Order Advisory Group, *The Priesthood of the Ordained Ministry*, and written against the background of ecumenical failures and division on the ordination of women. A debate on the theology of ordination had taken place in Synod in 1972, and more recently in 1984 it had been debated in both Convocations. My own reaction to the FOAG report was coloured by an informal gathering a year or two earlier of five Evangelicals and Catholics, invited by Dr Garry Bennett, one of the members of FOAG, at New College, Oxford, to discuss ministerial priesthood. In unhurried, thorough debate very substantial agreement was reached. It was something of a disappointment, therefore, that in the Synod debate on the report most of the opposition came from Evangelicals, among them personal friends.

Looking back at the speeches I get the impression that they may have come to the report looking for points to seize on - perhaps the very title disturbed them. If I am wrong I seek forgiveness. A more significant mistake was, I believe, to assume that every description or aspect of understanding of the ordained ministry must have clear warrant in the New Testament, and unless that were so it had to be eschewed. Testing everything by Scripture as our final authority under God must be our primary principle. But to quote Bishop Mark Santer in the debate, 'a rich and coherent understanding of the work of the ordained ministry..... certainly cannot be reduced to the bare language of Scripture .... but equally certainly (is) rooted in Scripture and is not contradictory to it'. There is here, it seems to me, a recognition of development of understanding of biblical truth that has gone on by the Spirit's continuing abiding with the Church. We have it in the ongoing understanding of the Trinity and of Christology. There has been the development of the ordained ministry, though not of the same order as those doctrines. I would be the first to agree that some aspects of the development do run contrary to Scripture, and it is right to repudiate them, but looking closely again at the chapter in the report that attracted most criticism I find it difficult to pin down unscriptural points, though I might have expressed some phrases differently. Another criticism was that it hardly mentioned the ministry of the laity, but the terms of reference did focus on the ordained ministry.

In a brief contribution to the debate I mentioned that, in 1983, in the Evangelical journal, Churchman, a key issue, perhaps the key issue for Evangelicals with regard to the ordained ministry was said to be whether it is to be conceived of only in functional terms or whether it has an ontological character. Rather than use the adjectives, 'functional' or 'ontological', I preferred three verbs, which are justifiable from Scripture and found full expression in the criticised chapter. The verbs were 'to enable, to represent and to signify'. To enable will not be in dispute. To represent the whole priestly body in functions should be acceptable. But to represent Christ to his Church may be difficult for some Evangelicals. Ordination is not just about the Church setting apart. To quote the book, *Growing into Union*, mentioned in a previous chapter - 'the ministry acts in the name of Christ as head of the Church'. I find that truth also in the *Book of Common Prayer*. In summoning reluctant communicants to the Lord's Table the priest calls them 'in the name of God' and 'in Christ's behalf'. The third verb, to signify, not the same as represent, points to the ordained ministry as a sign of the authority and headship of Christ over his Church, including the ministers themselves. There is no direct use of the word 'signify' in the New Testament but its truth may be inferred from the Epistles.

So the debate in 1986 did not contribute much to a consensus on the theology of ordination. One aspect that was never mentioned in the debate, but needs addressing, is the concept of indelibility of orders. It is firmly held in the Catholic tradition, but I question whether it should be regarded as an indisputable Anglican position. It is easy to say, 'once a priest always a priest'. But anyone who has served in the ministry, and no doubt many laity too, will know that clergy can prove absolute misfits, that it is questionable whether some individuals should have been ordained - a mistake was made - and some actually lose their faith and get out of ministry, or at least want to do so. I am not thinking of moral lapses, which may happen to a priest truly called of God. But where a priest is better allowed to depart, what is the point of hanging on? Catholics will say he has received a 'character' in ordination, which cannot be denied. Can that be true, if the Church, and possibly the priest, made a mistake? Christ is 'a priest for ever' after the order of Melchizadek, but we priests are not of his order. And one thing is for sure, we cannot take our priestly 'character', such as it is, to heaven when we die; there are no sacraments or priests, as distinct from all the believing people of God.

THE ORDINATION OF WOMEN

The cause of women's ordination goes back as far as the 1920s, or even earlier. Admittedly it was a small group in the Church of England campaigning at first, at variance with the climate of conviction across the Church. Although deaconesses were said to be in "holy orders" in the early decades of this century, and since 1843 had been "ordained by the laying on of hands", their ministry in worship was very strictly limited. Learned professors in the Convocations in the early 1920s debated what a deaconess might do in church. There was no question of taking a part in Morning or Evening Prayer. It was agreed she might conduct a service for women and children, provided, one, she did from the chancel steps, and, two, there was clear notice given in the parish - necessary, lest a man might inadvertently enter church and 'be turned on sexually' at seeing a woman at the front. The story of the Church of England's treatment of deaconesses in conditions of service, pay, pensions and general recognition till much later in the century is a matter of shame.

By the time the General Synod began, the lobby for ordination of women to the priesthood was considerably stronger. And it was no surprise that, early in the life of the Synod, a major debate took place. It was in 1972, stimulated by a request from the first meeting of the Anglican Consultative Council the previous year that member Churches should offer their views. The story of the struggle from 1972 to final approval of women priests in 1992 would fill a substantial book. Argument and counter argument occur again and again. Reading through the report of the debates one wonders how much listening, as opposed to talking, went on. But there must have been some changing of minds.

The Saga

It is possible only to chart the main stages of the twenty-year story in this chapter and then to offer reflections on the arguments on both sides. The 1972 debate was on a much-praised report on behalf of ACCM by Christian Howard setting out the issues. It was good-natured, a trailer for all to come, and generally mild-mannered.

Despite being a doughty, very experienced protagonist for the cause of women's ordination, Christian balanced the arguments admirably. Even some who later took a strong line against, could accept that the evidence from Scripture was not conclusive, that ordination was a possibility, that 'we should not be over-concerned with the sex of the Apostles or even with ecumenical relations'. These admissions notwithstanding, opposition was firm. Some less-than-respectable arguments were advanced, such as 'the priest before the altar is entirely sexless, and to be thinking of a woman in that place is quite wrong'. It would not be the last time emotion seemed to over-rule reason. The report was received in anticipation of later motions after careful reflection.

In 1975, on the penultimate day of the first quinquennium, the Standing Committee initiated a debate on the motion, 'that there are no fundamental objections to the ordination of women to the priesthood'. The debate was opened by two speeches by bishops, one in favour, one against. As in the rest of the debate, contributions were much more weighty theologically than two years earlier. One or two pointers to future developments were evident - a Conservative Evangelical support for ordination from two speakers, and a fear by one opponent (George Austin) that it might lead to only those in favour being made bishops. The vote in favour of the motion was positive in all three Houses, with the narrowest majority in the House of Clergy. On a following Standing Committee motion, the Synod was asked not to proceed with the necessary legislation, because it believed that the time was not yet ripe - stronger support across the Church was needed. The Synod rejected the motion - it was not content to do nothing. That opened the way for a member of Synod to move that legislation should be prepared. That motion too was rejected. Synod had found itself in a completely contradictory situation. I moved that when the bishops, in the light of developments in the Anglican Communion and in this country, deemed the time for action was ripe they should bring forward proposals. A further point was added to ensure consultation with ecumenical partners. The motion was approved.

In 1978, following the Lambeth Conference in that year, Bishop Hugh Montefiore, recently appointed to Birmingham, proposed the preparation of legislation for admission of women to the priesthood and the episcopate. By now there were already women priests in North America and elsewhere. The Lambeth Conference debate and resolution had fully recognised the divisive nature of the issue across the

Communion, and was generally thought to have bought time for continued debate. The bishop's motion was lost in the House of Clergy.

Support for women's ordination was building up in some dioceses, even to the extent of successful diocesan motions forwarded to General Synod. The Southwark diocese was head of the queue of eight dioceses, and in 1984 its bishop (Ronald Bowlby) presented its motion, this time only for ordination to the priesthood. It was approved in all three Houses, though with the Clergy and Laity there was nowhere near the two-thirds majority ultimately required. The following year the legislation to ordain women as deacons received final approval, though a further attempt to allow women ordained abroad to function as visiting priests in this country failed.

Legislation for women priests was now on its way. There could have been a one-clause Measure simply allowing the step, but because of the substantial minority against, both in the Synod and across the Church, it was decided to have more complex legislation to try to keep as many of those in conscience totally opposed within the Church of England. Dire warnings about the numbers who would leave were being sounded. A report commissioned by the Standing Committee on the options for shaping the legislation did not find favour; whereupon the House of Bishops in 1987 offered a unanimous report on how the Measure should be framed. That unanimity came from bishops for, against, and not sure about the step. What they were saying was, if it is to be, this is how it is best done. Despite a series of spirited attempts to prevent the legislation, or substantially change it, the Synod approved the suggested procedure in all three Houses, just falling short of a two-thirds majority with the clergy, but achieving it with the other two Houses.

The Bishops had been asked to do further study on the theological issues involved in the priesting of women, notwithstanding the Synod decision in 1975 that there were no fundamental objections. The Archbishop of Canterbury (Dr Runcie) in introducing their conclusions in 1988, could say that 'not one bishop appears to consider it (the ordination of women) absolutely impossible'. I recall a conversation at that group of sessions with Bishop Graham Leonard in which he told me he was not an 'impossibilist'. General Approval was given to the Measure and the accompanying Canons. At the Revision Stage the next year the Synod, in the words of Dr Runcie, went through 'two unusually taxing days of debate - the most taxing, I think, in terms of attention, detail and emotional investment that I have known in nineteen years as bishop'.

D Day

So the general Synod came to the most fateful day in all its history thus far, 11 November 1992, when Final Approval was sought for the Measure, Canons relating to it, and the Measure to make financial provision for priests impelled on grounds of conscience to leave the Church of England's stipendiary ministry. This time all was to be decided in one day, from 10.00 a.m. to 6.00 p.m. In the crucial vote, the major focus was on the House of Laity. As a result of the general election of 1990, and votes taken the previous July in the separate Convocations and in the House of Laity, it was believed beforehand that the House of Clergy, along with the Bishops would provide the necessary two-thirds majority, but that would not be the case with the Laity. Intense lobbying and persuasion had gone on in the intervening months. Towards the end of the afternoon, after a spell of silent prayer, as had become customary with such votes, the Registrar's ringing call to 'Divide' propelled the Synod through the voting doors. In silence the Archbishop of Canterbury (George Carey) announced the result. A two-thirds majority had been achieved in the House of Laity with just two votes making the difference. So it was approved in all three Houses.

The result was all the more devastating for opponents, mainly on the Catholic side, because they had expected defeat for the legislation.

Act of Synod

The burning question now was the extent of the secession of priests and laity to Rome, and what might be done to restrict it to as small a number as possible. The ball was in the bishops' court. They, or those who were willing, would be ordaining women, they are pastorally responsible for all in their diocese whatever their conviction, and some arrangements had to be made for bishops conscientiously unable to ordain.

Under the chairmanship of the Archbishop of York (John Habgood) with the agreement of his brother Archbishop, a group of bishops came up with proposals. They presented them in July 1993. The most controversial element was the idea of Provincial Episcopal Visitors, bishops specially consecrated to cover the two provinces, crossing diocesan boundaries to offer episcopal ministry to the priests and parishes who, under the Measure, had refused the ministry of women priests and opted for this special episcope. In 1987 Archbishop Robert Runcie, in a Synod debate, had expressed his belief that there was no way forward in parallel episcopates. He thought that 'Ecumenically it would be more disastrous to jeopardise the episcopal nature of the Church of England than to move towards the ordination of women to the priesthood'. Was the jeopardy being realised? There are parallel episcopates in some Provinces of the Communion, but they are specifically for cultures of indigenous peoples with a sense of isolation from the majority culture composed of people originally from other lands.

One formidable critic was Bishop John Baker, soon to retire from Salisbury. He drew attention to what he saw as the theological weakness. While it accorded with Christian charity to recognise the 'two integrities', those who said 'Yes' and those who said 'No' to women priests, and the aim to preserve unity as far as possible was right, there was inconsistency in saying the official teaching of the Church of England is 'Yes', but those who could not accept the ordination of women by their bishop as valid are on a par with all others in the Church. What undermining of a bishop's authority and role as a focus of unity would there be in having to admit a bishop from outside his diocese to minister to priests and parishes not accepting his own episcopacy in sacramental acts and ordinations?

In the event diocesan bishops have welcomed the 'flying bishops' to their staff meetings and to carry out their ministry. The Bishops' proposals were framed into an Act of Synod. In November 1993 it was overwhelmingly approved, only 26 out of a total of 434 voting against, and on 22 February 1994 the Episcopal Ministry Act of Synod was solemnly affirmed and proclaimed. Actual ordinations of women priests soon followed, somewhere round a thousand by the summer. In devising the Act of Synod and gaining its acceptance, a great debt of gratitude was owed to Dr John Habgood, who won the confidence of so many whose basic approach to women's ordination was different from his own.

How, and when, will the Act of Synod be able to be assessed? Perhaps not for a long time. The number of priests leaving the Church of England has so far been much less than the direst predictions. And some of these men have returned. The degree and extent of bitterness apparent in the American Church, though the division there is not confined to women's ordination, has not been matched in England. A difference of attitude towards the Act does exist, in that some hope it will be a temporary expedient because opposition to women priests will over time disappear, while opponents see that attitude as a threat to the provision for them in the Church as an accepted and continuing part.

PERSONAL REACTIONS

The women's ordination issue had exercised my mind for over thirty years. As already indicated, I had to begin with the headship principle because, as an Evangelical, that seemed the crucial point. But in various articles and booklets I needed to engage with other arguments for and against. From the Catholic side there seemed to be three main arguments. First, Jesus only chose men as his Apostles. To this I could only say I did not accept that he was thus ordering the pattern of ordained ministry for all time. Did he in fact during his earthly ministry before his death have in mind the structure of the Church at all? He promised the Spirit to guide in all things. And if, after the Resurrection, he taught many things including matters about the Church, the result after Pentecost was a proliferation of ministries through men and women. I believe that as his three-year ministry was predominantly towards Israel and its restoration for service to the nations, his choice of twelve men was to be a re-formed patriarchal band, comparable with the patriarchs of old, to serve the messianic community.

A second argument focused on the priest as an ikon of Christ at the altar. I had no problems with the ordained minister being a representative of Christ acting in his name. But there are two questions to face here. In what mode are we to think of Christ when we celebrate his Supper? Not Jesus still as he was in the upper room, surely, but the ascended Christ, having perfected our redemption. That is the Christ the whole Church now represents in the world. And in his ascended work he is not exclusively male but has taken redeemed humanity, male and female, to his Father's glory. A woman can say equally with a man: 'My redeemed human nature is there because I am one with him and he with me.' Why, then, may an ordained woman not represent Christ on earth?

The third argument was about the authority of one part of the Church Catholic to take unilateral action, and thus jeopardise Church unity moves. Dr Garry Bennett, in the discussions I have mentioned, in 1984 told me this was the only respectable argument left against the Church of England ordaining women priests. I recognised the force of the ecumenical considerations. But I recall some words of Father Gerald O'Collins in *The Tablet* quoted in 1975: 'If our ecumenical relations would be upset by recognising the full dignity of women in Church life (ie ordination) they are the wrong kind of relations. Ecumenical relations which would be harmed by the ordination of women are not worth having.' I do not pretend he had the authority of the Church to say that.

When Anglo-Catholics want to emphasise that Anglicans are but a small part of the Catholic Church, I question their definition of the Catholic Church. It must not be restricted to those Churches that have retained the three-fold order including episcopacy. All Churches committed to the Trinitarian and Apostolic Faith are part of the Church universal, holy, catholic, apostolic. Of that total body, Anglicans are indeed a small part, but they are not the only part to ordain women. True, other Churches do not intend to make priests in the Roman understanding, but neither do all Anglicans. They do intend them to be ministers of Word and Sacrament.

More particularly, on the question of authority, I would insist that any part of the Church Catholic has authority to do what it believes the Lord would want for his whole Church. It has an obligation to consult other parts, to listen carefully to objections and weigh them seriously, but it cannot be paralysed, waiting for some General Council unlikely to happen. The indisputable fact is that other Churches act as they think they should without being held up. That is certainly true of the Roman Catholic Church, and the Orthodox Churches. The size of those Communions, representing the greater part of Christendom, is not ultimately a deciding factor. In Christian history the majority has not always been right.

When I had satisfied myself on the headship issue, I found further positive reasons for the rightness of women's ordination. Over the past two hundred years or so, the expansion of the Church across the world has owed much to women, many unmarried, who have founded, nurtured and led many young churches in their early days. God had obviously equipped these women with gifts for his work, and meant them to be used. But also in the Church at home were women employed as Parish Workers, Deaconesses and then Deacons, who clearly had the gifts that would find fuller expression as Priests. As chairman of a diocesan Council for Women's Ministry, I had witnessed these gifts. Indeed, on my staff, along with a succession of male colleagues, I also had a woman who began as a Parish Worker. My first wife, Ruth, died in 1992, a year later I married my colleague, Brenda, then a Deacon. A year after that she was priested. All this, some may say, shows I am biased! But it seems, from the collective evidence of women priests since 1994, God has given them the requisite gifts.

Further, I take seriously the concept of development of revealed truths in the New Testament. Principles are introduced there that in due time bring new situations. The institution of slavery, still accepted in first century Christian minds, was after many centuries ended, as the implications of biblical truths were worked out when historic conditions were ripe. Opponents of women's ordination have said that step has no parallel with the ending of slavery. In one of the debates in the Synod in the 1970s I was standing in the hope of being called to speak. A lay man from the Norwich diocese just behind me passed a note which I still have - he did not think he would be called. It reads, 'My great-grandfather, Thomas F. Buxton, laboured for years to bring in his Act for the Abolition of Slavery. He had strong opposition from certain sections of the Church; their arguments were exactly the same - based on Scripture - as we have heard against the motion this morning [I have his papers and can vouch for this!]'.

In the last hundred years or so we have seen a revolution in conditions for women - in education equality, technological devices easing the burdens of housework, medical discoveries in family planning. It has resulted in hitherto unimagined enlargement of opportunity for women in a partnership with men in all walks of life. This context, surely part of God's purpose in history even if, as with all good things there can be abuses, is the matrix in which the New Testament principle of equality and complementarity (as in the created order) of women and men in God's Kingdom can be more fully realised. This is not to underestimate the distinctiveness of the sexes but to maximise their mutual contributions to a partnership. It seemed to me a most strange notion that a full partnership of women and men in the ordained ministry must be denied, when in society at large a full partnership is not only possible but welcomed by Christians. The Church is a sign and earnest of God's Kingdom, his New Order. Are women's opportunities for full use of their God-given gifts to be less there than in the old order in the world?

I turn back to another Synod debate in 1975 for another insight. It came from Bishop John Taylor. The original priesthood is that of humanity in the generic sense. As the culmination and crown of the created process he stands between the rest of creation, though part of it, and the Creator God. He is in a mediatorial role between God and creation, acting with and for God in the created order and articulating for the rest of creation the praise due to God. In that priestly role, humanity is created male and female. John Taylor maintained, 'Through the Fall Man forfeited his priesthood, but in Christ it was restored. Christ is true priest because he is true Man. And in him the way is opened for mankind to take up again its original priesthood.' He went on to speak of the Church as the *pars pro toto*, a royal priesthood, on behalf of the rest of mankind, and within the Church the ordained ministry as *pars in toto* to enable the whole of God's people to exercise its priesthood. The logic of this imaginative line of thought seems to me to be that, as in the original purpose male and female share together, so they should share in the New Order in all aspects of ministry.

I have sketched out the grounds on which my own support for the ordination of women priests has been based in order to offer some answer to the oft-repeated charge that supporters were in captivity to the culture of the modern age, unduly swayed by extreme feminism. Feminist demands and clamour for justice do not go to the heart of the matter in my judgement - however important justice is - the ordination of women must be a matter of theology, ecclesiology and the Kingdom.

CROWN APPOINTMENTS COMMISSION

Reflection on ten years on the Commission involving thirty-nine appointments (1982-92) must largely be confined to private thoughts under the constraints of commitment of confidentiality and respect for individuals in the processes. Nevertheless, there are general observations that may be worth recording.

A major question revolves round the possibility of further evolution of the process of appointing diocesan bishops - the matter concerning other senior appointments, suffragans, deans and provosts, archdeacons and cathedral canons has been under review, but the present Crown Appointments Commission could not cope with such added assignments. There can be no argument that the present system is both theologically and ecclesiologically an improvement on the pre-1977 way of appointing bishops. The Church now has a decisive voice, expressed by elected laity and clergy with the Archbishops and in conjunction with representatives of the vacant diocese chosen by its diocesan Vacancy-in-See Committee. In addition, the secretaries of the Prime Minister and the Archbishops consult widely in the diocese, both within the Church and in the wider community. Upon these consultations profiles of all nominated persons, whose names have been submitted by the Commission members and diocesan representatives, are prepared for the eventual selection meeting.

In the two decades of its operation, the CAC has adopted some refinements of a practical nature while remaining within its terms of reference. They have chiefly been to improve the profile information on nominees and to ensure that both names submitted to the Prime Minister are approved by the Commission - earlier there was sometimes an assumption that the name first offered with obvious preference would be chosen, whereas the Prime Minister has freedom to submit either name to the Sovereign or to ask for a rethink.

It is not minor refinements, however, that occasion widespread discussion. Should the process be more open? Should there be interviews, at any rate of a short-list of candidates? Should applications be allowed? Let it be said right away, a 'bit more open' process is not really practicable. There is no half-way house between the present full confidentiality and openness, in my view. Even if there were a move only as far as interviewing, say, three or four persons, leakage of information might be more likely. And each appointment would involve at least two meetings of the CAC. We must acknowledge, however, that in the world outside the Church, and indeed for some important church appointments, an interview system operates.

There are varied systems of appointment across the Anglican Communion where openness is the pattern. But it has to be said that they can afford scope for political intrigue, trade-offs between pressure groups, personal campaigns. That is not to say the Lord cannot overrule and good appointments not come through. What can be said about the strict confidentiality followed at present? It is claimed to protect possible candidates, their families, and possibly their dioceses, from unsettlement. Whatever the media and church gossip may do, no one is told they are on the list for consideration - unless an individual on the Commission is nominated for consideration. But should possible unsettlement of those under consideration be a major concern? Most moves in the church inevitably entail a review, with some degree of unsettlement, of present commitments. Again, most clergy seeking or exploring a move prefer to keep the initial stages confidential, presumably to avoid unnecessarily unsettling their congregation. If a serving bishop were known to be attending interviews for another diocese, would it be known and would the unsettlement on his diocese have more serious effects than in the case of a parish?

It is possible to make out a case for the CAC being able to interview a short-list. Almost inevitably at present, some on the full list of nominees - there can be fifteen or so - will be unknown to one or more members of the Commission, the eight permanent members and the four from the diocese. In that case there are only the profiles and general reactions of other members to go on. It is more likely that the diocesan representatives are at a disadvantage here.

Even an apparently modest reform of interviewing, however, immediately runs into a constitutional issue. The CAC system is based on an agreement between the Prime Minister and Leaders of the main Opposition Parties pre-1977 and the Church of England. In the negotiations Sir Norman Anderson, a distinguished Chairman of the House of Laity, Law Professor and former missionary, with service in the Church Assembly as well as Synod, played a leading part. The Sovereign was still to be the one who appoints bishops. The Sovereign acts on the advice of her Chief Minister. The Prime Minister, we are told, cannot be reduced to that of a postman simply conveying a message for the Commission to the Sovereign, hence, the provision for him or her to make a genuine choice between nominees, or to ask the CAC to think again. So, would the interviewing process tend to compromise the necessary confidentiality at this final stage of appointment? Short of disestablishment it may be difficult, or even impossible, to make changes of any substance.

I will admit to a questioning of the role of the Prime Minister in the process of appointments during my ten years on the CAC. In respect of two or three of the thirty-nine appointments, it seemed to me that political considerations may have played a significant part in the Prime Minister's choice between the two nominated. I emphasise it was guess-work on my part. We were not told whether the Commission's No.1 was approached, nor if approached whether he had declined. But where a strongly preferred nominee was not appointed, and where the political leanings of the other appeared to be nearer those of the Prime Minister, and was appointed, speculation arose. Without any doubt the Prime Ministers have acted entirely within their rights and obligations in the system.

Speculation on more than one occasion, then, raised for me the question whether advice to the Sovereign might go through some channel other than the Prime Minister. After all, there could eventually be a Prime Minister personally hostile to the Church, or much more politically motivated in making appointments. Church-State relations can result in a betrayal of the Gospel, as was seen in Nazi Germany. It can be argued that disestablishment would come in England before such a disaster, or that the ethos of this nation's establishment would keep Prime Ministers acting honourably. I wondered, therefore, if the conveyancing of the CAC's discussion on an appointment could be by the Archbishops, as members of the Privy Council, to the Sovereign. In a General Synod debate in February 1993, concerned with a way forward in respect of other senior appointments made by the Crown, opinion was divided between the impossibility of by-passing the Prime Minister and the desirability of further exploration.

I now offer some further general observations on the years on the Commission, before going on to a specific event. Speculation in the media, church and secular, about likely appointments or the reasons behind the Commission's choices, are often wide of the mark. The confidentiality process inevitably stimulates widespread speculation, search for leaks, and even book-maker's interests, the more so in respect of senior bishoprics. Very considerable misinformation, yet presented as authentic, surrounded, and still in the media surrounds, the appointment of the present Archbishop of Canterbury, for instance. Even years later journalistic speculation is wide of the mark. In my two terms on the CAC there was only one serious leak of information, to the best of my knowledge, and that I think did not come from the Commission's permanent members.

In the appointing process the role of the 'diocesan four' should not be underestimated. If they are agreed in opposing any nominee, the permanent members of the CAC accept their view. The composition of the four differs from vacancy to vacancy. Within their number there can be quite different perceptions of the suitability of a nominee to their diocese's needs. Sometimes the CAC has been criticised for not appointing strong 'characters' (meaning 'controversial'? 'eccentric'?) to the House of Bishops. It is here that the influence of the diocesan representatives can be considerable. Faced with a choice between a man likely to stir up controversy and, possibly, division in the diocese and a safer candidate, the temptation to opt for the latter is strong. I recall many cases where clergy morale in the diocese was reported to be low. So, a bishop who had considerable parish experience was asked for by the four.

I do not think the permanent members in my time thought a pastorally-minded bishop necessarily to be one with the bulk of his previous ministry in parishes. In fact, I recall one appointment where three of the diocesan four were not happy about the limited parochial experience of the person nominated. A year or two later, one of the three concerned admitted their fears had been unfounded; they were encouraged by their bishop's deep pastoral concerns. It has to be emphasised that, when attending the CAC meeting, the diocesan representatives are full members of the Commission with the same voting rights as the others. Vacancy-in-See Committees need to ensure that the four persons they send are as representative of the diocese as possible - clergy and laity, different traditions - but also capable of independent judgement. They are not delegates but representatives.

As with most elections of the four from a diocese, so with the five-year elections of three clergy and three laity from General Synod to the CAC, party traditions and churchmanship have a significant influence. I can say, however, that in my two terms on the CAC there was a healthy disinclination to divide simply on party lines. Mutual respect and a warm relationship can build up among permanent members crossing traditions.

In respect of Archiepiscopal appointments, of which there was one for each province in the years 1982-92, the process is more lengthy, the consultation more widespread, and additional members include chairpersons, appointed by the Prime Minister after consultation with the General Synod Standing Committee, who are prominent lay members of the Church of England. In the case of the Archbishop of Canterbury, consultation includes all the Primates of the Anglican Communion and is expressed in person through its Secretary-General. Instead of the Archbishops, one senior bishop from each of the Provinces of Canterbury and York joins the Commission for that appointment.

I turn finally to a specific event during my time on the CAC. In the summer of 1987, elections to the third term of the CAC took place. One of the three clergy appointments was Dr Garry Bennett. He invited me to New College, Oxford, to discuss the work of the Commission. In the course of a twenty-four hour stay I heard from him all the criticisms of the CAC and of Archbishop Robert Runcie's role in it that I was later to read in the famous *Crockford's Preface*, though he gave no hint at all of his authorship. I made it as clear as I could that on several important points he was mistaken, so far as my experience in the previous five years convinced me. In particular, I sought to correct his view that the Archbishop of Canterbury dominated discussions to ensure his favourites were elected. He expressed his deep concern at what he saw was a lack of strong Catholic leadership in the House of Bishops, in face of the threat to that tradition when the ordination of women to the priesthood came, as he thought it would. In my surprise, I raised the names of bishops then in office. Some, he said, would have retired or be about to retire; others he maintained 'had not proved themselves'. Of others he was bluntly critical. We agreed, however, that a stream of bishops firmly in that tradition was necessary, and I undertook to raise the matter at the first meeting of the new Commission the next month. It was to be a general discussion meeting with no particular vacancy on the agenda. I thought it might be easier for me to raise it than for him, though I pointed out how some diocesan representatives, following strong opinion voiced on their Vacancy-in-See Committee, and recorded in their Committee's statement, would turn against a known opponent of women priests, or would avoid someone strongly in favour. Garry Bennett expressed his warm appreciation of the way that first meeting went, and in particular of the support for concern for Catholic leadership. So we came to the first, and for him only, appointment meeting. It was, as he acknowledged to me, a good and harmonious meeting. Soon after came the tragedy of his death. The question that has haunted me is, did he come to feel he had earlier misjudged the CAC and the role of Archbishop Runcie, and was that a contributory factor to his despair? I cannot claim a friendship with him as close as others, but through these contacts, and earlier ones when invited to New College, I came to appreciate a relationship of trust. He seemed to me to struggle with some frustration and disappointment at being left so long in his Oxford post.

When the *Crockford's Preface* appeared, I tried to analyse the twenty appointments made in the previous five-year term. Acknowledging the difficulty of pigeon-holing bishops into churchmanship traditions, my conclusions were that five could be broadly Evangelical, seven broadly Catholic (though of those, three were against women priests' ordination) and eight described as Liberal or middle of the road. Finding a label for the last category is difficult, as some were conservative in certain matters. I also attempted to assess the criticism of undue influence of Archbishop Runcie in appointments. I concluded that five of the twenty had had close associations with him, five more had had some association but not much in the case of two or three, and with ten there had been no real association in the past. Archbishop Runcie continued with the Commission for another two years. Of the eight further appointments in his time as Archbishop two were Evangelical, three Catholic (two certainly voted against the ordination of women) and the other three middle of the road, if they could accept that description.

MISSION AND EVANGELISM

If ministry is a portmanteau word, as already suggested, the same is even more true of mission. It covers everything the Church is sent into the world to do. Reports concerning mission come to general Synod from the Board of Mission and Unity (now the Board of Mission) but the Board for Social Responsibility and the Council of Education, the latter particularly in relation to the Church's work among the young, also cover aspects of mission. It is not surprising therefore, that a series of reports over the years have largely dealt with the meaning of mission and the place of evangelism in it. Seldom have debates on the reports revealed emotional divisions as with other major issues. Indeed most speeches would be in praise of the reports, sprinkled with anecdotes in support. As a consequence, there was a tendency after initial stages in the debates for a substantial retreat to the refreshment room. With hindsight some of the reports would have lost nothing of their value by being referred directly to dioceses and parishes without prior debate in General Synod.

Archbishop John Habgood, in one debate, suggested, perhaps half seriously, a moratorium on the word mission. Because it was comprehensive in meaning and meant different things to different people, it would be better to use verbs - to witness, to proclaim, to serve, to change unjust structures, to heal, to be (as God wants his people to be). It is certainly helpful to think of mission in terms of verbs and evangelism as about a noun, the Evangel.

The first Synod debate on Mission and Evangelism was in 1974. Behind the report, *Evangelism Today*, was three years' difficult discussion within the BMU. Two attempts to get a report together failed. Criticism of the second draft landed me with chairing a small group to have another try. The background to the difficulties is worthy of note. In the early 1970s there was still a wide gap between those who saw Evangelism, and even the whole of Mission, as proclaiming the Gospel with the aim of personal conversions, and those who thought the Church's record in matters of justice, caring and service was too poor to justify preaching a Gospel. She needed to be a 'presence', a silent, serving presence in the world. Protagonists of both positions tended to indulge in verbal bombardments from entrenched positions. The divide was not confined to England, it existed world-wide. The 1974 report attempted to define evangelism within the totality of mission, an essential part within the whole range of mission responsibilities. The mid-70s saw three international documents converge on that same understanding. In the July before the Synod debate an International Congress on World Evangelisation (a gathering of Evangelicals) at Lausanne could say: 'We must repudiate as demonic the attempt to drive a wedge between evangelism and social action.' It marked a most significant development in Evangelical attitudes. In 1975 the fifth WCC Assembly in Nairobi on the theme Confessing Christ Today and Pope Paul VI's *Evangelii Nuntiandi*, (Evangelisation in the Modern World), issued as an Apostolic Exhortation, both emphasised the same message. It did not mean debate was over, but it became less sterile. Subsequent reports from the BMU carried forward the exploration of what mission meant in today's world. In this the Board was helped by a group for missiological and theological study. *The Measure of Mission* in 1987 was acclaimed as achieving a wider agreement on theological questions about mission and evangelism than had been evident in the Church hitherto.

Debating reports is one thing, taking action is another. In its first twenty-five years the Synod has twice been faced with decisions to make in regard to two major challenges on Evangelism - the Nationwide Initiative in Evangelism and the Decade of Evangelism.

The Nationwide Initiative in Evangelism

The request for the Church of England to take part in the NIE - at first known as the National Initiative in Evangelism - came from the British Council of Churches. Behind that initiative were different strands of thought and groupings. There was a wide range of Evangelicals chiefly focused in the Evangelical Alliance. Some of them were keen on another Billy Graham Crusade in Britain in 1978, some were not, but there was a general desire for some new initiative. Contacts with the British Council of Churches revealed a reciprocal feeling that the time was ripe for some initiative in 1978 or '79. It could be a national mission provided it was centred on the local church, it wanted to emphasise local churches working together, and the message was to be the Gospel in its wholeness. Under the chairmanship of the Archbishop of Canterbury (Dr Donald Coggan) a 'Lambeth Group' prepared proposals. The group had BCC, Evangelical Alliance and other Evangelical interests, and Bible Society representation.

Three stages were envisaged in the NIE. They were set out by the Bishop of Guildford (David Brown) as Chairman of BMU in introducing the debate on the Church of England's response in November 1977. The first stage was to be an evaluation of local evangelistic efforts, encouragement of new ones, and an exploration of convergence of Evangelical and ecumenical attitudes. Stage two was a proposed National Assembly on Evangelism in 1980, to reflect on the first stage and look forward. Stage three would be, it was hoped, more concerted ecumenical Evangelism through the 1980s.

The Synod agreed to a positive response to the BCC invitation, and asked the Standing Committee to ensure synodical representation on the Council to oversee the initiative. The Bishop of Guildford, Dame Betty Ridley and I were appointed. From the beginning there was a mixture of optimism and doubts. Many had a vision of what might come from the NIE, but their visions did not coincide. Even from the Evangelical Alliance, a mixed body of members from mainline Churches and others more independent, there were differences. As already mentioned, some saw another Billy Graham Crusade as an integral part, some were opposed to that. Some wanted a Church-growth programme 'to treble the numbers of convinced Christians in the country by 1980, and to have at least five percent informed Christians in every segment of our society'. Others eschewed the setting of numerual targets. And it was obvious there was some distrust of co-operation with the BCC, which could lead to 'weakening of the Gospel message'. From the BCC side and from the Roman Catholic representation, there was suspicion that the initiative could be driven by narrow Evangelical aims and the Kingdom imperatives in the Gospel be ignored. The Council of Reference set up an Initiative Committee, but the co-operation between the two failed at certain points.

Perhaps the most successful achievement in the process was the production of a convergence statement on The Gospel we affirm together. It covered seven affirmations, but it still could not be described as consensus, and so some suspicions remained on the Evangelical side.

The National Assembly took place at Nottingham in September 1980. Though it drew only about half the 1,800 people hoped for, it was a more representative spread of Christians at a large conference in England than ever before - and on Evangelism at that. As the Assembly proceeded, there was criticism of the lack of attention to the relationship of the Kingdom of God to Evangelism and the Church. An extra session had to be introduced to ventilate the concern.

The Initiative had owed much to the initial efforts and support of Archbishop Donald Coggan. On his retirement, the three of us on the Council of Reference conveyed its invitation to his successor, Dr Runcie, to replace him as Chairman. In the early days of his Primacy he did not feel he was able to do that, but undertook to give a major address at the Assembly. Following the Assembly, the work of NIE was expected to continue in a new Initiative Council replacing the Council of Reference and the Initiative Committee. Its demise in 1983 was occasioned as much as anything by the failure of participating bodies, including the Church of England, to provide funding beyond 1982.

Was the NIE a failure? The story of it, published by the BCC and Council of Churches of Britain and Ireland, was entitled, *An unwanted child?*. Despite all the frustration and disappointments, it opened up new possibilities in co-operation. It can be said to have contributed to the process of creating new ecumenical instruments in these islands, in which the Roman Catholics and other Churches not hitherto associated would participate. The BCC set up an Evangelism Unit. The Mission England project in 1984 owed a lot to the goodwill built up in NIE. And in the longer term the NIE contributed to the atmosphere in which the Decade of Evangelism was welcomed. The Decade must be a feature of the next chapter, launched throughout the Anglican Communion and originating not in English minds. When it was debated in General Synod in 1989, support for it was sobered as well as encouraged by the experiences of the NIE.

Faith in the City

Differences of approach in the NIE process had revealed continuing debate as to what must be included in the term Evangelism. Reference has already been made to complaints of neglect of Kingdom imperatives, social justice, compassion for the oppressed and so on. With justification, it could be argued that when Jesus entered his public ministry, preaching the Good News of the Kingdom, he covered more than personal repentance and faith in God through himself. What the debate had demonstrated afresh was the impossibility of keeping the various aspects of mission in distinct compartments. Mission is all of a piece and, while at certain times and circumstances one's attention and energies should be directed towards proclaiming the Good News of Jesus Christ crucified and risen for a verdict in individual lives, mission's other aspects must not be forgotten. A starving, oppressed person has prior needs. General William Booth told his Salvationist officers in the worst nineteenth century slums that their order of priorities was soup, soap and then salvation. Good News had to be seen in deed before being heard in word. The *Faith in the City* report in 1985 was concerned with the Evangel in deed.

Four years earlier, one of the firm challenges from the Partners-in-Mission Consultation had been to 'stand alongside the poor and to take steps to redistribute resources to further Mission in inner city areas'. Within two years, Archbishop Robert Runcie took the initiative to set up the Archbishop of Canterbury's Commission on Urban Priority Areas. He was influenced by a group of bishops serving largely industrialised dioceses, but in synodical terms the initiative was his. It did not arise from a Board or a Private Member's Motion or the Standing Committee, but was an example of episcopal leadership in a matter of major significance. The Standing Committee endorsed the initiative and the CBF found the funds, though it had not been originally in the budget.

The Commission's report had some adverse publicity before it reached Synod for debate. It touched a raw nerve in some government supporters because it was critical of failure of policy and action in urban priority areas - but it had also exposed the Church's failures. The report was even categorised as Marxist by one who should have read it more carefully. While others accused the Church of England of 'meddling in politics' - one or two voices in the Synod debate echoed the charge. The Synod as a whole warmly welcomed the report, including the proposal to set up a Church Urban Fund.

The establishment of the Fund, for which the dioceses raised in excess of £20 million, and subsequent allocation of a large number of grants for a wide range of projects, has been one of the great achievements of the Church of England in the past decades. The report had highlighted the difficulty felt by Black Anglicans - a term used to cover several ethnic groups - in getting representation on Church councils and synods. By a series of measures emanating from the Standing Committee's response to the report, and actions from individuals, remedies were sought. The problem, however, remains. In voting for representatives to all Church bodies a positive concern for ethnic minorities must be seen as a Christian responsibility.

Faith in the Countryside

In September 1990, an Archbishops' Commission in Rural Areas produced what might be seen as a companion to Faith in the City, Faith in the Countryside. On a superficial judgement there might seem little in common between deprived inner city areas and isolated rural communities. But the Commission drew attention to urgent rural housing needs to enable young families to remain in the country for such employment as was still available, to the need for programmes of care in the community, to the effects of dwindling public transport facilities, and real poverty amid apparent affluence for some. This time the report received a general welcome from government supporters.

The report highlighted a crisis for the Church in the countryside. With diminishing numbers of stipendiary clergy, the burden of maintaining old churches of historic interest, and as a result increasing difficulties in the relationship of the Church to the community, new patterns of ministry for both the clergy and laity were needed. Indeed, these were beginning to emerge with signs of encouragement.

The Archbishop of Canterbury, Dr Runcie, in welcoming the report in the closing days of his archiepiscopate, reminded the Synod that a similar Archbishops' Commission in 1920, a time of more settled country life, had recommended radical changes to meet rural needs. They included abolition of the parson's freehold, regular review of the parson's position in the parish, a significant rise in clergy pay, and a more creative part in church life for laity, particularly women.

The report was warmly received by the Synod. It supported its recommendations, and included a welcome for the Archbishops' initiative in appointing a Rural Officer to assist in the follow-up.

CHRISTIAN INITIATION

Throughout the life of the Synod encompassed by this chapter, it has failed to resolve differences of understanding regarding Christian Initiation. Is Baptism the complete rite of initiation? If it is, and the New Testament evidence appears to suggest it is, why the need for another rite, Confirmation, before admission to Holy Communion? Confirmation is undoubtedly valued as a necessary pastoral opportunity, even by those who do not regard it as an essential part of initiation. But what happens at Confirmation? Different answers are given within Anglicanism. One can remember, in early days in the ministry, presenting candidates for Confirmation and hearing the bishop tell them they were about to receive the Holy Spirit - just like that. What, then, was their baptism about? The fact that bishops' addresses are more restrained on that point may be due to a series of debates on the issues involved without resolving them.

In the first year of Synod's life, it debated the report of the Ely Commission on Christian Initiation. The Bishop of Ely, in introducing it described the subject as 'of paramount importance to the whole of Christian life'. Yet by that time (1971) the Church at the centre and in the dioceses had already been discussing and reporting on it for at least thirty years. It is high time to move on from here, he maintained. The Commission had researched Anglican history, but also the background to it in the western Churches. The practice of Infant Baptism was reaffirmed, but a Service of Thanksgiving for the birth of a child was advocated - a proposal that was later to come to fruition. Baptism with water in the Trinitarian name was accepted as the full and complete and only rite of Christian Initiation. This did not imply a denigration of Confirmation. It was and would still be a rite of adult commitment and commissioning, commitment to a well understood pattern of life in the Church and commissioning by God, the Holy Spirit, with grace given to measure up to the commitment.

In the debate, some of the research conclusions were challenged, and though the report was received, opposition to the main contention on Baptism as the complete rite was clearly voiced.

In 1974, debate on the Ely report was resumed. A motion that Infant Baptism should continue to be available to the children of all parents requesting it and willing and able to make the requisite promises - and that the new baptismal services should reflect this view - was approved. An attempt to include in the provisions that parents should afford some evidence of being able to fulfil their promises was defeated. A motion of more far-reaching significance accepted the principle that full sacramental participation may precede a mature profession of faith. On the basis of this, the dioceses were to be asked if they would support a reordering of initiation practice, either by admission of baptised persons to the Holy Communion at the discretion of the parish priest in consultation with the bishop followed later by Confirmation by the bishop, or by uniting the laying on of hands and/or anointing with oil to Baptism, followed after preparation by admission to the Holy Communion and, subsequently, where appropriate, by affirmation of baptismal vows with further laying on of hands.

Following the reference to the dioceses, I was required in 1976, on behalf of the Standing Committee, to test the Synod's mind on the possibility of allowing alternative patterns to co-exist in the Church. The mixed economy would preserve the traditional pattern as well as allowing admission to Holy Communion before a mature profession of faith. The Synod was put off by the prospect of different practices, even within the same deanery, although some dioceses wanted to accept the experiment. Instead it went for a motion inviting bishops to admit younger children to Confirmation, after consultation with their Synods, and to encourage a periodic renewal of baptismal vows in adult life. It was intended as a compromise.

In the earlier 1974 debate the Rev Peter Cornwell, later to join the Roman Catholic Church, had presented a working paper in which he suggested to the Synod that in face of competing solutions in the Church, we could seek a mediating position, but he saw no sign of it emerging. That being so, there were three courses of action - to do nothing, to seek to convert the majority to one point of view, to accept not only a pluralism of belief but also a pluralism of practice. The second option was not on. The third had its problems, but might be a temporary expedient. On the first option he guessed that if 'central authority did nothing, private enterprise would do a lot of things'. How right he was! Experiments admitting children to

Communion before Confirmation began in some parishes. Almost ten years after the compromise motion in 1976, to confirm younger children 'after consultation with Synods', no evidence was found of any bishop consulting his Synod. What did happen was the setting-up of working parties in dioceses - fourteen by 1985 - to consider Communion before Confirmation. As a result, a handful of dioceses adopted a policy of allowing the experiment, while a larger number granted permission to specific parishes for a period.

It was the Winchester diocese that raised the matter again in General Synod, with a Diocesan Motion requesting the change in certain dioceses for a period of twelve years as a pilot experiment 'in the light of the growing demand'. That was in 1980. It was debated in 1983. An amendment removed reference to the growing demand and the experimental provisions. As a consequence, the motion asked the Standing Committee to review the 1976 decision against the new pattern of initiation; and received a two to one vote in favour. A working party was set up under the chairmanship of the Bishop of Knaresborough, and its report appeared in 1985. It took evidence from dioceses and parishes. Unanimously the working party went further than the Winchester motion in its original form. They recommended a change in practice beyond limited experiments, based firmly on recognition that Baptism is the sacramental sign of full incorporation into the Church. Subsequent to the report's publication, but before its debate in Synod, there appeared the conclusions of an International Anglican Consultation on Children and Communion, responding to the 1968 Lambeth Conference call for an examination of the theology of initiation and admission to Communion. The conclusions were in line with the Knaresborough report.

The Synod once again revealed anxieties lest changes would downgrade the importance of Confirmation, but in the end it took note of the report as a launching document by a substantial majority.

In July 1991, the Synod returned to the subject of Christian Initiation. It was faced with a draft Canon relevant to the 1974 decision, that parents asking for baptism of their children should be able and willing to make the promises. Now the Synod rejected the 'being able' concept, not only on grounds that such ability could not be assessed, but also because most members were resisting a more rigid baptismal discipline. Immediately afterwards, a composite motion from the House of Bishops was presented to test the mind of Synod. It affirmed the traditional sequence of Baptism, Confirmation, admission to Communion as normative, re-affirmed the 1976 decision that within that sequence Confirmation could be at an early age, and urged that experiments of admission to Communion before Confirmation should be discontinued. The Synod rejected the latter point. A majority, including some bishops and many involved in religious education, wanted such experiments to continue. A following motion from the Rochester diocese, asking for the bishops to prepare regulations to enable children's admission to Communion before Confirmation was, however, defeated in the House of Bishops though gaining slim majorities in the other two Houses.

After nearly a century or working parties, reports and debates at diocesan and national level, the Church of England can still not make up its mind on Christian Initiation. It cannot agree on whether Baptism is, sacramentally, a complete act of initiation. And, though it accords a high place to Confirmation, insisting it is to be administered by a bishop whereas other Churches, Roman and Lutheran, leave it to parish clergy, the rite itself remains in a search for an agreed theology.

As I write, the House of Bishops has issued guidelines which allow the possibility of admission of children to Communion before Confirmation with the support of the bishop. At last a development that has sound pastoral implications may be officially approved.

MARRIAGE AND DIVORCE

If the Church of England cannot make up its mind on Christian Initiation, the same is true of its policy on Divorce and Marriage of those who have been divorced. Here we touch human nature at a deep level of emotions. The atmosphere in every Synod debate on the matter has revealed that. Indeed on all issues touching human sexuality there has been a similar atmosphere. Debates on homosexuality were fraught in a particular way - I will not comment on them as I have already offered observations in the previous chapter. Earlier debates on the Church's responsibilities towards those whose marriages had failed, drew out of many speakers obvious anxieties. If in any way, particularly in changes of attitudes and discipline, the Church appeared to be relaxing its commitment to marriage as a life-long, exclusive partnership, what would be the effect on our children's or close relatives' marriage? In the escalating divorce rate, marriages within church families were no more immune than others. As the years went by, and perhaps more Synod members had to come to terms with the break-up of marriage in their own extended families, realism, though continuing concern, seemed more evident. By the time the Synod debated Cohabitation, that appeared to be so.

The Situation before the Synod

Before briefly surveying the Synod's debates on Marriage and Divorce it may be useful to describe the position it inherited at the beginning of its life. The Church's commitment to life-long, exclusive partnership in marriage was undiminished. The Prayer Book service and then the ASB service together leave no doubts. There were, and still are, Convocation Regulations against the marriage of a divorced person in church during the life time of a former partner. These Regulations date from 1938 in York, 1957 in Canterbury, no earlier. Indeed, the Churches of the Reformation had almost all allowed divorce and remarriage. So have the Orthodox Churches. Before 1857, divorce was possible only by a private Act of Parliament, but remarriage in church was allowed to such divorcees, if a priest was willing. By an Act in 1857, divorce became open to anyone on grounds of adultery. This would cause a difficulty for priests unwilling to marry divorcees, because up to then all parishioners had a right to be married in their parish church. So, on grounds of conscience, a priest was relieved by the same Act from the obligation. Nevertheless some priests continued to conduct marriages of divorcees.

Why did the Church of England through its Convocations act to prevent such marriages? Between the World Wars the rate of divorce had risen steeply. The year 1938 was not long after the Abdication crisis and the subsequent marriage of the Duke of Windsor by an Anglican priest in France. It was also shortly after the A.P. Herbert bill making divorce somewhat easier. The possibility of increasing numbers of remarriages in church alarmed many church members. But, in addition to these factors, the concept of indissolubility of the marriage bond had gained ground in the Church of England, as compared with earlier centuries, due to the ascendancy of the Anglo-Catholic movement in the 1920s and '30s.

The indissolubility issue has underlain all the debates in Synod. All agree that the marriage bond, according to the divine will, ought not to be dissolved. The dissolution of a marriage is a falling short, a sin. The Catholic view is that the bond in fact cannot be broken. Dissolubility is impossible - hence, the Roman Catholic practice of invoking the nullity concept, even in cases where a marriage has produced children. Those of Catholic persuasion had not always taken the strict indissolubilist line, however. Edward King, Bishop of Lincoln and eminent Catholic leader, said in 1895, 'I am unable to accept the conclusions of those who make marriage absolutely indissoluble and so forbid the remarriage of those who have been separated under any circumstances'. It is much to be regretted that the media generally presents the Anglican position as indissolubilist. It is the position of some Anglicans, but it has never been the Anglican position.

Law and Grace

The witness of the Church to God's will for marriage must be undiminished, indeed it is needed all the more so in these days. There is, however, another witness laid upon the Church. It is the witness to the primacy and sovereignty of the Grace of God, redeeming, pardoning, renewing all who have fallen short of the standards of God's law when in penitent faith they turn to him. In his atonement, God acts towards sinners in Grace, not by setting aside the Law, nor by mitigating it, but at infinite cost to himself upholding his righteous law and making possible full pardon and renewal. The Church's pastoral discipline must witness to this Grace as well as God's will for marriage. Indeed, Grace must have the last word for all of us in all circumstances, or we are lost. So often, throughout the debates, it seemed as if the choice was between compassion and witness. Such polarisation is mistaken. Nor do I believe it is just and consistent with the primacy of Grace to tell a divorcee, penitent for the failure of a previous marriage and turning to God for his help in a new partnership, your past is forgiven, God will renew you, you are convinced you are marrying within his will, but for the sake of the Church's witness to marriage you cannot have that marriage solemnised in church - we will allow you a service of blessing in church after a civil marriage in a Registry. The signal given diminishes the witness to the primacy of Grace. This discipline also makes a member of the Church who has never married before suffer the deprivation of a marriage in church with the normal service in order that the Church shall witness to society. The Church suffers no cost for its witness, the innocent person does. Because of the Convocation Regulations, I did follow this line in earlier years, but with a heavy heart and regret. From the beginning of the Synod, however, it was my hope that the Regulations would be changed. Because they were not, and still are not, I, with an increasing number of clergy, decided not to follow them.

The Debates

In 1972 the Synod debated the Root report, opening up the meaning of marriage, indissolubility, divorce and remarriage. An attempt to ask the dioceses their will for a consideration and reassessment of the Regulations was rejected. The following year, a working party report set before the Synod, in a broad way, the main practicable courses of action open to the Church - retaining the present basic discipline, or changing it to allow marriages of divorcees in church in certain circumstances. Bishops took part in the debate in support of both options. Again a move to consult the dioceses on alteration to the existing discipline failed, but only because of a tie in the House of Clergy. The Synod, on a vote by Houses decided to remain with the Regulations.

Another Marriage Commission, chaired by the Bishop of Lichfield, presented Synod in 1978 with a further report, *Marriage and the Church's Task*. There were four dissentients from the Commission's findings - an indication of continuing opposition to revision of the marriage discipline, which the majority of its members advocated. It was the House of Clergy again that defeated the motion. The only positive moves to come out of that debate were, to ask dioceses to comment on the report and to seek an early opportunity to debate the admission of divorcees to Holy Communion - a step rejected by Synod in an earlier debate.

Three years later, in 1981, the responses of the dioceses having been received, another attempt to change the Regulations met with success. The motion recognised there were circumstances in which a divorced person might marry in church and asked the Standing Committee to set out a range of procedures for consideration. The majority in favour was substantial in all three Houses. The Standing Committee presented its proposals in July 1983. There was indeed a range of possible procedures, but only two seemed to get support, those known as Options F and G. The former would have left it to the parish priest's sole discretion as to which marriages might be in church. It was a simpler option but did not gain Synod's approval. Option G was more complicated. It drew the diocesan bishop into the decision-making process, thus making clear that the Church, rather than one man, was involved. The bishop would receive advice from a panel drawn from dioceses in the region. It was thought that indissolubilists could find an acceptable procedure within Option G, in that they might see a case for nullity in some applications. The Synod voted in all three Houses for Option G, asking that the Convocation Regulations be rescinded and replaced by an Act of Synod, and that a Handbook to accompany it be prepared, the new procedure to be implemented, if possible, by Easter 1984.

I was invited to chair a working party on Option G. It had to work fast to meet the suggested timetable. Between July and November 1983 it produced a draft Regulation and, among other documents, a proposed Handbook offering a Code of Practice. The November Group of Sessions seemed to be going along with the proposed Regulation. A large number of amendments were considered and some approved. Time ran out, however, and the intention was to continue the debate in February the next year. That was not to be. Bishops consulted with their clergy about Option G in the intervening period and discovered considerable opposition. One of the suggested documents was an application form intended to elicit facts which would help a panel. That occasioned a negative response. Whether or not the time for informed consultation at diocesan clergy level was sufficient, given that many clergy would be coming to the matter suddenly, is open to question. What is not really in doubt was the complex procedure and documentation offered in Option G. There was a reason for much of the complexity. On the working group, both indissolubilists and those of a different view were represented. There had been a real attempt to produce something that both could accept, even though it was thought the former would not vote in favour at the end. The suspicion proved correct.

The result of the bishops' investigations and further thought was to ask the Synod, in February 1984, to set aside Option G and to allow them to bring forward their own draft Regulation, making the bishop and parish priest responsible for decisions, with advice from a diocesan panel if requested by the priest or the couple. In the light of the opposition to Option G, and because of my own unease with what we had produced, I gave my support in the debate to the bishops' motion. They were asked to bring a draft Regulation to the next sessions in July. This they did and, despite evidence in their House that some would wish to explore a nullity approach if the Regulation proposed did not succeed, the Synod gave support with substantial majorities and asked it to be referred to the dioceses for their response by mid-January.

When the bishops came back to the Synod in February 1985, they reported that there was clearly not a sufficient majority for change in the dioceses, and so the Convocation Regulations remained the primary statement of the Church of England, despite continuing difficulty in holding to them. They asked that clergy exercising their right in the law of the land to conduct 'second' marriages should seek advice of their bishop on the factors to be observed. The Synod agreed, in spite of attempts to rescind the Regulations. One point from the Regulations was rescinded - the prohibition of any public service in church for those who have contracted a civil marriage after divorce. This officially permitted 'services of blessing' in such cases.

A Position of Credibility?

What has happened since 1985? A growing number of clergy have conducted marriage services of divorcees in church, using the authorised services without variation. This has involved one or both partners making identical vows as in the previous marriage. Throughout the debates, this possibility has been offensive to many. Others, including myself, would say that vows, of course, ought to be regarded with the utmost importance and a full intention to keep them. But fallen human nature can lead to the breaking of vows and land individuals in circumstances where they can no longer be kept. They are made in the sight of God and his people, but they are made by the couple to each other. So when they are broken and can not be reactivated, the New Testament emphasis, 'where sin abounded, Grace does much more abound', becomes operative to those who repent. I have to confess real difficulty, anyway, in the Church appearing to elevate marriage vows above all other vows - baptismal vows, ordination vows, and so on - which are made directly to God.

In many dioceses guidelines are offered for priests willing to conduct these marriages. This puts a bishop in an anomalous position. He recognises the clergy's right in law, seeks to guide despite the Regulations and yet, because of his responsibility as bishop, cannot himself marry a divorcee out of loyalty to the Regulations. As I left Synod, I hoped the House of Bishops would seize the initiative, present a new Regulation to Synod with provision for the consciences of priests against these marriages. They now seem to be engaged in that exercise. Let them seek the General Synod's approval, but not go through the process of official referral to dioceses and deaneries, unless they can be sure of more informed and responsible debate at those levels than has been the case in the past.

Having witnessed Diocesan Synod debates, and myself gone round deaneries on a range of matters referred from General Synod - Marriage and Divorce, Church unity moves, etc - it has been sad to see how ill-prepared with good information, for and against, very many members have been. I am totally committed to the Anglican belief that authority for the government of the Church is committed to the whole people of God, as I will make clear in the next chapter, but for that authority to be exercised responsibly two things are necessary, episcopal leadership and an adequately informed body of representatives of the rest of the people of God. Until the bishops act - and the ball is in their court since they urged the retention of the status quo in 1985 - the Church of England will lack credibility on its discipline for divorcees wishing to marry in church. When the Church lacks credibility it reflects on its Lord.

RELATING TO OTHERS

Throughout the history of General Synod so far, the Church of England's relations with other Christian bodies have resulted in a succession of lengthy debates - with the Methodists, with a group of Free Churches in Britain, with the United Churches of the Indian Sub-continent, with the World Council of Churches, with Roman Catholics through ARCIC reports, with Lutheran and Reformed Churches in Europe and with fellow Anglicans in the Communion. A review of the reports and debates on them would require a book in itself. I will only offer a few observations.

Through all the Church unity schemes, a major stumbling block has been failure, generally in the House of Clergy, to agree on the meaning of ordination and its relation to the episcopacy. The Anglican-Methodist scheme, coming up to the last hurdle as Synod began, is a clear example. Attitudes to the scheme featured prominently in the General Election to Synod in 1970. Much progress had been made between the two Churches. Understanding of the Christian Faith appeared to be no problem. The sticking point for many Catholics and Evangelicals was the Service of Reconciliation. In the uniting of both ordained ministries, Catholics believed it did not sufficiently clearly convey episcopal ordination on Methodist ministers and make them priests. Evangelicals objected for the opposite reason. The imprecision of the words accompanying the mutual laying-on-of hands cast doubts on the existing status of Methodist ministers as true ministers of Word and Sacrament. Neither party, apparently, could leave the outcome of the uniting act to God. Carried along with the majority Evangelical view, I voted against the scheme in May 1972. A two-thirds majority in each House and an overall 75 per cent majority were needed. Only in the House of Bishops was the required result achieved, and the overall vote was just under 66 per cent.

I have reflected on my own vote. I think, with the hindsight of twenty-five years, I should on balance have voted in favour. The Methodists voted overwhelmingly in favour. Would the mission of the Christian Church in this land have been helped if that scheme had gone through? Different answers will be given, but here we are now having again to consider unity moves with Methodists and other Churches.

Within a year of the collapse of the Anglican/Methodist scheme, the United Reformed Church, itself recently united, invited the Church of England to join with other Churches in exploring the possibility of a united Church. So began eight years of negotiations - talks about talks - in which I was involved, the Churches' Unity Commission which produced the Ten Propositions, accepted by Synod in 1978 as a basis for a Covenant, and the Churches' Council for Covenanting. It ended in 1982 with a failure to achieve a two-thirds majority in the House of Clergy, the requisite majority being realised in the other two Houses. Again, disagreements on ordained ministry and episcopal ordination featured largely in debate and decision.

The same issues were the main points of contention in decisions about entering into full communion with the United Churches of the Indian Sub-continent. The Church of South India, in which Anglicans had been one of four uniting Churches, came into being in 1947. At the time there was strong opposition from the Catholic wing in England to entering into full communion, with a threat that 3,000 priests would resign. Their objection was that, in the uniting of ministries, episcopal ordination was not conferred on non-Anglicans. Around that time, notices could be seen in church porches in England which said, 'Members of the Church of South India may not receive communion in this church'. There could be no clearer evidence of the poor way the CSI was being treated. Internal debates in the Church of England were being conducted at the expense of a Church far away that had dared to obey Christ's call for unity in its mission to the world.

It was not until 1984 that a favourable response came to the CSI's request for full communion. And yet, the motion passed in Synod expressed only the desire for, not a declaration of, full communion. The reason behind an apparent hesitation was that full communion, if it entailed complete interchangeability of ministries, was not possible. There were four male presbyters in the CSI who remained alive from before the inauguration in 1947 and had come from the non-Anglican Churches. The prospect of these aged men coming to England and wanting to preside at a eucharist was indeed remote, yet if they had, Canon Law would prevent them because they were not episcopally ordained. The CSI also had women presbyters. They, too, would be excluded by Canon Law then prevailing. Here was an instance of the uncertainty of what full communion means, a problem that has plagued Anglicans for a long time and is still exercising them throughout the Communion.

The Church of North India and the Church of Pakistan - the Church of Bangladesh could not be contacted at the time - were accepted as in full communion in 1972 by an overwhelming majority, though there were over forty abstentions. The latter, though keen for full communion, had doubts about the Act of Unification. The two United Churches had sought a way of uniting ministries that avoided the problem met by the CSI. Each participating minister would be told he was called and ordained in his former Church to ministry in the Church of God. Then after the mutual laying-on-of-hands in which bishops took part, they would be regarded as episcopally ordained. It was the inference of two kinds of ordination, that seemed to be coming down on one side of a theological debate among Anglicans, which influenced the abstainers. The majority were inclined to believe that the reconciling ministries in the Act of Unification had the essence of conditional ordination, where the outcome was left to God.

It has been my own regret that a principle proposed at the first meeting of the Anglican Consultative Council at Limuru, Kenya, in 1971 has not been followed in union schemes. The principle is that non-episcopal ministers may be accepted in full orders of the episcopal Church by virtue of coming into full communion with the bishop. If that were clearly declared as the basis of integration of ministries, laying-on-of-hands with prayer ought not to create divisions. After all, Anglican priests at any licensing or institution to a new appointment have hands laid on again with prayer.

Talking with Others

By far the most time given by the Synod to the two-way talks with other world Communions - Orthodox Churches, Lutherans, the Reformed Churches, the Roman Catholic Church - until the last few years, was with the latter. The Anglican/Roman Catholic International Commission has been meeting throughout the lifetime of Synod so far. In 1979, the Synod agreed that the Commission's Agreed Statement on Eucharist, Ministry and Authority was 'sufficiently congruent with Anglican teaching to provide a theological basis for further dialogue'. Further dialogue are important words there. Questions of considerable importance had been raised in the debate, and in order to satisfy other concerns, a study of the doctrine of the Church was requested. Furthermore, the hope was expressed of a stage-by-stage progression to full communion. The latter seems as far off as ever.

In 1986, the ARCIC reports giving elucidations on the Eucharist and Ministry and Ordination were approved by each House, though with substantial minorities in the House of Laity. The report on Authority in the Church received a rougher ride. It was not satisfactory, in the eyes of a substantial number, in maintaining the role of the laity. It leaned too far still in the Roman direction, concentrating authority in the Pope and bishops. The most trenchant criticism came from a Catholic layman, Oswald Clark, a man of great eminence in the General Synod and the Church Assembly before it. He and I managed to include amendments to the final motion. Mine asked that, in further talks, the role of the laity and the relation of laity, clergy and bishop should be given greater attention. Mr Clark's amendment. coming from Catholic convictions, not only emphasised the role of the laity, but asked for more adequate treatment of the Marian and Infallibility dogmas and the case for a universal primacy at Rome and the claim that the Pope is the Vicar of Christ on earth. Mr Clark's Catholicism has always been wholeheartedly Anglican.

1989 saw another ARCIC document, Salvation and the Church, being debated by Synod. It was generally welcomed and sent to dioceses and deaneries for study and comments. Whatever the dioceses and deaneries had to say was not put on the Synod's agenda for debate in the next five years.

Talking and Acting

If talks with the Roman Catholic church have been just talks so far - and it is impossible to disguise the disappointment of Anglicans at the Vatican's response to ARCIC I - talks with Churches of the continent of Europe did lead to action. They began with Churches in West and East Germany before the unification of the two countries. In the West, the Evangelical Church, comprising twenty-five member Churches, Lutheran, Reformed and United, and in the East the Federation of Evangelical Churches, were our partners in the initial stages. By 1991, the Synod entered into closer relationship with the Evangelical Church of a united Germany. This was on the basis of the Meissen Declaration, a doctrinal understanding. Approval was by proclamation of an Act of Synod. It was celebrated by services of commitment in both countries.

By that time, similar encouraging progress was being made in talks with the Nordic (Scandinavian) and Baltic Lutheran Churches. Agreement between the Anglican Churches in the British Isles and these European partners was achieved in the Porvoo Statement. At the last Group of Sessions in the 1990-95 quinquennium, the Declaration was finally approved in all three Houses. The report of the House of Bishops in its preface by the Archbishop of Canterbury (George Carey) maintained that 'the Porvoo Common Statement contains the single most important ecumenical proposal to come before us for many years'.

Since just after World War II, relations with the main Churches in Britain were sustained through the British Council of Churches. In 1990 it gave way to the Council of Churches for Britain and Ireland, with which Churches Together in England is associated. In the new Ecumenical Instruments, the Roman Catholic Church and a wide range of other Churches came in to join those previously in the BCC.

Relating to Fellow Anglicans

In 1982 Archbishop Ted Scott, Primate of Canada. was invited to address the General Synod. He was on the Standing Committee of the Anglican Consultative Council and the Moderator of the Central Committee of the WCC. In the course of his address, which clearly revealed his affection for the Church of England, he gently suggested it sometimes gives the impression it owns the Anglican Communion. I would add that at times it does seem not to want to know. In introducing a debate on the Anglican Consultative Council in 1983, I asked why we had such a thin house when ACC is debated, and reflecting Archbishop Scott's remarks said, 'Insularity still inhibits the fulfilment of that unique role which the Church of England should play and which the rest of the Communion wants to see'. The point was reiterated by other speakers. The Archbishop of Canterbury stressed the mutual need of the Churches of the Communion. A year later Canon Sam Van Culin, appointed in 1983 as Secretary General of the ACC, was invited to address the Synod. In a wide-ranging address he spoke of the contribution the Church of England could make to the Communion. Among its features was England's experience of conflict in the life of the Church, which he believed could be more ecumenically useful. If the unity God willed for his Church was one of 'reconciled diversity', then experience of synodical strife, and the agonies of conscience which lie behind it, would ultimately be good for the Anglican Communion and also the wider Christian family.

I would add that there are resources in the Church of England which can benefit the whole Communion. I am not thinking of personnel and money which for many years have gone overseas. Nor have I in mind our experience of synodical government - other Churches have much longer experience, the American Church since the late eighteenth century. But in theological studies we have facilities of value world-wide. Our Doctrine Commission and successive Faith and Order Advisory Groups have produced substantial reports. Many Anglican Provinces do not have the facility to set up such commissions. In recent years there have been Inter-Anglican Theological and Doctrinal Commissions set up for the whole Communion, but because we can provide the money and have the will to continue with our own commissions, what they produce can be fed into the common treasury of Anglican theological study.

To share the Church of England's resources with the rest of the Communion may be the easy part. To receive from all the rest may be much harder. There is the temptation to believe others cannot really understand our situation, they will offer simplistic solutions. Fifteen years' involvement with the Anglican Communion leaves me in no doubt we have much we could profitably learn.

SOME PARTING THOUGHTS

I miss General Synod, but not in a grieving way. To be part of it has been a privilege, a demanding yet worth-while experience. Some people, viewing it from afar, think it is only a talking shop. Others say we can do without it, especially when it does what they do not approve of. Leave it to the bishops, they may suggest. But they too would sometimes disappoint them.

The General Synod is necessary because it is the legislative body of the Church of England. So long as it is the Established Church it will need to conduct legal business along Parliamentary lines and satisfy Parliament in legislating. And even if the Church were disestablished, a legislative body would still be needed, as every other Anglican Church knows. Furthermore, a national council of the Church is needed to decide on the allocation of central resources to the dioceses and parishes, to ensure a fair distribution, and to promote the Church's national responsibilities in mission. The Synod is also a voice of the Church of England in the nation - not the voice, but a voice. The media is more inclined to pick up pronouncements of bishops or archbishops as they seem newsworthy, and present them as the voice of the Church. But over the years one can remember responsible and worthy debates in Synod, like the Church and the Bomb, on Capital Punishment, on social and moral issues facing the nation. Very many valuable reports have emanated from the Synod's Boards and Councils on major concerns for the Church's own life - on mission, worship, work with children and education in general, marriage, dealing with problems of ageing, bereavement and facing death, and so on.

In his Presidential address on his retirement, Archbishop John Habgood reminded the Synod of two major concerns. The first concerned the public role of the Church in society, so much in need of moral and spiritual guidance. Extreme financial stringency could rob the Church of resources at the centre in meeting its responsibilities. The second concern was the way the Synod in particular interprets the Christian inheritance in today's world. All too often there can be simplistic appeals to 'biblical truth', as though quotation of a text or two can suffice. He hoped that in the future life of the Synod there would be a real effort to grapple with Hermeneutics. My hope is that the Archbishop's message as he left the Synod will be borne in mind in the years ahead.

Chapter 5
The Anglican Communion
1981 - 1996

In 1981, while serving on the Appointments Sub-committee of the General Synod I was asked to leave the room for a few minutes. On my return I was invited to serve on the Anglican Consultative Council as the Church of England's clergy representative. As one of the larger Churches of the Communion it has three representatives, one bishop, one priest, one lay person. It is a truism to say a moment or two can change one's life. Those few moments changed mine, though little did I realise it at the time. I was expected to serve for three meetings of the Council, that is, till ACC-7 in 1987. In fact I came off in October 1996 at ACC-10.

It is not just the opportunity of being in eighteen different countries, some of them two or three times, that has had such a profound effect on my life and course of ministry, but rather the sharing in the experience of Anglican dioceses and parishes in so many of the cultures of the Anglican Communion. There are now approaching forty separate Churches in the Anglican family, covering one hundred and sixty four countries. Going to eighteen of them may not seem a big deal, but at all the international gatherings of the Communion, ACC, Primates' Meeting and Lambeth Conference, all the Churches are represented. Before 1981, I thought I knew something about Anglicans in other lands by reason of serving on a missionary society council. But what I experienced from 1981 was tantamount to a conversion experience.

It is easy to identify the problems of transplanting a Christian tradition native to and shaped by centuries in England into a multiplicity of other lands and cultures. I am not unmindful of the distinctive traditions of the Scottish Episcopal Church, the Church of Ireland or the Church in Wales in Anglican mission across the world.

The freeing of the essence of Anglican faith and practice from the English cultural accretions in which it first came to a land and people has been a lengthy process in many places. But now, to share in the rich diversity of expressions of Anglicanism in worship, witness and fellowship, gives a new dimension to one's understanding of the Catholic Church - a little insight into the contribution of the redeemed of all nations in the worship of heaven.

Again I must emphasise, I am not attempting a history of the Anglican Communion during the years I served on the Council and its Standing Committee. A comprehensive account would require a book rather than a chapter. I will offer reflections and assessments of developments and the problems and opportunities they present. I have contributed to part of a work much nearer to a history of the years 1958 to 1990 in the Anglican Communion. Bishop John Howe was Anglican Executive Officer from 1969, and then the first Secretary General of the ACC till 1982. On his retirement he became the first ACC Research Fellow (1983-4) and was asked to write on the developments in the Anglican Communion from 1958 to 1982. His work was published as *Highways and Hedges*.[1] Subsequently I was asked to continue the story up to 1990, whereupon the combined work was issued as, Anglicanism and the Universal Church, by the same publisher in 1990. Some of my reflections will echo the latter part of that book but will not cover all the same ground. And, of course, much has happened from 1990 to 1996 to develop judgements made earlier.

DO WE NEED THE FAMILY?

Every family knows the changes that must come from time to time when the children are little, through the turbulence of teen-age, to when offspring are adult. Happy is the family that can come through the decades to a situation where adults and their parents are bound by loving relationships in which trust and interdependence are combined with freedom of each to be fulfilled. To a remarkable degree the Anglican family of Churches has come through to that situation. To be sure, there are disagreements, serious disagreements, as can happen in the best of families, but to be heavily involved in the affairs of the Communion is to be thankfully aware of the bonds of affection.

John Howe, writing fourteen years ago and describing twenty-five years, could identify two watersheds for the Communion. The second will feature in a later section of this chapter. The first was the transition

---

1. Published by the Anglican Book Centre, Toronto, 1985

from earlier time when older Churches established younger Churches overseas, the latter still much dependent for resources, financial and in personnel, on the former, to the time when the younger become Provinces or national Churches in their own right, self-governing adults in the family. To adopt the metaphor used by John Howe, the transition was from head office with branch offices overseas to a worldwide family of autonomous but related companies.

Since the late 70s a divisive issue has arisen in the family. First in Hong Kong, then in the Episcopal Church in the USA (ECUSA), and after that in a succession of Churches, women were ordained as priests, and are now bishops. While it is hardly a surprise now to hear of another Church or Province deciding to follow this pattern, there remains strong opposition within the Communion. In some Churches those opposing may be few in number, in others a substantial minority, while some Churches as a whole are not willing to take the step, at any rate as yet. The result is an impaired state of full communion. For the latter there should in principle be complete interchangeability of ordained ministries. Every ordained Anglican priest ought to be acceptable to preside at the Eucharist anywhere in the Communion. If a woman priest or bishop is barred by the canon law of any Church or Province, full communion is impaired. The issue has been a major concern at the last two Lambeth Conferences in 1978 and 1988, and the subject of commissions at international and provincial levels, and meetings of the ACC. It has yet to be seen how it will affect the Lambeth Conference in 1998, when women bishops will be present for the first time.

A more recent, but possibly more divisive, issue concerns homosexuality within the Church. That there are considerable numbers of homosexuals, self-declared or anonymous, in the Anglican and other Churches is not in dispute, though the reaction of some Provinces appears to suggest it is not true of them. Two concerns arise in this matter. First, given that some homosexuals wish to make a public act of commitment in a same-sex relationship, can the Church offer them a service of blessing? As yet the incidences of parishes and priests willing to do this are very few in the Communion. But the possibility of an increase, as some countries provide in law for such public acts, poses for most Anglicans a threat to the Christian witness on marriage and sexuality. The second concern is the ordination and continuation in ministry of practising homosexuals. The emphasis is on the word practising. The ordination of homosexuals as such has probably gone on throughout Church history, and the idea that none were involved in homosexual genital activities is not credible. But with homosexuality now much more evident in the public domain, its relation to the ordained ministry has come to the fore. The threat of a major split among Anglicans grows, not only within Churches of the First World, but between sympathisers with homosexual activity and Third World Churches. A clash at Lambeth between some American and some African bishops seems, at this stage beforehand, inevitable. When, as in the case of a few bishops, this 'new morality' is accompanied by sympathy toward a 'new age' religion and syncretism, the divide is indeed stark.

On both the divisive issues outlined above - women's ordination and homosexuality matters - widely different attitudes to Scripture lie at the root of the problem. At extreme ends of the spectrum a literalist, fundamentalist approach conflicts with a cavalier 'pick and choose' treatment of Scripture leaning more towards insights found elsewhere. Most loyal Anglicans may be found between the extremes. On them rests the responsibility of arriving at a faithful and credible understanding of the truth of the biblical revelation interpreted in today's world. As indicated in a previous chapter, the homosexual issue is particularly difficult in that it touches deeply the human emotions.

While this is not the first era in which Anglicans have been divided - the first Lambeth Conference in 1867 met amid strong disagreement on the teaching of the Bible - over the last fifteen years or so there have not been wanting those voices which question the worthwhileness of trying to maintain the unity of the Anglican Communion. Impairment of full communion has led some, admittedly a small minority, to declare themselves out of communion with those parts whose actions they cannot accept. And all Anglicans who take a responsible interest in the world-wide family must recognise it takes much effort, care and mutual trust to hold together so many autonomous Churches in many nations and cultures. Is it really worth it? Every Church and Province may believe it has enough to do to maintain its witness and mission in its own land, so far as possible with other Christian traditions. So, is maintenance of an effective unity with other Anglicans across the other side of the world a priority - as compared, for instance, with such connections as may be with other Churches in the World Council of Churches?

Fifteen years' immersion in Anglican Communion affairs convinces me beyond any doubt that it can and must hold together, that whatever the stresses and strains the family must be united, not just for its own sake, but for the wider Church of Christ. Sometimes one hears statements to the effect that it does not ultimately matter if an Anglican Church, say the Church of England, disappears, God's Church will prevail. I appreciate some truth there, but I detect a too narrow perception. We cannot foretell the future during even the next century, but now as we approach it I believe no good will come from letting Anglican unity slip away. To join with other Churches in United Churches, as in the Indian sub-continent, is a worthy, glorious goal. But it is most significant that those United Churches want to remain members of the Anglican consultative bodies. The name Anglican is of secondary importance, but a world-wide family preserving all that is good in that tradition, and preserving it, in fact, for the whole Church of God across the world, is at this time a priority. We can only be responsible for our duty in our own day, and leave the future to the Lord of the Church. I must give reasons for this assertion, and will proceed to do so. They fall under three headings - Mission, Ecumenical Relationships and the Anglican Contribution to the Catholic Church.

Mission

Mission is one throughout the world. That is because God's mission is one from the creation to the consummation of his purposes in the new creation. At its heart was the sending by the Father of the Son to reveal and redeem. After his resurrection, Jesus said, 'As the Father sent me, even so I send you'. The Church is thus caught up in God's mission, sent into the world to do all he wills to do through it. It is now recognised that all Churches across the world are in a missionary situation. For much of the last two or three hundred years, during the missionary movement of the oldest Anglican Churches, that recognition was not widespread. Mission was something done overseas. But now the oldest Churches find themselves in as difficult a situation for mission as any in Church history, while in terms of making Christ known, the evangelistic thrust in mission, younger Churches drive forward. It has been suggested there are 3,000 new Anglican Christians on average every day.

The oneness of mission has been leading to a greater sharing of resources across the Anglican family. At the second meeting of the ACC in Dublin in 1973, as has been mentioned in an earlier chapter, the growing impulse to sharing resources in mission was encouraged in the following statement 'The responsibility for mission in any place belongs primarily to the church in that one place... this mission must be shared in each and every place with fellow-Christians from each and every part of the world with their distinctive insights and contributions.' The meeting went on to advocate replacing the erstwhile idea, that there were givers who had nothing to receive and receivers with nothing to give, with the truth that we are all both givers and receivers. Of course, sharing of resources ought not to be just an Anglican exercise, but the fact is that, as a general rule, structures are needed to enable it to happen. And the co-ordination of structures of different Christian denominations is very difficult, with each having its own authorities and decision-making bodies. Inter-denominational co-operation happens in relief agencies such as Christian Aid, but the transfer of money and personnel with expertise from one Anglican Church to another normally takes place within the structures of inter-Anglican partnership. For mission, the Communion needs to retain its family unity. Thus the burdens and joys of each part will be shared by the whole in informed prayer and exchange of gifts in relationships of mutual trust.

Ecumenical Relationships

A major development of the last fifty years in Christianity has been the growth and progress in ecumenical relationships. The number of United Churches coming to birth has been disappointingly small. But multi-lateral and bi-lateral talks between separate Churches, at international and national level, have proliferated. Fifty years ago, the World Council of Churches was founded. The impetus for this can be traced back to the Edinburgh Conference in 1910 when Churches, faced with the mission challenge across the world, saw their divisions as an obstacle to the presentation of a gospel of reconciliation.

The same spirit that imbued the WCC stimulated bi-lateral talks between world Communions, all in the hope of coming closer together with the ultimate aim of Church unity. Both common ground and remaining disagreements have been explored. Thus the Anglican Communion has been in conversations with the Roman Catholic Church, Lutherans, the Reformed Churches, the Orthodox and Oriental Orthodox Churches, the Methodists, and possibly soon there will be talks with Baptists and the Pentecostal Churches. In various parts of the Communion, these international commissions are mirrored at national level.

The ecumenical scene, therefore, demands a co-ordinated Anglican response. Our world Communion partners are entitled to a unified presentation of Anglican reactions, including differences as well as agreements among us. Furthermore, a high degree of consistency from the Anglican side across the inter-Church dialogues is required. And this consistency must be sought between Anglican thinking at the Communion, international level and more localised, national dialogues. Putting it simply, Anglicans must try to talk to their neighbours as one family.

The Anglican Contribution

The Anglican tradition, expressed through all its member Churches, has a distinctive contribution to make to the universal Church. In its separation, an Anglican Church is part of the the one, holy, catholic, apostolic Church. It exists, therefore, not for its own sake; its motivation must not be merely self-preservation. Archbishop Michael Ramsey, in his book, *The Gospel and the Catholic Church*, spoke of Anglicanism as 'pointing through its own history to something of which it is a fragment' (p.220). There is thus a provisionality about it as a Christian tradition as it looks forward in faith to the Church one, holy, catholic. The same provisionality, however, must be applied to every other Church, including the Roman and Orthodox, despite their absolutist claims. But recognition of provisionality in no way diminishes the truth that Anglicanism has a contribution that is unique to make, now to the treasury of all the Churches, and in future to any united Church. It has much to offer out of its history, its ethos and its understanding, particularly of the Church itself.

Anglicanism represents Catholicism renewed by the Reformation and influenced by subsequent movements, notably the Enlightenment and the Romantic movement, and by the Evangelical, Catholic and Liberal traditions. As with all movements in the history of the Church, there can be both beneficial and baneful effects, temporary and more lasting results. But Anglicanism as it is, at the close of the millennium, is not as it was in the sixteenth century or centuries following but what it has now become, a body of Christians world-wide, with warts but dependant on the Grace of God.

The ACC in 1984, at its sixth meeting in Nigeria, sought to define the Anglican ethos thus: 'The Communion seeks to be loyal to the apostolic faith and to safeguard it and express it in Catholic order always to be reformed by the standards of Scripture. It allows for a responsible freedom and latitude of interpretation of the faith within a fellowship committed to the living expression of that faith.' It went on to emphasise the commitment to Reformed Catholicism and 'a way of thinking and feeling that has developed over the centuries which calls for an acceptance of measures of diversity, an openness, tolerance and mutual respect towards others'. Mention now of tolerance and mutual respect illustrates the fact of development in Anglicanism; those qualities were not as evident in former centuries as today. Some Anglicans seem to regard any developments from, say, the Reformation Settlement, as regrettable, but only a dead tradition remains static.

Because it spreads across on hundred and sixty-four countries the ethos of Anglicanism, dominated for long by English history and culture, has had over two centuries to adapt to other national cultures, some of them never within the British Empire. The process of inculturation of Anglican worship, traditions of spirituality and styles of government, varies from place to place. Other historic Christian traditions emanating from Europe - Roman, Lutheran, etc - have likewise needed to be inculturated across the world; but each experience has been different and, more significantly, shaped by its own understanding of the Church. For instance, while Anglicans share with Roman Catholics the historic episcopate, they believe the bishop exercises authority in council with laity and other clergy, as well as by virtue of his own office. In the relationship between the local and the universal Church, there is a considerable difference between Anglicans and the Roman Catholic Church with its hierarchical structure stemming from the singular authority of the Pope.

In the past, some Anglican theologians have inclined to the belief that Anglicans have no distinctive or special doctrines of their own. Their point has been to emphasise Anglican commitment to the teaching of the Catholic and Apostolic Faith as found in Scripture, summarised in the Creeds and in the General Councils of the early centuries. In a recent book Bishop Stephen Sykes[2] has, to my mind, convincingly contradicted the claim of 'no special doctrines', showing that there is indeed a distinctive Anglican understanding of the Church. It still needs to be clearly articulated, but all the ingredients may be perceived. When we differ in the way we organise and exercise authority in the Church from the Roman, Methodist, Presbyterian, Congregationalist and Baptist ways we are working on distinctive Anglican principles.

Out of Anglican experience a particular view of Authority has emerged. The primary function of authority is to maintain the unity of the Church in truth. The unity of the Church is grounded in the unity of the Trinity but, given that the Church is a company of fallible and sinful human beings, how may it be kept united in truth? We reject the Roman way of submission to the Pope. In all Anglican statements on authority, the starting point is Scripture, but how can

---

2. *Unashamed Anglicanism,* Darton Longman Todd, 1995

Scripture be rightly understood and applied? Anglicans emphasise the place of Tradition, what the Church has learned over the centuries, and Reason. But there is more to be said.

A report presented to the 1948 Lambeth Conference, but not actually endorsed by it, speaks of authority, as inherited by Anglicans from the undivided (ie early) Church, as single in that it is derived from a single divine source, reflecting within itself the richness and historicity of the divine revelation, and distributed among Scripture, Tradition, Creeds, the Ministry of Word and Sacraments, the witness of saints and the consensus fidelium (general agreement of the faithful). The uniqueness and supremacy of Scripture is affirmed, but what is addressed there is the need for Scripture to be rightly understood and applied in the Church, avoiding the dangers of a multiplicity of private interpretations. The report continued on the nature of authority: 'It is thus a dispersed rather than a centralised authority, having many elements which combine, interact with, and check each other; these elements together contributing by a process of mutual support, mutual checking and redressing of errors or exaggerations, to the many-sided fullness of the authority which Christ has committed to his Church.' The exercise of authority in the Church, according to Anglican understanding, therefore, is not juridical, by pronouncement from some central body or person, but by a process.

The 1948 statement further emphasised two instruments in the process as valued by Anglicans - episcopacy as the source and centre of our Church order, and a common standard of worship in which the dispersed elements of authority come together. At the time, the *Book of Common Prayer* in its English or Scottish form dominated Anglican worship across the Communion, but even now that liturgical revision with cultural influences has led to many forms, a unitive influence is still apparent. The essential principles of the *Prayer Book* are still followed.

Something further needs to be said about the role of episcopacy. Bishops have a distinctive responsibility for worship, doctrine, unity and mission. As Anglicans we are episcopally led. But we are also synodically governed. In synod, bishops act in council with laity and clergy. There are therefore two principles in the government of the Church - the bishop, or bishops acting collegially, and the bishop in council. If either side of the equation gets out of balance with the other, trouble ensues. That is so because Anglicans see the authority of Christ over the Church committed to the whole people of God, the laos. Bishops are part, a special part, of the laos, but not apart from the rest. We only get our understanding of bishops right, or the other clergy, or the laity, when we see the Church as above each.

I have attempted to give reasons why the Anglican Communion should hold together - for Mission, for its Ecumenical Relations, for its distinctive contribution to the world-wide Church. I will later outline how I have seen developments in those areas during the last fifteen years.

ONE FAMILY, MANY CULTURES

A human family may or may not struggle with different cultures. Parents themselves may be from different sub-cultures within the same nation or different nations. The nuclear family has then to cope with influences, or even pressures, from the extended family. Further, within a family originating in the same culture, children growing up can opt for a sub-culture their parents could not entertain. The Anglican family, however, must live with a multiplicity of cultures, living with them not in a passive, tolerating way, but positively embracing them.

When the first Inter-Anglican Theological and Doctrinal Commission was set up, to consider questions concerning the Communion as a whole, special reference was made 'to the diverse and changing cultural contexts in which the Gospel is proclaimed, received and lived'. In pursuance of that part of the task, the Commission produced the report, *For the Sake of the Kingdom* (1986). It was a study of Church and Kingdom in creation and redemption.

Culture is an integral part of God's creation and therefore partakes of all his provision for humankind. Creation is, however, marred by sin; thus all cultures are affected by injustice, selfishness and greed. In God's redemption, a new creation is established through Christ, a kingdom of love, joy, peace and righteousness, already present through Christ's death and resurrection but still to come in its fullness. God's kingdom has both continuity and discontinuity with creation and its cultures, being native to it yet transcending it. So, in his kingdom, Christ affirms what is good in all cultures and challenges and seeks to redeem what is evil. As the Church is a sign, foretaste and instrument of the kingdom, it must serve those purposes with the Holy Spirit's guidance and aid. But the Church is made up of sinful, fallible members, though redeemed, and by nature conditioned by the culture they live in. The constant danger, therefore, is of the Church being in captivity to the culture, adopting standards and ways contrary to the

Gospel. The challenge is to be of and sharing in a culture in all that is good, and to be a counter-culture in all that is not. Captivity to culture is a possibility for all religions. Through their culture people discover and preserve their identity. Religion, whether already part of their culture or drawn in to support it, can be subordinated to the needs of that culture, at the expense of inner spiritual realities. That can be true of Christianity, perhaps more with some people in western democracies than elsewhere; it is also true of Islam, Judaism, Hinduism and other religions.

It was almost inevitable that Anglican missionaries taking the Gospel to other lands, mostly British colonies, or chaplains going out to serve their fellow-countrymen, would take it in English cultural wrappings. So, on foreign soil we find English-style church buildings at odds with traditional architecture of their area. The same is true, of course, of other buildings built in the Empire. When evangelism produced young churches, worship became 1662 Prayer Book translated, and whatever ritual and style the missionaries came with. As already mentioned, the inculturation of Anglicanism away from Englishness has been a lengthy process, still incomplete.

In 1983 I recall attending a village church in an African country, far away from any large city. It was to witness a wedding. The bride entered in a white gown with train, accompanied by seventeen bridesmaids all dressed in similar dresses, just as in any English parish church. The service was 1662 translated. At the conclusion, from the back of the small mud-walled church came a group of women singing in lovely African harmonies and swaying to the rhythm. I asked afterwards what was happening. It was the local Mothers' Union with an anthem to marriage comprising Scriptural verses. It seemed to me that only at that point did the event come alive in terms of African culture. I have reason to believe it would be different in that area now. Not long afterwards, I was present at a cathedral service in another African country. It was wholly in the style of an English cathedral - large robed choir, English hymn book and chants rather drearily sung. A few days later, I was in a parish for Sunday worship many miles into the country. Morning Prayer was in the local language, but the canticles were sung with lovely swinging tunes and much bodily gyrations. Afterwards I asked the priest why the service was so different from what I had observed in the cathedral. Apparently, the younger members had recently presented him with an ultimatum - African tunes and worship style must be brought in or they would join the Pentecostal church.

I have emphasised earlier the twin principles of Anglican government - episcopal leadership and bishop in council, synodical government. The Churches of the First World are at home with those principles, but do they really fit all other Churches of the Communion? Again I take Africa as an example. The traditional form of government in most African cultures is of a chief consulting with the tribal or village elders. He may listen to them all day, each elder having his say as the 'talking stick' is handed to him. At the end he pronounces the decision. Synodical government, as it is conducted in the older Churches, akin to parliamentary procedures, does not seem appropriate. A bishop in council, with a smaller body representing the Church might be more natural. It seems to me that it would be helpful to have an international study of the way episcopacy should be exercised in widely differing cultures, the only requirements being the recognition that it is to the whole Church that authority is given, and episcopacy be exercised according to leadership principles in the New Testament, servant authority in leadership.

What is beyond doubt is that the style of debate in synods and councils in Anglo-Saxon cultures is quite foreign to many others. This has been painfully obvious at previous Lambeth Conferences and ACC meetings. Serious efforts to rectify this fault are now in hand. It would be unfair to suggest that all missionaries were insensitive to the need for inculturation. Many years ago I knew a pioneer missionary who, from the founding of a church, encouraged the new Christians to govern the church themselves. He sat at the back of the meeting, only contributing when asked. It would take a very long time to decide what he might have decided in a few minutes, but that was not the point. With some others, he had adopted the principles of Roland Allen for the church to be self-governing, self-supporting, self-propagating. I know myself, however, how one can inadvertently be insensitive in situations even with friends of other cultures. Amid the pressure of debates and business-arranging, to deal with others as might be normal in one's own culture is sometimes to cause upset without knowing it. I can think of instances I now regret.

Conduct of theology needs to take account of diverse cultures. For centuries, Christian theology has inevitably been in the domain of the older Churches - and particularly all done by men, at that. Anglican groups for study of theological and mission issues over recent decades have included representatives from a wide range of Churches, men and women. The report, *For the Sake of the Kingdom*, maintains, 'there is no human culture in which Christ and the Gospel of the Kingdom cannot be received, and therefore there is that in every culture which answers to Christ'. Thus, what the Church in any one place may receive of good from its culture through the working of the Holy Spirit contributes to the many-splendoured glory of Christ and his kingdom.

HOLDING THE FAMILY TOGETHER

It is one thing to present a case for the Anglican Communion to hold together, it is something other to find a way of achieving it. The realities to be faced can appear intimidating. The autonomy of each member Church and the multiplicity of cultures have already been mentioned. The responsibility of each Church to conduct its mission and explore the imperatives and implications of the Gospel relevantly in its cultures cannot be denied. There is indeed one Gospel revealed in the Scriptures, but the Gospel contains varied though complementary dimensions and must relate in affirmation, judgement and redemptive power to each human condition and context. How the Gospel is applied at any one time in a given situation will be quite different from other times and places; herein lies a source of disagreement between Christians. New Testament study, however, reveals considerable disagreements within the early Church, and different emphases of the one Gospel in major centres of Christianity influenced by leading Apostles. Furthermore, Anglicans have no centralised juridical authority, as in the Roman Catholic Church, though the Vatican itself is finding increasing difficulties in gaining submission across its Communion - evidence of a world-wide impatience with any authority imposed from above. Nor do Anglicans have a Confession of Faith establishing historically the basis of their Church. The Thirty-nine Articles were never that, though they are recognised in the Church of England as a determining part of its heritage. Other Anglican Churches have no similar commitment to them.

There are undoubtedly bonds of affection within the Anglican family, of which every international gathering of Anglicans affords evidence. Reference has been made to an Anglican ethos, emerging and developing from a shared history. And each member Church regards itself as in communion with the See of Canterbury. The Archbishop's authority, however, is moral not juridical. It has been a great privilege to have close relationship with both Dr Runcie and Dr Carey in my time on the Standing Committee of the Anglican Consultative Council and as Vice-Chairman and Chairman. I have had ample opportunity to witness the affection and moral authority they have earned across the Communion. But something more than the Archbishop of Canterbury's link with the Communion, bonds of affection and shared ethos is needed to hold the Communion together in face of the realities just described in a rapidly changing world. That something more begins with a willingness of the member Churches to talk together and to pray together, and the structures to facilitate that Christian exercise.

Over twenty years ago, Bishop Lesslie Newbigin, in justification of the World Council of Churches wrote, 'If the Church is to be a reality in a place, its members have to meet. If the Church is to be a reality in the life of a nation, there has to be some kind of national synod or assembly. Equally, if there is to be any reality in the claim that the Church exists as a global community, if there is to be any reality in our claim that Jesus Christ transcends nations and cultures and ideologies, then there has to be a place and a time when men and women of clashing cultures, nations and ideologies actually meet and test the reality of this claim in a personal encounter. Without this, it becomes merely a slogan repeated from within the walls of a ghetto.' All this can be applied, indeed must be applied, to the Anglican Communion if its claim to be a world-wide community is to be credible. Historically, this has happened in the Lambeth Conferences, beginning in 1867, in occasional Anglican Congresses, in the ACC and in the Primates' Meeting.

It is over thirty years since there was an Anglican Congress bringing together large numbers of bishops, clergy and laity. Another one is proposed for the year 2001, to which every diocese will be invited to send representatives. In celebrating the Christian faith together, the unity of the Communion as it moves into the next millennium could be greatly strengthened. The normal, regular means of maintaining Anglican unity, however, have been recognised over the past twenty years as our 'Four Instruments of Unity'.

Instruments of Unity

The office of the Archbishop of Canterbury as one of the instruments has already been mentioned. He is a focus of unity with presidential responsibilities towards the other three instruments. He need not be English by birth, as past history shows. However, because of the Archbishop's constitutional position in England, so long as the Church of England is by law established, any non-English person might need some years' experience of life within the Church of England in order to lead it effectively, and, further, be qualified to take the royal oath. The rest of the Communion's members may feel the latter factor alone constitutes a convincing case for disestablishment. But even if disestablishment were to come about, the Archbishop would still be Primate of All England. There is no reason why bishops from other Provinces should not be appointed to English dioceses - it has already happened - and be available for appointment to Canterbury.

The Lambeth Conference

The Lambeth Conference, the oldest of the other three instruments, was first held in 1867. It is convened by the Archbishop of Canterbury; of late it has been thought helpful to speak of the Archbishop 'gathering' the bishops to the Conference, a richer word than 'inviting', bringing out his moral leadership role. From the start any legislative authority was eschewed and, ever since, resolutions agreed at its meetings, while having moral weight, varying according to the significance of their content, are commended to member Churches for their consideration. The point is amply illustrated by the resolution at Lambeth 1968 to set up the Anglican Consultative Council. Because the Lambeth Conference is normally called at ten-year intervals, the need for additional structures between meetings in order to respond to rapidly changing situations had already been recognised. This, coupled with appreciation of the role of laity and clergy other than bishops in the exercise of authority in the Church, led the bishops to suggest a body, smaller in number than their own Conference, drawing together bishops, clergy and laity from each member Church and meeting more frequently. But the Conference itself could not set it up, only the member Churches could decide. A two-thirds majority of Churches in favour was sought by October 31st 1969. In the event, support was unanimous. The first ACC meeting took place in Limuru in Kenya in 1971.

There are those in the Communion who are less than enthusiastic about the continuation of the Lambeth Conference, preferring to see an enhanced and more effective ACC - although I have not known of any invited bishop refusing to attend the Conference. Their argument is against a 'bishops-only' gathering in days when synodical principles underly Anglican practice. I have heard the claim by some that decisions in their Church are not now taken by bishops alone. Taking human nature into consideration, and the rightful responsibilities of bishops, I wonder how literally the claim should be taken. My own conviction, based on the twin principles of episcopal leadership and bishop in council with laity and clergy, is for the continuation of the Lambeth Conference.

In all gatherings of human beings, there is always room for improvement in process and participation. The Lambeth Conference is no exception. In 1988 the bishops were asked 'to bring their dioceses with them', the implication being that they each consulted widely beforehand in their diocese on the main topics of the Conference. Listening to the debates, I wondered how many dioceses had been given the opportunity. I was more dubious as to the extent preparatory study material had been read. And, although the sixth and seventh meetings of the ACC in 1984 and 1987 had by design produced good material on the four main sections of the Lambeth programme, many bishops seemed unaware of it, even though the reports had been sent to them. But the same can be said of members of the ACC, although in some countries postal inefficiencies can be to blame. What can be said for the Lambeth Conference is that preparation beforehand is becoming very thorough. It was true of the 1988 Conference and will prove to be even more so for 1998.

The ACC

The ACC has strengths and weaknesses. Its numbers are small enough for all the members to get to know one another at a meeting. The larger Churches are represented by a bishop, a priest or deacon and a lay person; smaller Churches have one or two representatives. Normally, each representative attends three meetings, covering a period of approximately nine years, the exceptions being the elected chairman and vice-chairman who go on for two meetings from their appointment. These latter two cease to be representatives of their own Church and try to spread their concern over all member Churches. There is, inevitably, a turn-over of at least a third of the membership at each meeting. While this introduces new blood, it also contributes to a recurring problem at ACC meetings - the tendency to 'reinvent the wheel'. In tackling important current issues, excellent work done at previous meetings is forgotten or unknown unless someone stirs the memory. This is not to say new insights and better expressions should not be encouraged. Nor is it to claim that everything done and written in the past is of good quality. I could point to written material in the past fifteen years' meetings (ACC-5 through ACC-10) which is less than inspiring. But what is done in the present should build on the best in the past. One example should suffice.

In 1984 at ACC-6, a very good definition and exposition of mission was presented - I will refer to its contents in due course. In 1987 there was a preparation seminar for the Lambeth Conference the following year. As mission was a major part of one of the sections scheduled for Lambeth, members of the seminar were giving serious thought to its meaning, but they appeared not to know of the ACC-6 work. They were glad to be informed of it, and it went on to receive substantial support at Lambeth. In 1990, however, ACC-8 saw ways of building on and improving the 1986 definition. Preserving the memory within Anglican consultative bodies is an important factor in producing the best possible material for the Communion, indeed in discovering God's will in relation to contemporary needs. The Anglican Communion Secretariat and ACC members who have served for some years, have chief responsibility for this concern. Here I pay tribute to the devotion and hard work under pressures of the Secretariat, led by the three Secretary-Generals I have known, John Howe, Sam Van Culin and John Peterson. The Communion should know the debt it owes to what is, by comparison with other International Church bodies, a very small staff.

The effectiveness of the Churches' representation on the ACC remains a major problem. For one thing, it is questionable whether the representatives a Church appoints or elects all have appropriate access to centres of real authority in their own Church - the bodies where policy, priorities and finance provision are decided. Without that access, ACC resolutions and resources can hardly get across to member Churches, bearing in mind the ACC has no legislative powers. A further concern relates to the agenda for ACC meetings. During the fifteen years I was on the Standing Committee, all the Churches were asked to submit items of importance to them before each meeting. The response was always poor. The request went to Provincial Secretaries and to ACC members. Were the latter unable to present the request or to persuade the relevant authoritative body? When meetings took place, as often as not, individual members would want a resolution debated by the whole Council on a matter of great concern for their Church but quite inadequately serviced with background material. This contributed to a meeting ending up with a plethora of resolutions, far too many, as I judge, for effective influence within the Communion. Happily, the latest ACC-10 meeting[3] managed to avoid earlier problems. One could argue that the effectiveness of resolutions from the ACC and from the Lambeth Conference is in inverse proportion to their total number.

---

3. The official report - *Being Anglican in the Third Millennium* published for the Anglican Communion by Morehouse Publishing (1997)

Such criticisms as I have offered are aimed towards making a good and necessary instrument of unity better. Major responsibility for the success of the ACC lies with the Standing Committee served by the Secretariat. In electing the Committee, the Council ensures a fair representation of regions of the Communion, of the orders of bishops, clergy and laity, and, as far as possible, of men and women. The latter point is not easily achieved because member Churches appoint more men than women. The Standing Committee meets every year, usually preceded by the Inter-Anglican Finance Committee meeting. By the ACC Constitution - the ACC is the only body with a constitution - the Standing Committee acts for the Council between meetings. With the staff, it prepares the agenda for the Council meetings. The process was helped in respect of the latest, ACC-10, meeting in October 1996 by a small Design Group drawn from the Standing Committee. However thorough the preparations for an ACC meeting there has to be a readiness to alter the programme during the meeting if the demand from members is convincingly strong.

The Primates' Meeting

At Lambeth 1978, the idea of a fourth instrument of unity was conceived, the Primates' Meeting. From 1908 onwards, small meetings of Primates took place from time to time with the title, Lambeth Consultative Body, to assist the Archbishop of Canterbury before, after and between Conferences. When the ACC was set up in 1971, the Primates' groups ceased. By 1978, the need for all the Primates to meet regularly was becoming apparent. The Archbishop of Canterbury needed their advice and support in the Communion. Primates themselves, often in exposed and stressful situations, could benefit from mutual support. Beyond matching those needs, the purpose of a regular Primates' Meeting was not made wholly clear at the time of the Conference, as Bishop John Howe, Secretary General of the ACC, indicated in Anglicanism and the Universal Church. The role of the ACC, now getting well established, was recognised. Indeed Archbishop Donald Coggan expressed the firm hope that the Primates' Meeting would work in close partnership with the ACC.

Beginning in 1979 the Primates' Meeting, convened every two or three years, has proved increasingly valuable to the Communion. Pressures on Primates have grown - one only has to think of Desmond Tutu in recent years, and Robin Eames in Ireland, as examples. The burden on the Archbishops of Canterbury increases. And, I would argue, because of the Anglican emphasis on episcopal leadership in tandem with synodical consultation, there should be opportunity for the principal bishops of all the Churches to consult together on those matters where bishops have a particular responsibility. It has to be said, however, that the Primates' Meeting was set up without reference to the synodical structures of member Churches, unlike the decision concerning the ACC. At first its cost was not a call on the ACC budget but now, along with a considerable proportion of the Lambeth Conference costs, it is funded by the comprehensive Inter-Anglican Budget levied on all churches.

Dr Coggan's hope for close partnership of the Primates with the ACC did not see fulfilment for over ten years. During the 1980s, the Primates and the ACC Standing Committee met twice back-to-back with a one day overlap for joint discussion, and it happened again in 1991, but the occasions could hardly be described as effective partnership. The Primates, having finished their own business, were anxious to be off home; some indeed had gone.

Developing Relationships

Lambeth 1988 gave consideration to the instruments of unity and their closer co-operation. There was renewed confidence in the role of the Lambeth Conference, and the ACC was affirmed in its role as defined in its constitution and clarified as a result of an evaluation process initiated at ACC-5 in 1981 and welcomed at ACC-6 in 1984. Attention to the ACC's role was prompted at the Conference by its own members present as non-voting members with the help of two or three bishops. It might otherwise have been overlooked.

At the Archbishop of Canterbury's invitation, the ACC Standing Committee submitted proposals to the Primates, meeting with it in Cyprus in 1989, for clarification of the respective roles and co-operation of the four instruments of unity. The proposals included a programme of meetings up to the next Lambeth Conference in 1998, to include joint meetings of Primates and the ACC in 1993 and 1996, with some provision of time for the Primates' own business. By this time, the Primates had felt the need for a Standing Committee of its own to meet annually. This Standing Committee was to meet jointly with the ACC Standing Committee. The Joint Standing Committees, in 1992, planned for a first joint Primates and full ACC meeting in Cape Town in 1993. For reasons outside the control of the planners, the experiment was not wholly successful. The Primates did not have enough time for their own business. Being in South Africa at a crucial time in its history, the planned programme was interrupted, and with profit it must be said, to participate in events of the Church of the Province. One of the strong points in favour of the ACC has been its ability to meet in different places throughout the Communion, as opposed to the fixed location hitherto of the Lambeth Conference. This has resulted in much appreciated support and encouragement for the host Church.

I was particularly disappointed, however, that the joint meeting in Cape Town did not prove fully satisfactory. Over previous years, there had been signs of a possible divergence of policy between the Primates and the ACC, meeting at different times. One instance concerned the Anglican Centre in Rome and its continued support from the Inter-Anglican Budget. The Primates had assumed responsibility in what was, admittedly, a delicate situation. Their solution was at variance with a general view on the ACC. Tension was avoided only by the ACC backing down. I was convinced of the necessity for joint meetings of the Primates and the ACC if such divergence of policy was to be avoided. And, indeed, the joint meeting of the Primates and ACC-9 in Cape Town afforded examples of successful agreement on important issues. One, in particular, stands out. It related to the opposing attitudes to the ordination of women within and between Churches, and how the 'two integrities' as they had become known, can be respected. Primates and ACC members together reached a harmonious agreement. One can imagine the damage if the two bodies, meeting separately, had diverged in policy.

After Cape Town, it was obvious that the Primates needed to have their own separate meetings, and so they decided during 1993. But the Joint Standing Committees, in April 1994, agreed to continue to meet together. The responsibility now rests on their members to ensure that both their parent bodies keep on the same track. The concept of dispersed authority has for many years been claimed as an Anglican strength. Different perceptions will arise in the meetings of the instruments of unity, but close partnership can prevent conflicting policies and ensure unity of purpose.

The experience of ACC-10 in Panama, in October 1996, confirmed that the Council meeting with the Primates' Standing Committee is the right solution for the immediate future. It was a harmonious meeting. All business was conducted without due haste, thanks to the planning of the Design Group. Indeed, it was the best of the ACC meetings I attended. What enhanced the success was the tremendous warmth of hospitality and help, in all manner of ways, of the diocese of Panama. And it was abundantly clear that the presence of representatives of all the Provinces, with the Archbishop of Canterbury, in their relatively small but vibrant diocese was a great encouragement to Anglicans there.

BEING A COMMUNION

Emphasis has already been laid on the Anglican family being multi-cultural and embracing widely differing convictions on some issues currently within the Church. And if attention is fixed only on these issues, the question as to whether the family can hold together understandably arises. I have sought to describe structures, the consultative bodies, by which unity can be sought. But basic to structures must be an understanding of what a Communion is. Mechanisms require an underlying philosophy. What is our concept of being a Communion? I will conclude this chapter with another fundamental requirement for the Communion, but for the present time I remain with the question just posed.

We have a choice. Either we have a Communion based on a clearly defined and detailed Confession of Faith and universal Canon Law, and a structure of authority stemming from some over-arching, controlling body, with legislative powers or sanctions; or, we strive for Unity in Diversity. Anglicanism has rejected the former option. Since the break with the Papacy in the sixteenth century its ethos has moved in the other direction. As the Communion has had to face divisive issues, particularly women priests and bishops, and has had to define Anglican understanding of authority in dialogue with other world Communions, a series of Commissions has grappled with what it means to be a Communion. What were named the Grindrod and Eames Commissions' documents, and successive Inter-Anglican Theological and Doctrine Commission Reports - the latest one being The Virginia Report already discussed at ACC-10 and going to Lambeth 1998 - have all revealed a developing consistency. The Virginia Report certainly carries forward Anglican thinking on what it means to be a Communion. Basic to its conclusions is the belief that Communion of the Church on earth is rooted in and sustained by life in the Trinity. We are one because we are baptised into the dynamic life and love of the Triune God.

That does not entail uniformity, any more than it would be appropriate to attribute uniformity to the Persons of the Trinity. And if God has made humankind to live in a multiplicity of cultures, and every member of the human race to have personal characteristics, uniformity becomes an unrealistic fantasy. Any Church striving for it is doomed to disappointment. So Anglicans believe in, and indeed experience, Unity in Diversity. A study of New Testament documents shows the early Church with diverse emphases and responses to situations while united in the Body of Christ. The report then explores ways in which the Communion's four instruments of unity may more effectively aid Unity in Diversity. Debate and assessment of the report will be a major concern of Lambeth 1998.

Inevitably, of course, the question arises of how much diversity can be sustained. Does anything go? Among some individual Anglicans, quite way-out ideas are held, such as 'Christian' atheism or New Age concepts. In Anglicanism and the Universal Church, John Howe discusses the matter of acceptable limits of faith and practice in the Anglican Communion. He calls agreement on that a watershed yet to be crossed. One watershed, he says, has already been crossed - the transition from dependant out-posts of older Churches to autonomous Provinces throughout the Communion. John Howe clearly repudiates the idea of a universal, total and therefore imposed Canon Law, but felt the need for some agreement on limits of interpretation, and consequently of practice, in Anglicanism. I have described how, later in that same book, from before the ACC-7 meeting in 1987 the idea of a Common Declaration was suggested, encapsulating Anglican emphasis on tradition and development. A tentative draft, based on the Chicago-Lambeth Quadrilateral, was drawn up and, after further revision, incorporating phrases from past Lambeth Conference statements, was submitted to Lambeth 1988. The Quadrilateral focuses on Scripture, Creeds, Sacraments (the two Dominical Sacraments) and Ministry in the Episcopal Succession. Around the time John Howe was commenting on Anglican diversity, Bishop Stephen Neill, in a study paper for ACC-6 maintained, 'If the Communion is to hold together, outward signs of unity must be supplemented by a succinct and straightforward statement as to what it is that the Anglican Communion stands for as a witness to the truth'.

The draft Common Declaration got a general welcome at Lambeth 1988, but the bishops asked for study by a future Theological and Doctrinal Commission. Since then the idea has run out of steam. Clearly some Provinces are unenthusiastic, probably anxious about possible movement towards a theological straight-jacket. Nevertheless, there seems to be widespread agreement that Anglicanism is essentially committed to the Lambeth Quadrilateral, even though in one at least of its four clauses it is open to different interpretations. It defines Anglicanism as committed to the Scriptures as 'containing all things necessary to salvation and as the rule and ultimate standard of faith'; the Apostles' and Nicene Creeds; the two Sacraments ordained by Christ (with unfailing use of the words of Institution) and the elements ordained by him; and the Historic Episcopate, 'locally adapted to... the varying needs of nations and peoples'. It is the fourth clause that has particularly occasioned differences of interpretation.

I firmly believe that any Church or Province, as opposed to groups or individuals, clearly departing from the Quadrilateral's affirmations would forfeit the right to be defined as Anglican. For instance, abandonment or material alteration of the Creeds, or dispensing with the Sacraments or changing their intention would require action by the rest of the Communion. What that action might be, and how it would be taken, is not clear. It is not individuals, be they clergy, laity or even bishops, who are in mind. Action deemed necessary because of heresy, immorality or other unacceptable behaviour, is the responsibility of the Churches or Provinces concerned. The issue relates to member Churches and Provinces. A Church, like any individual, may call itself Anglican. Its claim, it may be assumed, is based on accepting a tradition and affirming an ecclesiology. But it is another thing to be recognised by the Communion as a constituent member. At present that involves two main requisites, acceptance on to the schedule of Member Churches in the ACC Constitution and recognition of being in communion with the See of Canterbury. It is because the ACC is the only international Anglican body with a constitution - essential, among other things, to guarantee its charitable status and employ personnel - that a definition of recognised members can be established. As this is the way a Church or Province can be officially recognised as Anglican, it is conceivable, though one hopes not likely, that a Church could be removed from the schedule of membership. Presumably the basis of criteria would be the Lambeth Quadrilateral.

In recent years, there has been something of a rush of parts of the Churches and Provinces to become Provinces in their own right. The reasons may be political, a wish to be distanced from other parts of the same Province, or even perhaps personal - the desire of some bishop to become a Primate - while it can also be a logical development. What is not in doubt, in some instances, is the failure to observe all the guidelines agreed over the years by the ACC, with the support of the Primates, for the creation of new Provinces. Full consultation with the ACC throughout the negotiating process, a minimum of four dioceses for a Province (unfortunately, in my judgement, not followed in one or two cases recently), the completion of a suitable constitution for the Province and the prospect of financial viability, are among the guidelines. Unless the Communion is to lapse into some disorder, observance of the guidelines is necessary. At the recent ACC-10 meeting in Panama, the guidelines were clarified and re-affirmed.

During the ACC-9 meeting in Cape Town, I was strongly urged by representatives of the Church of England in South Africa to seek the Archbishop of Canterbury' approval for that Church to be recognised as in the Anglican Communion. I had to point out that he alone could not achieve that aim. The approval of the Primates and the ACC was essential. This would not be given so long as their Church and the Church of the Province of Southern Africa were not in full Communion. Despite a series of earnest attempts by leaders on both sides and the then Archbishop of Sydney (Donald Robinson) a substantial number of the CESA laity had opposed closer relations with the CPSA.

Reference to the schedule of membership in the ACC Constitution raises a further question about the Anglican Communion. Are not its boundaries getting blurred? Looking down the schedule we come to the united Churches of the Indian Sub-continent - CNI, CSI, the Church of Pakistan and the Church of Bangladesh. They are most welcome fellow-members of the ACC, their bishops will all be at the Lambeth Conference and their Moderators attend the Primates' Meeting. But they do not call themselves Anglican, nor does anyone else, though former Anglicans are found within them. Every indication shows them happy with the Lambeth Quadrilateral. After they came into being it was on their own request that they became associated with the Anglican Communion, even though the establishment of communion with Member Churches took some time, a very long time, particularly in the case of the CSI and England to England's shame. From the Anglican side there was a concern not to diminish the United Churches' fellowship with other world Communions to which, before union, non-Anglicans had belonged, Methodist, Reformed, Lutheran, etc.

Further developments in other parts of the world are likely to blur the edges of the Anglican Communion. These developments, mainly between Anglicans and Lutherans, represent the brightest and most encouraging part of the ecumenical scene. In the United States of America, a Concordat between the Episcopal Church and the Evangelical Lutheran Church in America, agreed to by the General Convention 1997 of ECUSA but not yet accepted by the Lutherans, aims to bring both Churches into communion. In Canada, the Anglican Church and the Lutherans are looking towards full communion in 2001. Progress between Anglicans and Lutherans in parts of Africa are encouraging. The Anglican Churches of Britain and Ireland have entered into the Porvoo Agreement with Baltic and Nordic Lutheran Churches, aiming at full communion. The Church of England is on course for the same goal with the Evangelical Church of Germany (Lutheran, Reformed and United Churches).

These, and possibly other moves in other directions, notably in Brazil, Namibia, Southern Africa and Tanzania, are between individual Anglican Churches and other Churches, not between the whole Anglican Communion and sister Communions. What should, and will, be the consequences for participating in Anglican international consultative bodies, Lambeth Conference, the ACC and the Primates' Meeting, if individual Churches and Provinces enter into full communion - that is, if the partners wish to participate? Blurring of the boundaries of the Anglican family should be a welcome price to pay for the creation of United Churches and even establishment of full communion between separate Churches. Perhaps we should bear in mind that when marriages take place in any family the boundaries are extended beyond blood ties. Regional ecumenical progress is to be warmly welcomed, but for smoother movement towards working out the issues for the whole Communion, as indicated above, close monitoring and consultation between regions will be increasingly necessary.

OTHER ECUMENICAL RELATIONS

Each of the encouraging developments already referred to are with Lutherans, and in mainland Europe with Reformed and United Churches as well. As has been maintained, the Anglican-Lutheran scene is most encouraging. For over 60 years, however, Anglicans have been at a half-way stage towards full communion with the Old Catholics, a break-away Church from Rome. There is a sharing of sacramental fellowship, agreement on essentials in faith, though not necessarily all details, mutual participation in episcopal consecrations. But they are still two separate Communions. Since 1993, however, the two Churches have been pursuing the path to closer unity.

Progress towards communion with the Orthodox and Oriental Orthodox Churches is slow. Some agreement on the nature of the Church has been established; its unity is seen as grounded in the Trinity into which the baptised are drawn. But one obstacle is illustrated by the fact that Anglicans see our divisions as within the Church of Christ, whereas the Orthodox believe that their Church is the One Church of Christ which, as his Body, is not, and cannot, be divided.

Since Lambeth 1988, joint dialogue with the World Methodist Council has been through an international commission whose Interim Report was submitted for comments in both Communions. On the basis of reactions, a further report went to the World Methodist Council in 1997 and goes to the Lambeth Conference in 1998. Likewise Lambeth 1988, following a report in 1984 of the Anglican-Reformed International Commission, encouraged the ACC to consult with the World Alliance of Reformed Churches to establish a continuation committee for further progress. It met for the first time in 1996 and its report was prepared for the respective bodies, the World Alliance and the Lambeth Conference in 1997 and 1998.

What can be said of dialogue with the Roman Catholic Church? Details of the work of ARCIC I (Anglican-Roman Catholic International Commission) and ARCIC II are probably more widely known across the Communion than those of other ecumenical dialogues. Official talks with Roman Catholics at world level have been going on for thirty years. Considerable agreements have been reached, indicating convergence in the search for 'the restoration of complete communion of faith and sacramental life' (as the Common Declaration of 1968 envisaged). Space forbids any detailed observations on the achievements thus far. The Anglican-Roman Catholic Commission has been meeting every year - more often than our other international dialogues. Even if at times Anglicans have felt the Vatican's response to its reports has been slow and less than enthusiastic, we must recognise the great change that Rome has had to face from former centuries.

Having recognised the progress, however, I now offer some observations on the gulf still to be bridged. They are personal but I imagine they reflect the views of many Anglicans. A major and fundamental difference on authority in the Church is unresolved. It radically affects two aspects of the Church's life - what is to be believed, and how the Church is to be governed. Anglicans are committed without question to the supremacy of Scripture in its role as the rule and ultimate standard of faith. As has already been noted, they see the interpretation of Scripture in every age as assisted by Tradition and Reason within the collective experience of the Church. They do not see the Church in its teaching office as being able to determine what must be believed for salvation, particularly on matters neither clearly taught in Scripture nor even mentioned in Scripture. Thus Anglicans as a whole cannot be committed to the Roman Marian doctrines, whatever individual Anglicans may accept. Further, Anglicanism cannot be committed to one understanding of sacrifice in the Eucharist, even if some Anglicans approximate to or fully accept the Roman position. It was because Rome, in the nineteenth century, judged Anglican ordination services to fail in intention to create sacrificing priests according to its own understanding, that Anglican orders were declared null and void. Full communion between our Churches must not only recognise our orders but allow that diversity in unity which can be the only basis for unity.

How is the Church to be governed? It has already been maintained that Anglicans believe that the authority of Christ in governing the Church's life is devolved to the whole people of God, laity, clergy and bishops. A hierarchical structure derived from a Pope through Conferences of Bishops is unacceptable to Anglicans. At local level in many places, laity are being brought more into decisions in the parish, as indeed they are in its ministry, but the authority system remains. Whether it will continue under a less conservative, reforming Pope, if such is elected, is still to be seen. The exercise of authority of Pope John Paul II in imposing bishops of his own views, even contrary to the wishes of dioceses, and creation of like-minded Cardinals, is not the way Anglicans can accept.

What of the Papacy itself? Irrespective of its occupancy at any time, could Anglicans see a role for a universal primacy? In Anglican/Roman Catholic talks the prospect has been raised. I would say it all depends on what the role is. The Archbishop of Canterbury is *primus inter pares* among Anglican Primates. He, with the other consultative bodies, is a sign of unity, but he has no jurisdiction over the Communion, his influence being moral not legal. Anglicans have every reason to value such a role. If that were the nature of a universal primacy, complete agreement would be possible. But could Rome develop, we might say reform, along those lines? And could the Orthodox Churches accept it? It is my growing conviction that no one person should be placed in the authoritative role of the Papacy as it is. I do not believe the Petrine claims can be pushed to support that position. I see no evidence in the New Testament for one Christian leader being given such authority over the whole Church. I do not think it is good for any man, particularly for his spiritual health, to be in a role that is accompanied by such adulation and reverence as the Pope receives on his travels and in Rome.

Having expressed these serious reservations, however, I want to welcome the increasingly good relations with Roman Catholics at local and diocesan levels. The friendship and co-operation in many things are a great encouragement, especially when the situation thirty or more years ago is remembered. I greatly desire the day when we will have full sacramental fellowship.

COMMUNICATING IN THE FAMILY

I earlier maintained that for the unity of the Anglican family, talking together is essential. But communication cannot be only through the meetings of consultative bodies, however valuable the face-to-face relationship of representatives from the Churches. Nor does the facility of letters by post, E-mail and Internet, or telephone conversations, exhaust the needs of communication, though these modern technologies have enormously helped. The visits of the Secretary General and other members of the Secretariat, supplementing the greatly appreciated visits of the Archbishop of Canterbury to the Provinces, have a binding value. And a host of visits and ministries across all the dioceses, many based on diocesan links, contribute greatly to a sense of unity.

In the last two or three years, and particularly from a meeting of the Joint Standing Committees in 1995, a much increased emphasis has been placed on the production and promotion of the excellent *Anglican World*, its quality and style being affirmed throughout the Communion. Great credit is due to Canon James Rosenthal and his assistants in the Communications Department of the Anglican Communion Office. The Joint Standing Committees gave warm backing to the programme of getting the periodical widely distributed across the Communion, not least to those who might not be able to pay for it. It was recognised that considerably greater finances would be required than were at present available in the straightened Inter-Anglican Budget. Until other sources could be tapped, and subscription income increased, John Peterson as Secretary-General undertook to raise extra-budgeting income.

PAYING FOR IT ALL

Mention of the finance needed for building up Communications prompts reference to a continuing, and as yet unresolved, problem of inadequate funding for Communion activities as authorised by member Churches through their representatives. The plain fact is that all Churches do not pay in full the requested quota. With some it may be due to genuine poverty, with others lack of will and conviction that contributing to the Communion's needs is a priority. Through my years on the Standing Committee and its Finance Committee, I can say without any doubt that most stringent budget preparations have applied in every year. The needs of a small staff are severely scrutinised and controlled. Some very substantial cut-backs have been necessary. Without the generous help of institutions such as Trinity Church, Wall Street, New York, in pump-priming finance, and Virginia Theological Seminary, USA, in funding the meetings of the Doctrine Commission, and groups of individuals in raising funds for the office of the Anglican United Nations Observer, much of value would not have been accomplished.

The office of the Anglican UN observer demands special attention. Thus far, apart from a very small token contribution from the Inter-Anglican Budget agreed at ACC-10 in 1996, the considerable financial burden has been borne by American contributions, encouraged and assisted by the Archbishop of Canterbury. This is not a satisfactory situation. If the Anglican Communion as a whole believes the observer and his office (with staff) meets a need in its world-wide mission not met in any other way, it must begin to shoulder the burden. Fund-raisers may still be needed for the short-term, and possibly medium-term, future, but the total Inter-Anglican Budget would increasingly have to meet the costs. At ACC-10 it was decided to instigate an evaluation of the Office. If the outcome were to prove positive, a basis of confidence would be laid for future support. If there is not a conviction that the Office is a major priority, bold and urgent decisions are required. In straightened circumstances, establishment of priorities is essential. After more than one rather unsuccessful attempt to find a good way of prioritising, a satisfactory method has begun to operate from the ACC-10 meeting in Panama.

When disasters occur in Provinces - genocide, earthquakes, hurricanes, famine or huge refugee problems - other world Communions respond swiftly with financial help. The Anglican Communion has no such facility. Individual Churches may initiate help, as the Church of Canada did for Rwanda, and individual Anglicans and their parishes can contribute through Christian Aid and similar relief organisations. But it would mean much to local Anglicans in disaster areas if their Communion could be seen to be sharing in the help. They are justified in asking what it means to be in a family if the family cannot help members in need. In response,

Archbishop George Carey has sought the help of international financiers in setting up an Anglican Investment Agency through which wealthy Anglicans and Church finance bodies may invest capital in accordance with assured ethical criteria. Part of the broker's fee will be given to a body of trustees responsible for dispensing grants to meet extraordinary situations of distress and other needs not met by the Inter-Anglican Budget. Another scheme recently launched is the Compass Rose Society, through which individuals or parishes may contribute to a range of activities within the budget, selecting what particularly appeals to them.

It is recognised that in a small minority of cases, Provinces do not meet the requested quota to the budget because they are not in favour of the whole programme of activities. If all being done accorded with their own priority, they would pay up. I myself have little sympathy with a pick-and-choose attitude to church financing whether at parish, diocesan, national or international level. It seems to me a failure of Christian fellowship, unless it can be demonstrated that some funded activity runs contrary to Christian standards. It is, however, understandable that some parts of a Communion's programme may appeal more than others.

A particular need for extra-budgetary funding at present concerns the Personal Emergencies Fund, set up on the initiative of Archbishop Donald Coggan. It aims to make grants, albeit of modest amounts, to clergy or their families in need of financial assistance, almost always for medical emergencies. It applies obviously to Third World countries. Each application has to be supported by the bishop or archbishop. Income from investment and donations is insufficient to match all needs. Maybe, when the other new ways of funding get going, this fund could be better provided for. At present it is administered by three people - Archbishop Robin Eames, Bishop Simon Barrington-Ward and myself - who conduct their business mainly by telephone. The stories, and subsequent expressions of gratitude by recipients, make the enterprise abundantly worthwhile.

When all is said on financial deficits, tribute must be paid to the Provinces in extreme difficulties who pay their quotas. At the ACC-9 meeting in Cape Town the Secretary General, Sam Van Culin, and I were approached by two representatives of the Church in the Sudan, a Church in persecution within a long-running civil war and with many displaced Christians. Their journey to South Africa had been fraught with difficulty, taking a long time and involving for one of them a severe beating before he left the Sudan. They were coming to us to hand over a cheque for their Church's contribution to the Anglican Budget. At ACC-10 they again brought their quota. During the same meeting we received a message from the Church of Nigeria. Despite the value of their currency falling to less than 1 per cent of its 1986 value, political instability and oppression, they were sending their full 1996 contribution and giving a commitment to meet the 1997 quota in full. In addition, their Church is to train four Rwandan priests in Nigeria. Having in the past sent missionaries to and trained priests for the Church in the Sudan (some of whom are now bishops) they are now to train another priest for that Church and to support him and his wife for three or four years. May Sudan and Nigeria be a challenging example to all member Churches!

UNITY IN WORSHIP

In a submission to the Lambeth 1948 Conference, the *Book of Common Prayer* could be described as a powerful bond of unity across the Communion. Since that time, in the processes of liturgical revision Anglicans, like other Communions, have brought in a range of services in modern language and adapted to the cultures of their Provinces. Inculturation of worship is entirely justified. Amid the changes, a concern has been to ensure the worship is authentically Anglican and can still be a unifying bond. At my first ACC meeting in 1981 in Newcastle, England, I wondered if the liturgies from a number of Provinces were tending to divergence, particularly in respect of the Eucharist and its intention. And it must be admitted that, at local parish level, one can witness worship that appears to sit loose to Anglican norms.

In more recent years, a greater similarity between liturgies has emerged, at any rate in the basic elements of the Eucharist. That was apparent In the most recent ACC meeting in Panama, yet cultural expressions, not least in songs and hymns, were appreciated. Much of the credit for these welcome trends must go to the members of the International Anglican Liturgical Consultation, who also take part in an ecumenical liturgical body. The original members of the IALC, covering their own expenses, wished to draw in representatives of Provinces who could not afford travel costs. They asked the ACC to set up an Anglican Liturgical Commission funded from the core budget. It proved financially impossible at the time, so the IALC members undertook to continue finding the necessary expenses for themselves and a wide range of representatives from the Provinces. It would report to the Primates and the ACC. There has followed a series of forward-looking, valuable reports on matters like Inculturation, Christian Initiation, Eucharist and sacrifice. In all of them, agreement between the main Anglican traditions is evident. Anglican liturgy is still a bond of unity, though quite different from 1948.

MISSION TOGETHER

If the Church is not wholeheartedly engaged in mission it is not the Church of Christ. Jesus himself came into the world to fulfil the crucial part in the *Missio Dei*, the Mission of God. What God did through his life, death, resurrection and ascension establishes, brings into effect and energises that Mission. The Church, as the first fruits of the mission, is inherently caught up into its purpose. If its members fail to see that truth or to commit themselves to it, they forfeit the name of Church and become merely an exclusive club doing religious things.

Mission, then, is what Christians do, personally and corporately. Primarily it is done in local contexts, local situations and in personal relationships, although local should not be interpreted in too narrow terms. A Church has a mission at national or provincial level, addressing the powers that be, speaking to society and working for the principles of God's kingdom. A diocese has a mission to a regional community and the many strands that make it up. And these wider responsibilities can undergird the mission of a parish and its baptised members. So, in what ways can and should a world-wide Communion be involved in mission? Should Anglican bodies like the Lambeth Conference, the Primates, the ACC assume a role, or leave it all to the local level?

I believe there are two necessary tasks to be fulfilled at the world-wide Communion level. One is to reflect upon the meaning and development of mission in all the world. The other is to assist in sharing of resources and insights across the Churches and to stimulate obedience to mission. Both these tasks need some further comment. The ecumenical dimension must not be overlooked. Other Churches, and associations of Churches like the WCC, explore the meaning and development of mission. Co-operation in mission with all Churches that are willing for it is not only a demonstration of the Gospel but a demand of the Gospel. However, that, as I see it, does not remove the obligation for each Church to do all it can for its own members to be obedient to mission, while encouraging such ecumenical co-operation as can be. The sharing of resources and insights from a multiplicity of cultures should be, as far as possible, ecumenical, but the plain fact is that so long as Church structures, synodical and voluntary, and resource-gathering mechanisms are separate, the bulk of this responsibility will be denominational. So, the Anglican Communion must have a central agency for mission.

Anglican Developments in Mission

One would not want to suggest that such developments are only in modern times - they have been going on for centuries. My concern is really with the last fifteen years as I have witnessed what has happened.

In 1984 ACC-6 received a report from a working group on Mission Issues and Strategy - MISAG I. It began with these words: 'Though there are notable exceptions, the dominant model of the Church within the Anglican Communion is a pastoral one. Emphasis in all aspects of the Church's life tends to be placed on care and nurture rather than proclamation and service.' A shift of emphasis was called for. The Church's task was 'making known the truth about God revealed in Christ through what Christians say, what they are and what they do'.

The ACC at that same meeting sought to amplify this definition of mission in four clauses:

1. To proclaim the good news of the Kingdom
2. To teach, baptise and nurture the new believers
3. To respond to human needs by loving service
4. To seek to transform unjust structures of society.

This definition thus presents a holistic view of mission - evangelism in the sense of witness and proclamation, nurture of the baptised, loving service, social action. It represented a convergence of previously narrow and conflicting attitudes to mission being welcomed across all Churches. In 1990 at ACC-8, following a growing concern, a fifth clause was added - To strive to safeguard the integrity of creation and sustain and renew the life of the earth. The definition has been accepted and valued across the Communion - an example of the Communion worldwide helping its member Churches, dioceses and parishes in mission.

In 1985 the ACC Standing Committee set up a continuing Mission Issues and Strategy Group (MISAG II) to develop and implement the ideas of its predecessor. At Lambeth 1988 the momentous decision to launch a Decade of Evangelism was taken, largely stimulated by African bishops but also catching a mood in other Churches, such as the Roman Catholic. The Lambeth Fathers called for decisive changes to shift the emphasis "from mere maintenance to wholehearted commitment to Evangelism, understood within the holistic view of Mission".

MISAG II reported to ACC-9 in Cape Town in 1993. One of its chief recommendations was for the establishment of a continuing Commission for Mission (MISSIO) drawing together representatives of Churches, particularly in the 'South' or the Third World (any definition has its difficulties), mission agencies and consultants. A feature of recent years has been the exchange of missionary personnel and resources across younger Churches previously only on the receiving end from older Churches. This had led to two 'South to South' Conferences, arranged by the relevant Churches in which the exchange was developed.

During the past fifteen years, a welcome development has been the establishment of Networks across the Communion. Although authorised by the ACC, and reporting to it they have had an independence. Each is concerned with some aspect of mission - Peace and Justice, Refugee and Migrants (temporarily in abeyance), the Family, Youth, Indigenous Peoples. People with expertise and special concern from the Provinces have formed the Networks which, apart from small grants from the Anglican Budget in some cases, are self-funding. In December 1995, representatives of the Networks met with some of the ACC Standing Committee - the first time this had happened. It was soon evident that the Networks desired closer communication with one another and a more meaningful relationship with the ACC. Guidelines for that development were drawn up and accepted by ACC-10. I believe it is necessary for the Joint Standing Committees to work out with the Networks a more detailed pursuit of the goal. The Anglican Secretariat has had a Mission and Evangelism Department. As has been right, the Decade of Evangelism and its promotion across the Communion has taken up time and energies, particularly of its Secretary, Dr Cyril Okorocha. While Evangelism must continue to be a priority beyond the Decade, it seems right now to explore ways of relating the Networks, as they are concerned with mission, more effectively with the ACC. This should not inhibit their scope for initiatives, but a better partnership could increase harmony of thought and action. And it could lead to funding assistance from the Inter-Anglican Budget.

It should be noted that the Anglican Observer Office at the United Nations has a concern and connection with issues dealt with by the Networks, so collaboration with that Office needs developing.

The Decade of Evangelism

Can there ever be an objective and balanced assessment of the Decade of Evangelism till well into the next century, until Church historians can look back? A judgement during the 1990s can only be provisional. The lasting effects must be assessed eventually when it can be seen if its impact went beyond the year 2000. I have taken the view that the analogy of a large tanker at sea is appropriate. If a change of course is needed, it will take several miles to effect. The Decade is nothing less than a change of course. A major responsibility for the Lambeth Conference in 1998 will be to judge whether the signs are clear enough to forward the ship on the same course.

I believe it is a mistake to think of the decision at Lambeth 1988 to launch the Decade as the result of a sudden whim, though it may be some bishops lacked conviction but could not vote against Evangelism. As has already been shown, for several years before 1988 there was a growing concern across the Communion that a shift of emphasis was needed 'from mere maintenance to wholehearted commitment to Evangelism understood within the holistic view of Mission', to quote the Lambeth Fathers' own words.

When the Primates and the ACC met together at Cape Town in 1993, they heard reports of how the Decade was going, well in some places, not so well in others. They called for a Mid-Term Review in 1995. A good idea, it might be judged. Unfortunately, no financial provision was made or planning group appointed. Therein lay the cause of much difficulty in preparation for the Review. Early attempts to organise, chiefly by Cyril Okorocha, the Mission and Evangelism Secretary, ran into difficulties through no fault of his own. In November 1994, I began to chair a planning group hastily drawn together. At once urgent questions had to be faced. How was a major conference to be financed? Could we ensure that delegates from all Churches in the Communion would be drawn in - many of whom needed to be paid for? Would all approaches to Evangelism across many cultures be represented? Time was short. In March 1995, only six months before the projected Conference, there was difficulty in persuading the Primates' Meeting and the Joint Standing Committees that it was wise to go on with plans. The answers to the questions posed above could not yet be given. As chairman of the planning group, I was tempted to think we might be risking a disaster. Although with Cyril Okorocha, and a few others, I believed in the project, to fail badly would set back the Decade.

In the event over four hundred people came together in September at the Kanuga Conference Centre in North Carolina - two hundred and fifty of these being present for part of the time as observers but also contributing their insights as well as finance. Churches in more than sixty countries sent delegates. By the end of the Conference, a budget of over £150,000 had been met including a balance to produce a report[4]. This provision, owing a great deal to Cyril Okorocha's efforts in convincing potential donors, came from a large number of individuals and institutions. Delegates told their stories of advances within their cultures. A most significant feature was the consensus that Evangelism had to be seen and prosecuted in the context of the totality of mission. Indeed, it is when it is perceived by the outsider as reaching out to him or her in all felt needs that the proclamation of Good News becomes credible.

The results of the Conference, known as Global Conference on Dynamic Evangelism beyond 2000 (G-Code 2000), have been fed into the MISSIO Commission, which in turn was asked to make recommendations to the Design Group for Lambeth 1998.

Although other Communions, notably the Roman Catholic, have in varying degrees taken up the idea of a special emphasis on Evangelism leading up to the official commemoration of Christ's birth 2,000 years ago, the Anglican Decade of Evangelism has been a most significant and distinctive contribution to world Christianity. The Roman Catholic Evangelisation project seems generally to have been directed to lapsed Catholics, particularly in Europe. The Anglican development, though clearly more effective in some areas than others, has primarily been concerned with challenging and enabling dioceses and parishes to be more effectively engaged in bringing Good News to their communities, and ordinary church members to be witnesses of God's saving love to their friends and neighbours. To this end, many dioceses have appointed Advisers in Evangelism. Where progress has happened, the impact will not end with the Decade.

A CONCLUDING WORD

It has been a great privilege to chair the ACC since 1990. I was in considerable doubt as to whether I should accede to invitations to allow my name to be submitted. Earlier that year, before ACC-8 in Wales, I had gone into print stating that I did not think the Chairman should ever be from England - the Archbishop of Canterbury was English, the Anglican Communion Office was in England. Ought I not to stand by

---

4. Published in 1996 as *The Cutting Edge of Mission*, Anglican Communications Publications.

that judgement? Pressed by several members, I went off on a free afternoon during the meeting in Wales to a quiet beach on the coast.

I laid my confused thoughts before God. I was sixty-seven years old, within three years I would retire from my parish, in eighteen months I would leave our General Synod. If elected, I would expect to serve for six years. My wife, who had sustained a heart attack sixteen years before, was deteriorating in health - what would be required of me? And I was fully aware that the centre of gravity of the Communion was no longer in the older Churches like England. As I tried to be open to God's guidance, my attention was drawn to a round stone on the beach. As I held it, I reflected that here was a minute piece of the cosmos that had existed millions of years before I was born. It had once been part of some greater whole, in the early ages of this planet, but had broken off and been smoothed and rounded by the seas over vast periods of time. In some way it was part of God's creative purposes. My life, too, was within his purposes, and indeed was the object of God's saving purposes through Christ, redeemed at infinite cost in the Cross and Resurrection. The word seemed clear, leave the result of the election to the chair in the Lord's hand!

As I prepared my mind for my last ACC meeting in October 1996, and my last act as Chairman at the closing Eucharist - I had been asked to preach - I wondered what theme to take. My thoughts were on the next few years facing the Communion, with much to encourage but with heavy problems through deep divisions on current issues. Our structures for consultation were in good shape and heart. But I increasingly felt that structures alone were not enough to get us through any stormy seas. My mind was drawn to the opening verses of Philippians 2: 'Consider others better than yourselves, look out for one anothers' interest, not just your own'. I had to ask myself if I had followed this injunction in divisive issues I had lived through. In the ordination-of-women saga, had I looked on opponents in that way? In these verses, St Paul appeals for oneness of mind, lowliness of mind, mutual regard. All this is the path to the unity of God's people. But is it practical?

St Paul obviously does not advocate abandoning of convictions carefully arrived at, but rather a due regard for the convictions of others and concern for their well-being. Basic to the mutual regard that must undergird unity in diversity, is the willingness to accept deep within us that we do not ourselves possess the whole truth. However strong our belief that 'we have got it right', there is the possibility we are forgetting or ignorant of something. The section of Paul's letter is crystallised in his advice, 'Let this mind be in you that was in Christ Jesus'. His humiliation, self chosen, led to four steps down - Heaven's glory, Bethlehem, Galilee and Gethsemane, Golgotha. To have his mind in the years ahead in all the Communion's affairs will be even more important than efficient structures.

Chapter 6
What next?

Retirement is great! I have heard of clergy feeling their lives are empty once they have retired. I suppose that, bereft of their pastoral relationship with their congregation there is a big gap to fill. It is important, I am convinced, that they retire in a parish where they will feel spiritually and emotionally at home, however much or little they are called upon for duties. My wife and I are grateful to be in a team ministry where the worship is congenial, the preaching is good and the friendship warm. As will be apparent from previous chapters, retirement for me, however, as for many pensioners, has been busy and fulfilling. But, inevitably, advancing years, if I am spared, will curtail activity. Then what? Mortality enters more into one's consciousness, and so it should. St Paul could say, 'For me to live is Christ, to die is gain'.

To face death with that confident hope is the inalienable right of every Christian believer. The Gospel puts death in its proper place as the gateway from life in Christ on earth to more glorious life in the immediate presence of the triune God. I believe that truth, even though I would wish to go on for some years yet in this life, if it is God's will. I do not think I am being inconsistent. There is still so much to enjoy of the good gifts of a heavenly father in creation, in the Church, in marriage and the family, with children, grandchildren and friends. As the title of the book indicates, 'to Grace, how great a debtor daily I'm constrained to be'. I have no desire to turn the clock back, to revert to an earlier age in life. I am content to be where I am, even if I now reflect sometimes that every passing second is one nearer the day of transition from this world. So, what am I expecting when that day comes? What is next?

THE CERTAINTIES

There are some great revealed truths in the Gospel of Jesus Christ of which I have no doubt. They cannot be proved, but they are of the essence of the Faith which, as I have indicated in an earlier chapter I have tested as critically as I can and found to be a convincing basis for living. The certainties I am holding in regard to the life to come may be fewer than some Christians seem to hold. For instance, some take the prophetic language and imagery of the Scriptures regarding heaven, and indeed future events in history, more literally than I believe is justified. In my early years, I heard speakers outline in detail time-tables of coming events on the world-stage before, during and subsequent to the Return of Christ. It was fascinating, and captured the imagination of those who believed it was a true exposition of Scripture. But the language of eschatology, the doctrine of the last things, has to be handled with great care. In both Old and New Testaments, symbols and metaphors abound in the apocalyptic literature. At times it is abundantly obvious that a literal understanding is quite unrealistic, at others perhaps not so obvious, but how to distinguish between the symbols is a problem without solution. The only way to talk about heaven, an entirely different dimension, is to use images of what is good and precious in this world of space and time, but no stress can be laid on the scenery of the life to come. So the certainties I hold - certainties of hope born of faith - are less in number than those held by some, yet they are firmer and mean more now than ever before after a life-time's reflection. Hope as a concept seems by definition to rule out certainty, but the New Testament is able to speak of a 'sure and certain hope', based on the absolute reliability of God's promises. This chapter, then, will indicate what I am certain about as I look forward. But I will also reflect on what I think the implications of those certainties might be. This will involve speculation, no more than that, and there must be a reverent agnosticism in the conclusions. But God-given reason may be employed to take up hints in Scripture in order to think around the cardinal elements in our Christian hope. Such an exercise may at least help to avoid unjustified assumptions.

The Resurrection of Christ

There can be no doubt that the crucifixion of Jesus resulted in physical death. Strange ideas that he swooned, later revived and left the country to live out further years elsewhere - apparently no longer in touch with his family and friends - must be discounted as idle tales conceived for some purpose associated with drawing attention to the interests of some person or groups or locality. So, his corpse was placed in a tomb. Within forty-eight hours that tomb was empty. If it was not, the proof could easily have been demonstrated. Either the body was removed, taken away by friends or enemies, or some other explanation is demanded. What possible reason enemies of the Jesus sect could have for removing the body stretches the imagination beyond belief. They might have wanted to prevent the tomb becoming a shrine. But when his followers within weeks were adamant in public that he was risen from the dead, it would have been possible to refute the 'dangerous' assertion quite easily. If friends removed the body and hid it elsewhere, then, for one thing, they were fools to go public with a story of a risen Jesus. But the records, which bear the ring of truth, show several things that militate against the preaching of a resurrection based on deception. The friends were clearly not expecting a resurrection. When the report first came they were sceptical. But then they were transformed from disillusioned, despairing and very fearful people, expecting persecution and possibly martyrdom, to bold, confident, joyful witnesses to a risen Jesus they had met.

Mention of an empty tomb does not seem to figure prominently in Apostolic preaching, though it would be wrong to suggest it was forgotten, because the Gospels, finalised some decades after the Resurrection, carry the account. But the Gospel to be preached was not really about an empty tomb; it was Christ crucified and risen. An empty tomb could not save.

A story from the time of the French Revolution, whose truth I cannot vouch for, concerns Talleyrand, previously a Roman Catholic bishop but excommunicated by the Pope. He was visited by another Frenchman, M. Lepeaux, who had been trying to launch a new religion. He believed he could provide an improvement on Christianity, but was disappointed at the response he had met with, despite all his efforts. He asked Talleyrand's advice. Talleyrand is supposed to have replied that it was indeed difficult to found a new religion. He did not know what to suggest. However, after a few moments thought he offered a suggestion. 'There is one plan which you might at least try. I would recommend you to be crucified and rise again the third day'. The enduring foundational truth of the Christian Gospel is the Death and Resurrection of Jesus Christ. But for those twin indivisible facts, the Christian Church would never have begun, what was perceived as a discredited sect in Judaism would have soon died out; and there would never have been a world-wide and growing Church two millennia later. Of course, no world religion based on a body of ideas and teachings can be demonstrated to be absolutely true. The Christian faith, however, is based on a life lived at a certain point in history, a death and rising again to life at a point in history, the evidence for which convinced and transformed sceptics.

There is one further strand to my certainty of the Resurrection. I know the risen Christ. I know about him, of course, but it is more than that. I know him in a personal relationship. I have told, in an earlier chapter, how as a child of five and a half I asked Jesus to come into my life, and through nearly seventy years since I have known the prayer was answered. Later, I was to understand more of the significance of that childhood act of faith. Across the New Testament is the firm assurance that the risen Christ dwells by his Spirit within the life and personality of those who trust in him. I cannot claim that every moment, every hour I am conscious of his indwelling. Preoccupations of daily life make it impossible, but through a myriad experiences in situations grave or joyful, perilous or peaceful, critical or plain ordinary I have known him with me.

The critic may say it is all fanciful; I have conditioned myself to believe it and imagine it. I have already acknowledged the almost infinite capacity of the mind to believe what it wants to believe. But I have to say that the presence of the risen Christ within effects changes which do not, I am sure, spring from my own will or feelings or imagination. Peace replaces anxiety. Guidance breaks through confusion, guidance which later proves to have been sound and right. Pardon and assurance of forgiveness follow penitence and confession. And the remarkable fact about all this is that I am constantly coming across other Christian believers whose experience of the risen Christ within their lives entirely matches my own. If I had never through all the years found anyone else claiming what I have known, I would have cause to wonder whether it was self-delusion. But millions upon millions of Christians down the ages, and still today, have not been the victims of self-hypnosis. Christ is alive, he lives within my heart and within multitudes of his followers. I quote from one of my favourite hymns.

I know that my Redeemer lives:
What comfort this sweet sentence gives!
He lives, He lives, who once was dead!
He lives my everlasting head.
He lives, triumphant from the grave.
He lives, eternally to save,
He lives, all glorious in the sky,
He lives, exalted there on high.
He lives, my kind, wise, constant Friend;
Who still will keep me to the end;
He lives, and while He lives I'll sing,
Jesus, my Prophet, Priest and King.
He lives to bless me with his love,
And still He pleads for me above;
He lives to raise me from the grave,
And me eternally to save.
He lives within my heart to dwell,
And save me from the power of hell;
To comfort me when'er I faint,
And soothe my heaviest complaint.
He lives my mansion to prepare;
And He will bring me safely there;
He lives, all glory to His Name!
Jesus unchangeably the same.

A very personal, perhaps individualistic, statement of faith! But it expresses beautifully my own testimony.

The Resurrection Body

'He will bring me safely there' says one line of that hymn. The certainty of the Resurrection carries with it the certainty of the Resurrection of the believer. Baptism into Christ's death and resurrection guarantees not only experience of his risen life in this world but a full share in the final resurrection. What that means is not just the continuation of the life of the human spirit made perfect, but also the resurrection of the body. The ultimate goal in our hope is not a heaven of disembodied spirits. The human people God has created are a unity of body, mind and spirit. They cannot be redeemed, perfected human people in heaven without the restoration of that unity, severed in their physical death. But what is the nature of the resurrected body? We rightly affirm our faith in it in the Apostles Creed. Having said, therefore, that the resurrection of the body is a certainty I hold, some reverent speculation may be allowed.

In his first letter to the Corinthians, St Paul speaks of the resurrected body as a 'spiritual body', at first sight a contradiction in terms. He must mean a body perfectly suited to spirits made perfect. But how to conceive of such a body is impossible for mortals constrained by this world of time and space. The only body we know is in its essence subject to change, decay and death from the moment of conception. At the moment we die, time and space and their constraints cease to have relevance. There is a further issue that bears on our speculation. People we know, and indeed our own selves, are known through a continually advancing age process, from birth and even before. It is impossible to think of the resurrected body as of any particular stage in that age process. Let us think of a loved parent now departed. The last we saw of them was in old age, losing their powers, finding life a burden, even suffering Alzheimer's disease. A resurrection to that state is quite unthinkable. But they were once an infant, a growing child, before we ourselves were born. Sentiment, and it is mere sentiment, would prefer to think of them 'at their peak'. But that too is unrealistic. What of a beloved dead child, even an infant, we committed to God's grace? Would that child remain as such in eternity?

There is, incidentally, relevance in these thoughts to a hotly-disputed debate - the abortion issue and when human personhood begins. Medical science indicates that as many as 30 per cent or more of conceived embryos abort naturally, mostly without the mother knowing she is pregnant. Where can they fit into God's purposes for resurrected persons? It seems to me perfectly proper to speak of an embryo of a few cells, or even in the early stages of gestation, as human life - it cannot be life of any other category. But, I would submit, God relates to people. When can a foetus be known as a person, not just a potential person? Is it when the capacity for separate, individual existence arrives? I do not think the emergence of the central nervous system and the capacity to feel sensations can be the decisive stage in development to personhood - the animal foetus also passes through such development. I relate these thoughts and questions to the resurrected body reflection. Has a child dead before birth, or even dying in the birth process, a place within God's purposes in the resurrection? I wish to be entirely sensitive to the need for the parents to grieve over their lost children. I believe a religious service with opportunity to commit that thwarted life to God and seek his comfort is most appropriate. But can there be eternal life for a potential person that has never known life after birth in this world? I emphasise I am not here referring to children who have lived and then died. God's love towards them is clear in the Gospels.

All this seems to me to emphasise the need for agnosticism on the nature of the resurrection body, while holding firmly to the credal statement of belief in that regard. But do we not have all the indications we need to know of its nature in the accounts of Christ's appearances after his resurrection? There was some continuity of a kind between the body Jesus had expressed himself through before his crucifixion and what they were now seeing from time to time. And this was in line with St Paul's later teaching about being sown a natural body and raised a spiritual body, using the analogy of sown seeds and subsequent plants - a quite different mode but nevertheless a continuity. Yet with the risen Jesus there was considerable change. He appeared, and just as suddenly disappeared. People who had known him intimately, even prepared his corpse for burial, did not at first recognise him. He ate in their presence, yet that could not have been because his body needed food. There is no blood circulation, digestive process, or nervous system in a resurrected body. Life beyond death is not subject to decay or change or hunger.

What are we to make of Christ's resurrection appearances? Can we best speak of them as Christophanies, instances of real appearances in terms the only terms, in which mortals can perceive with their five senses? I do not doubt, as I have said, that the tomb was empty. A miracle, no less, must have completely transformed his mortal remains into an entirely different dimension. Sceptics, governed only by the natural laws known to science, may reject miracles. But if we do not reject God's power to do what is miraculous - and the Resurrection is the supreme miracle - such a transformation is, to me, the likely approach. Certainly the resurrection was not merely the resuscitation of a corpse, similar to the raising to life of Lazarus. Subsequently Lazarus, and others restored to life by Jesus, died again. Jesus was raised 'after the power of an endless life', with the victory over death in his grasp; he has 'the keys of death and hades'.

After such a miracle the only way the disciples could know he was risen, even though the tomb was empty, was by convincing contact with him, seeing him, hearing him, touching him. A ghostly apparition would not have sufficed. He had to be seen as if brought back to life in this world, though with obvious evidence that it was not that - hence the differences from their former knowledge of him. The appearances make it abundantly clear he was not back with them as before. God, I would say, was accommodating himself to their mortal perceptions in the manner of theophanies of earlier times. The last appearance of the risen Christ in this way was the Ascension, the one that said, 'This is the last time; I am exalted to the Father's side, the place of authority, of intercession, of representation for my people, of guarantee that they will follow'.

Despite the factors in the Christophanies that emphasised the changes from life in a physical body - we can speak of a corporeal resurrection without implying a physical body - the appearances were so convincing as to change lives and create a witnessing Church. And it was not just for a handful of his closest disciples. St Paul mentions those disciples of whom we read in the Gospels but adds that 'up to 500 at once' saw him. If he was romancing, there were still plenty alive at the time of the first letter to Corinth to contradict him. But, significantly, he adds, 'last of all he was seen of me', and marks the uniqueness of that post-Ascension appearance by comparing it to a birth long after a normal gestation period. Did he mean that his meeting with the risen Jesus was just like the meetings in the forty days after the Resurrection?

I have emphasised the differences in the resurrected body. It is most instructive, however, to reflect on the marks of recognition. There seem to have been two ways in which, after initial failure, the disciples recognised Jesus. One was by hearing him speak to them in a certain way. To Mary, outside the tomb, it was in addressing her by name. I hardly think the significant factor was a tone of voice; the two on the road to Emmaus conversed for quite a time without recognising him. In addressing Mary by name he was awakening, or re-awakening, a relationship of trust. In addressing the dispirited fishermen by the lakeside, and calling on them to cast their nets again, he was awakening the memory of the event three years before when he called them to follow him in faith. So far as we can be sure every resurrection appearance was to those, and only those, who had put their trust in him. This may say that the risen Christ is known only to faith, not to imagination. It is interesting that, outside Damascus, Saul appears not to have recognised Christ by voice, for he needs to ask, 'who are you, Lord?' In any case, Saul had probably never heard Jesus speaking before the crucifixion. Faith follows identification in his case, but we may surmise that from the time of Stephen's martyrdom the

Spirit was already working in Saul's heart. He was told he could not go on kicking against the goads.

The other way of identification was by the wound-prints. In the upper room he showed them his hands and his side. A week later the sight alone, rather than the touch he was invited to make, was sufficient to dispel all Thomas' doubts. When the two on the road to Emmaus reached their destination, and fearing to lose contact with the remarkable stranger invited him in for a meal, it was not till he broke bread that they knew him. We do not know if they had been at the Last Supper and had seen what Jesus did there. But he could not have broken bread for them without them seeing the print of the nails.

William Temple in his *Readings in St. John's Gospel*[1] says the showing of his scars 'was proof of identity'. He continues, 'this, however transmuted, was the Body which had hung on the Cross and was laid in the tomb. But the scars are more than this; they are the evidence not only that what they see is the Body of Jesus, but what is the quality for ever of the Body of Him whom they know with ever-deeper understanding as the Christ: 'the Son of Man must suffer.'" 'The wounds of Christ are His credentials to the suffering race of men'. Temple quotes a poem by Edward Shillito, written shortly after the suffering of the Great War:

Jesus of the scars

If we have never sought, we seek Thee now;
Thine eyes burn through the dark, our only stars;
We must have sight of thorn-pricks on Thy brow,
We must have Thee, O Jesus of the Scars.
The heavens frighten us; they are too calm;
In all the universe we have no place.
Our wounds are hurting us; where is the balm?
Lord Jesus, by Thy Scars, we claim Thy grace.
If, when the doors are shut, Thou drawest near,
Only reveal those hands, that side of Thine;
We know today what wounds are, have no fear,
Show us Thy Scars, we know the countersign.
The other gods were strong; but Thou wast weak;
They rode, but Thou didst stumble to a throne;
But to our wounds only God's wounds can speak,
And not a god has wounds, but Thou alone.

---

1. Published 1950 by Macmillan & Co., London., pp. 384, 385.

Amid all the symbolic images of heaven in the *Book of the Revelation*, the most powerful must be, 'A Lamb as it had been slain', at the heart of the eternal home. If what has been offered hitherto as reverent speculation is anywhere near the truth, we cannot dogmatise on the resurrection body of Christ in heaven, nor on our own, but he must surely be known as the one who was crucified for us and be thus perceived in that essential, abiding presence. A hymn in poetic language speaks of 'those wounds yet visible above in beauty glorified'. In the chorus of another song, though no great poetry, I can express my own conviction and certainty:

I shall know him, I shall know him,
When redeemed by his side I shall stand;
I shall know him, I shall know him,
By the print of the nails in his hand.

The Parousia

I use the term Parousia, instead of Second Coming, to refer to the final act of Christ's redeeming work, for a particular reason. 'Second Coming' is not a New Testament writer's expression. 'He will come again' is, and Jesus himself spoke of his coming again. But that promise, like references to the Day of the Lord in the Old Testament, is capable of different interpretations. In one sense, Jesus' promise to come again was fulfilled in his Resurrection appearances, in another sense still in his coming to individual believing souls. But all these interpretations, however legitimate, do not detract from the hope foremost in the minds of the Christians of the first century of a Personal Return of Christ to complete his work of redemption. In the early days, expectation of its imminence had to give way to recognition that the time was not yet, even though alert readiness was still called for. 'Coming again' may lack precise meaning, Parousia leaves no doubt as to what is meant. Ever since the last Resurrection appearance, the Ascension, the hope of Christ's Return has been at the heart of the Christian faith. He came first in humility, he will return in glory. His appearing will finalise salvation and usher in the Day of Judgement. Beyond that, how dogmatic can we be? We can be certain that the struggle between the Kingdom of God on earth and the Kingdom of evil will go on till the End. Much of the apocalyptic language and imagery makes that clear. But what is the End to be like? In answering that question, Christians have come up with various answers, depending on their interpretation of eschatological language. They cannot all be right.

So much has been made of the thousand years, the millennium, in Revelation 20:2ff. Taking it literally as a thousand years, an unjustifiable interpretation as I believe, Christians have argued as to whether the Parousia will precede or follow the millennium within the time-scale we exist in, and what its true nature will be. Full weight must be given to the symbolism of the language of any apocalyptic literature, and that rules out any literal interpretation of the thousand years or other numbers found in the Book of the Revelation. Without attempting any description of the conflicting theories, or possible meaning of the symbols, I state my own conviction that God will return to complete his saving work of bringing his people to their final destiny, to judge everyone, alive or dead, to complete the triumph over the kingdom of darkness and evil.

The Scriptures also speak of the end of creation as we know it and of a new heaven and earth, but what that means we cannot say. Any new creation cannot be subject to the physical laws of this universe with beginnings, change and decay, and death. I do not know what the relationship of the Parousia will be to the time-sequence and world of space we are now bound by. We note phrases like 'the clouds of heaven', 'being caught up in the air', 'the trumpet shall sound', and 'every eye shall see him', but again one needs to recognise symbolism and imagery. With those who applied a literal interpretation, it was for a long time a puzzle to reconcile a Return at some spot on this earth, say, the Mount of Olives, with every eye seeing him, when this round earth is populated through six continents. The idea, now suggested by some of television being the answer I find quite unconvincing. It illustrates the problem and endless argument that too literal interpretation can land Christians in. Of the fact of the Parousia I have no doubt, of the manner I am agnostic. As a footnote I recount an incident at Keele 1967.

I had been asked to chair the section on 'The Church and its Message' to go in the Congress Statement. Approximately ninety clergy and laity had chosen the section. They were divided into four sub-sections, each chaired by a person with theological expertise. After each sub-section had done its work, I worked with their chairmen to produce a draft of the Message. The last paragraph was on The Christian Hope. It contained the phrase, 'the promised personal return of Jesus Christ'. When the draft was presented to the whole section, one member proposed the additional words, 'in this world of time and space'. In the early hours of the next morning, I took the draft with that possible addition to the group editing the whole Statement. The group was clear, the additional words should not be included. Subsequently the complete Statement was presented to a plenary session of the Congress, almost 1,000 members. No one asked for any amplification of the original phrase.

The Intermediate State

That expression is the best we can use in speaking of the state of souls between death and resurrection at the Parousia. From our perspective while alive, we can only think in terms of the time process. But at death, time ceases to be a constraint; it is as is space, part of the present created order from which death removes us. Throughout history, however, human beings, unless convinced that death is simply extinction, have not been able to avoid speculation on an after-life. Discoveries of ancient civilisations show elaborate preparations and rituals for the continuing existence of the departed. Different religions have their own beliefs - including reincarnation, an absorption into a de-personalised state of being, paradise, and a shadowy underworld. What has the Christian faith, emerging from but distinguishable from the Hebrew faith, got to tell us? Not a lot on the intermediate state. There are hints in both Old and New Testaments, but they hardly add up to a firm picture. Is it a conscious or unconscious existence? Dead believers are described as 'asleep in Christ' and certainly at rest. Sleep, however, might be focusing on the death of the body, and the spirit dead to this world. Rest does not necessarily imply inactivity. The blessed dead rest from their labours. Whatever they may be involved in will not entail such toil as tires and inflicts pain on earth. I don't believe we can use the parable of Dives and Lazarus to build certainties about the after-life. When Jesus taught in parables, every detail did not have to bear the same weight. He had a truth to get over in a story or in familiar scenarios of the day. Lazarus' rest and blessedness 'in Abraham's bosom' related to current understandings. Conversation between Abraham and Dives takes place despite a gulf between them. We are not being given here a kind of tourist brochure of heaven. What Jesus was teaching was the responsibility of the haves to the have-nots, and the need to heed God's revealed demands in this life while there is still time.

Undoubtedly the believer may look forward to being with Christ which, St Paul said 'is far better' than life here and now. There are always aged and infirm Christians, tired, disabled and distressed by pain, who say they wish the Lord would take them home, but St Paul, we may assume, had not reached that stage. On the Cross, Jesus promised the penitent brigand, 'Today, you will be with me in Paradise'. It is interesting, but not very helpful, to speculate why Jesus laid emphasis on 'today', when the Resurrection was not till a third day, and as the Creed affirms he was to descend to the dead, to Hades. However, 'with Christ in Paradise' hardly suggests an unconscious state.

So, from our point of view in time we have to speak of an intermediate state because death is a fixed point in time and the Parousia we look for is to us in the future. Whether the faithful departed in a conscious state are waiting, thinking of a future, is, to me, an unanswerable question. I recognise the *Book of the Revelation* seems to indicate a positive answer, but, again, how far can we press the imagery? A major question, however, revolves round the departeds' knowledge of the world they have left behind. Does death foreclose any continuing knowledge of, let alone contact with, what is going on?

Mere sentiment, particularly strong at a bereavement, governs the attitude of many people to such a question. Clergy visiting a bereaved family before a funeral are often aware of it. There is an assumption that a loved one has gone to heaven - 'he or she was such a good person and never did anyone any harm!' - and will be able to 'watch over' those who are left. As the days go by, one may be told that the loved one is still present, unseen, especially in the home. Even, at half-waking moments, in a time of sickness or at the imminence of death, a vision of that person may be claimed. Rational thought based on Christian teaching may dismiss all this as wish born of emotional need. The question of the departed's possible knowledge of continuing life on earth, however, needs further consideration. There is no justification, in Christian theology, for the kind of contact Spiritualists claim is possible, whereby the departed address the living. There is, however, the Communion of Saints, belief in which is expressed in the Creed. If, within that Communion, contact one way, from them to us, is ruled out, what of the other way, from us to them, through prayer?

Prayers and the Dead

Although the Christian Church has long had a tradition of invocation of saints, from the Virgin Mary downwards, so to speak, I seriously question the practice and find no place for it in my life. Incidentally, I wonder if I am right in thinking that after Mary, and possibly Joseph, it is lesser-known saints who are more invoked than the Apostles? In obituary notices and similar personal acknowledgements, I cannot recall St Paul and St John getting very much attention.

I am convinced that prayer to the Father through saints, Mary included, is not only unnecessary but based on wrong assumptions. There is one Mediator, the Son of God, our Brother and High Priest, through whom alone we approach the throne of grace. Any idea that he needs persuasion by his Mother, or anyone else who has gone before, to receive our prayers is unfounded. That is not to say the saints at rest do not pray. It is to say no extra mediation is needed. Anything that detracts from the sole sufficiency of Christ's High Priestly work is to be abhorred. Due honour of the Virgin Mary, gratitude for her obedience and example as the Mother of the Son of God incarnate, should not lead to any idea of her being Co-Redemtrix or Co-Mediator.

I return to the question of saints in heaven having knowledge of life now on earth. I find it most difficult to believe they can be at rest if they do know what is happening on earth. To be aware of the awful tragedies, oppression of innocents, cruelty among the nations, and to be at rest, seem to be incompatible ideas. Or, to bring it to a more personal level, if they are aware of the troubles, anxieties, failings and sins, with their shame, that their loved ones are still experiencing, it would surely disturb peace and rest. It may be a nice thought to imagine they are aware of our joys and successes, but we cannot have the smooth without the rough.

Having said all that, I want to affirm the continuing worth and effectiveness of the prayers of our loved ones offered while in this life. I know that, even before my birth, my parents and other close friends and relations prayed for me, right up to their death. Those prayers did not cease to be effective when the Lord took them home All they asked for in accordance with his will the Lord still honours. As I think of my children, and particularly the grandchildren as they grow up in the modern world, I pray for their well-being in every way, as I pray for many others. When I am gone, I believe those prayers offered while in life will still be used by God.

It is not possible to reflect on the intermediate state without thinking about prayers in respect of the departed, our prayers for them, not to them. I will state positively what I do believe and do in this matter. At the time of death I believe it is entirely appropriate to commit a loved one into God's keeping, with added assurance if they are known to trust in Christ. That committal to the Lord, as the body is committed to the ground or fire, is an expression of faith and a way of letting go from this world. On occasions thereafter, on anniversaries for instance, it is good to give thanks that the loved one is with the Lord at rest. But there is more content for the prayer, I believe. I best indicate this by my practice in the closing section of the prayer of intercession in the ASB Communion Service. 'We give thanks, O Lord, for all who have departed this life in your faith and fear, and especially for those through whom we ourselves have been blessed. We give thanks for their present rest in your presence and for the glorious hope of resurrection and reunion at the Return of Christ. Bring us with them to the fulfilment of your loving purposes'.

Protestant, evangelical attitudes to prayers for the dead have been nervous, if not downright hostile, in reaction to Roman Catholic ideas of the afterlife. Positively, evangelicals have wanted to emphasise the doctrine of assurance, that it is possible to know one has passed from death to life and so be assured of glory. Negatively, they have shunned the idea of changing the standing of the departed before God by intercessory prayers, or masses for the repose of the soul, particularly related to what they regard as the unscriptural concept of Purgatory. But fear of error ought not to inhibit full affirmation of the truth. Prayer in regard to the faithful departed should not be an uncertain attempt to persuade God but a confident expression of our faith in him and his purposes and gratitude for his promises.

As we look to the future and contemplate the intermediate state, we recognise there are purposes of God still to be fulfilled, as I acknowledge in the prayer example above. Even the most devoted of God's servants leaves this life still far to go towards perfection, holiness is incomplete. We all need to be changed, not only during our earthly pilgrimage but beyond. Purgatory has been the Roman Catholic answer to this quest. The New Testament suggests, rather, a more instant transformation. 'We shall be changed, in the twinkling of an eye', says St Paul. 'When Christ shall appear, we shall be like him, for we shall see him as he is', we are told in 1 John. Transformed by beholding is a concept first indicated with Moses on Sinai but taken up in the New Testament. In Romans 8, St Paul states that those chosen, called, justified, glorified, are to be conformed to the image of God's Son. The how and the when can be left to God. We need only to know it will be, in the beatific vision.

The Communion of Saints, then, is a truth to be cherished, but not embroidered by ideas owing more to human emotional needs than divine revelation. The Church Militant here on earth and the Church at Rest in heaven are one, awaiting to be the Church Triumphant, indwelt by the Holy Spirit who bonds them into one communion, worshipping the same Lord. Militant here on earth, Triumphant at last, though traditional descriptions, have their shortcomings. The Church is indeed in conflict with the powers of darkness in this world and looks forward to the complete victory over evil when the Kingdom of God is complete, but on earth the Church is also the Servant Church, following its God, the Servant King. A great moment in the Eucharist is when we offer our praise and worship 'with angels and archangels and all the company of heaven'. In that action we experience the Communion of Saints and anticipate the heavenly consummation of our salvation.

The Judgement

Deep within the human psyche, except perhaps with those who seem to have capitulated to evil, is a conviction that evil should be judged and punished. The conviction may sometimes be mixed with revenge, but the basic moral instinct is that good should be rewarded and evil punished. The idea that the universe is amoral and concepts of good and evil only the product of our biological and sociological development is still, as I believe, a minority view based on an atheistic philosophy.

The credal statement, 'He will come again to judge the living and the dead', crystallises the plain teaching of Scripture. The God of the universe is a Holy God, his justice must triumph. What, then, will the Day of Judgement mean? We must start by recognising that 'all have sinned and come short of the glory of God'. No one deserves to be let through the divine judgement on the basis of character or deeds they may present. The heart of the Good News of Jesus Christ, as I have tried to emphasise in Chapter One, is that full atonement for the sins of the whole world, an objective atonement made within the Godhead and presented complete to humanity, was accomplished in the Cross. There sin was judged to a destruction to be completed at the return of Christ. As someone has suggested, Calvary was the D-Day when the decisive battle was won, the Parousia is V-Day when the victory is completed, the war ended. In a human court the symbol is the scales of justice, on which evidence for and against is weighed. The most appropriate sign on the Day of Judgement is the Cross.

The New Testament is clear that there is 'No condemnation to them that are in Christ Jesus' (Romans 8:1). Many other references can be adduced in support. The Christian believer may face the Day of Judgement without fear. His or her conviction may be expressed in Charles Wesley's hymn:

No condemnation now I dread;
Jesus, and all in Him, is mine;
Alive in Him, my living Head,
And clothed in righteousness divine,
Bold I approach the eternal throne,
And claim the crown, through Christ, my own

Problems remain, however. What of those who lived before Christ, in the Hebrew race and in other nations? Or those who have lived since, to whom the Good News of Jesus Christ has never come, or of other faiths whose commitment to their own beliefs shuts out a hearing of the Good News? For myself, I can only leave the issue with God who, as Abraham indicated, 'will do right' as the Judge of all the earth. There are hints in Scripture that God deals with individuals according to their lights. What I am sure is not in doubt is that all accepted by God will be on the basis of that objective atonement at the Cross. It was for the whole world. It has cosmic efficacy, covering history before and after its action on the actual day on Calvary.

A further problem for us concerns the outcome of the Judgement, not so much in respect of those covered by the salvation wrought in Christ who enter heaven's glory, but any who in God's justice are not saved. Christians have long been divided over whether the latter depart into an unending conscious state of separation from God, hell, or cease to exist. Passages of Scripture can be adduced on both sides of the argument. No one person could hope to resolve the argument. There are, however, considerations to be borne in mind.

Does the Bible teach that the human being is inherently immortal, that every soul born into the world is bound for eternity with or without God? Death is conceived of in two different ways - the death of the body, and spiritual death which involves separation from God because of sin. When the consequences of sin are said to be death, it can only relate to this separation from God. Death of the body is something humanity shares with all creation - we live in that kind of universe. Any idea that if man had not sinned, physical death would not have resulted is out of the question. The human body is inherently mortal.

Salvation in Christ, while holding out the promise of a resurrected body not subject to mortality, begins by addressing the spiritual death caused by alienation from God, and brings eternal life by healing the separation and bestowing the life of God within the human person.

Eternal life is essentially God's life and, though also described as everlasting life, emphasis should be laid on its quality more than its duration. God is unending, but time and its passage as we know it is not what eternity is about. We remind ourselves that a human person is not complete without a unity of body and spirit, and that in heaven, whatever the form of the body, it will be the vehicle of the spirit made perfect. For those judged by God not to be saved, can there be a resurrected body? It is considerations of this kind that have led some to reject the idea of an inherent immortality in mankind and to speak rather of conditional immortality, immortality depending not on an inalienable right for all but a gift of God ('the gift of God is eternal life') won by Christ's death and resurrection. It is only right to recognise, however, that the New Testament has many references to eternal judgement and, using language and expressions of this world of time and space, seems to envisage unending separation from God, even suffering. Again we have to struggle with our understanding of eternity, recognising that categories of time and space do not apply, even though at present our thinking is constrained by them.

Many Christians, trying to cope with apparently different eschatological ideas, go for a universalist conclusion - in the end the sovereign love of God will win over every human being and all will be saved. And there are New Testament passages favouring that view. It is said that it is God's will that all men (people) shall be saved, and he will reconcile all things in heaven and earth in Christ himself. But, equally, there are many references to divisive consequences on the Day of Judgement, the saved and the lost and their destiny. And we need to remember that, in creating the human race, God willed to give freedom to trust and obey or reject him, with the self-limitation that involved. What is not in doubt is the repeated call and challenge for all who hear the Good News to respond in faith to Christ as Saviour while there is time in this life

One aspect of the Day of Judgement not touched on, concerns those accepted by God, justified by grace through faith. They are delivered from condemnation of their sin, but the Scriptures talk about rewards for service. We have no idea what they will be. St Paul likens our service for Christ and his Kingdom to amassing gold, silver and precious stones, or wood, hay and stubble, the latter to be burnt up, the former of lasting worth. The quality of Christian service differs from person to person and from time to time in the same person. Apparently this will be recognised, not, surely, so that any may glory in what they have done but that they may offer everything good in worship of God.

Another hymn of Charles Wesley, may express the truth in this regard.

Changed from glory into glory,
Till in heaven we take our place,
Till we cast our crowns before Thee,
Lost in wonder, love and praise.

Whatever our crowns or achievements or worthwhile service, we owe it all in the first place to God's grace, and to him must be the glory.

AMAZING GRACE

I began with the lines that well express my reflections on life and ministry;

O to Grace how great a debtor
Daily I'm constrained to be.

Life has so far been full, with blessings too numerous to recount. As for anyone else, there have been dangers, sorrows, trials, days of darkness, times when the ways of God were hard to understand and he was hidden. Sins and failures were many. But the grace of God in Christ through the Spirit has never failed me. Another favourite hymn says;

With mercy and with judgement
My web of time he wove;
And aye the dews of sorrow
Were lustred by his love;
I'll bless the hand that guided,
I'll bless the heart that planned,
When throned where glory dwelleth,
In Immanuel's land.

A Christian must believe the best is yet to be. Even though powers may fail and burdens increase, the future is bright. John Newton's hymn, whose title heads this final section, sums up my story;

Through many dangers, toils and snares,
I have already come;
'tis grace hath brought me safe thus far,
And grace will lead me home.